Recreation Guide
to **CALIFORNIA**
NATIONAL FORESTS

By George Stratton

FALCON PRESS®

Falcon Press is continually expanding its list of recreational guidebooks using the same general format as this book. All books include detailed descriptions, accurate maps, and all information necessary for enjoyable trips. You can order extra copies of this book and get information and prices for other Falcon books by writing Falcon Press, P.O. Box 1718, Helena, MT 59624. Also, please ask for a free copy of our current catalog listing all Falcon Press books.

Cover Photo: by Ed Cooper of Tioga Lake in the Inyo National Forest.

Stratton, George.
   Recreation guide to California national forests / by George Stratton.—1st ed.—Helena, MT : Falcon Press, c1991.
     vi, 258 p. : ill., maps ; 23 cm.
     "A Falcon guide."—P. [4] of cover.
     ISBN 1-56044-012-0 : $9.95

     1. Forest reserves—California—Recreational use—Guidebooks. 2. Forest Reserves—California—Guidebooks. I. Title.
GV191.67.F6S77   1991   917.94—dc20   91-70767
                                      AACR 2   MARC

ACKNOWLEDGMENTS

United States Department of Agriculture Forest Service personnel up and down the state of California were uncompromising in their cooperation for the writing of this book. They devoted their time to talking with me, showing me the forests, and checking each chapter for facts. Special thanks go to Jean Hawthorne, Mike McCormick, Bob Henley, Jack Darnell, Dave Reider, Ron Anderson, Dave Peters, Inez Robbins, Wallace McCray, Steve Waterman, Gary Hines, Bashford York, Gail vander Bie, Lesley Whisler, Ramiro Villalvazo, Ed Gornowski, John Ruopp, Bob McDowell, Dick Warren, Kathleen Myers, Bill Britton, Nancy Gardner, Duane Lyon, Garry Owen, Dick Gibson, Phil Horning, Al Ashton, Heidi Binneweis, Barbara Cooper, Michael Scialfa, and Barbara Croonquist.

A grateful acknowledgement goes to my wife, Thelma, for her encouragement and loving support. Thanks also to editor Chris Cauble for his help, and publisher Bill Schneider.

To Bill Wilson and all his friends who have shared their experience, strength, and hope with me through the years, and without whom this book could never have been written.

CONTENTS

MAP LEGEND

Interstate	**00**	Peak & Elevation	▲ 0000
U.S. Highway	00	Lakes	
State or Other Principal Road	000	River, Creek, Drainage	
Forest Road	0000	National Forest	
Main Road		Wilderness	
Secondary Road		Refuge	
Pass or Saddle		Parks	
Visitors Center	VC	Foot Trail	·········>

California's National Forests present visitors with a dizzying array of sights and sounds. Middle Falls of the McCloud River in the Shasta-Trinity National Forests. Royal Mannion photo.

INTRODUCTION

"In the administration for the Forest Reserves it must be clearly borne in mind that all land is to be devoted to its most productive use for the permanent good of the whole people, and not for the temporary benefit of individuals or companies. . .where conflicting interests must be reconciled the question will always be decided from the standpoint of the greatest good of the greatest number in the long run."

This quotation is from a letter written by Secretary of Agriculture James Wilson to Gifford Pinchot, Chief Forester, setting down the guidelines and charter of a new forest agency in 1905. The new agency, the Forest Service, was signed into being by President Theodore Roosevelt to provide leadership in the management, protection, and use of the Nation's forests and rangelands.

The National Park Service, under the Department of the Interior, is charged with preserving natural features in their pristine state for all time. The United States Department of Agriculture Forest Service, on the other hand, is dedicated to multiple-use management of their lands for sustained yields of renewable resources of water, forage, wood, wildlife, minerals and recreation. Agency objectives are to provide the best combination of uses for the American people; to make sure the land stays productive and of high quality for future generations.

Consequently, when you visit one of the national forests you may see logging trucks on the roads, or come across beef cattle in high mountain meadows, as well as campgrounds and visitors information centers. Recreation is only one of the uses of the forests.

This book lists the various kinds of recreational opportunities available in each of the National Forests of California. In each chapter you will find a description of the natural and human history of the forest, most of the campgrounds, a section on hiking trails and wilderness areas. There are descriptions of auto tours you can take on each forest, a listing of special places to stop and enjoy such things as museums, visitor centers, spectacular views, or quiet spots among the trees in a special grove.

There are descriptions of the major lakes and streams and the boating activities you can enjoy on them. Fishing and hunting are covered as well as off-highway motoring and bicycling. Some forests will have sports such as target shooting and hang-gliding, and many have both summer and winter resorts. Skiing, downhill and cross-country, is covered as is the opportunity for snowmobiling and snow play. Each forest will have its own unique recreation for your pleasure, from mushroom hunting and spelunking to the latest mountain biking.

At the end of each chapter there's a chart with each developed campground on the forest, showing how large it is, and whether or not there is piped water, R.V. space, fishing, swimming, or other activities. Some group campgrounds are not listed on the chart, however.

Every forest in the state offers group camping, usually by reservation. There are group campsites that will accommodate up to 300 people at one time. Most are smaller, ranging from sites for 25 people up to 75 or 100. To reserve

All ages enjoy the beauty and solitude of camping in the California National Forests at campgrounds like Pinecrest in the Stanislaus National Forest. Steve Bailey photo.

a group campsite for your organization, call the Forest Supervisor's office for the forest you'd like to visit.

Reservations for camping spots are the exception, rather than the rule on the National Forests. However, some places are so popular that a reservation system had to be installed. Beginning in 1989, you can make reservations for those campgrounds that accept them through Mistix, 1-800-444-PARK. The charts at the end of each chapter will tell you which sites accept reservations. At the end of the book, you'll find a list of telephone numbers and addresses for each forest as well as additional sources of information. Another list gives the names and addresses of packers and guides who have permits to operate on the forests.

In California, the national forests account for 54 percent of the forest and rangeland recreation. The National Parks and other federal, state, county and private lands together account for the remaining 46 percent. Sixty-two percent of the 6.3 million acres of wilderness in the state is on the National Forests, along with twenty-two of the thirty-three major downhill ski areas. The forests also have more than 2,400 lakes and reservoirs, 13,000 miles of maintained trails for hiking, horseback riding, and off-highway vehicles, and 1,800 miles of Wild and Scenic Rivers.

More people come into the forests each year. The Sierra National Forest, for example, adjacent to Yosemite National Park gets the same number of visitors as the park. Altogether, the number of visitors in California's national forests amounts to 25 percent of the national forest recreation use nationwide. When you add up all the opportunities and all the people who take advantage of them, the national forests are the largest providers of outdoor recreation in the world.

Within California you'll find eighteen national forest supervisors' offices, with responsibility for the supervision and management of nineteen national forests, including Lake Tahoe Basin Management Unit.

Also within the state are portions of three additional forests headquartered out of state. Of these three, only Toiyabe National Forest on the east side of the Sierra Nevada has enough acreage in California to be considered in this book. The other two, Rogue River and Siskiyou, are Northwestern Regional Forests headquartered in Oregon and hold only small amounts of territory in the state.

Each of the national forests is divided into three to six ranger districts, and it is personnel from the district ranger stations that you are most likely to come in contact with on the forest. They're there to supervise all of the activities on the forests, form volunteer interpretive associations to timber cutting. The ranger stations are the places to pick up information that you'd like to have about that forest. These are the folks responsible for summer

The multitude of lakes in the California National Forests provide recreationists with a variety of activities. Bathers enjoy the beach at Lake Tahoe in the Lake Tahoe Basin Management Unit. Jean Hawthorne photo.

season programs such as campfires, nature walks, and junior ranger programs for the kids.

It's at the ranger stations, too, where the permits you need to accomplish certain things on the forests are obtained. If you want to get off the beaten track and you're not going to camp in one of the developed campgrounds, for example, you must have a campfire permit before you can cook—even over a gasoline stove or charcoal brazier. And, in some areas, campfires are prohibited outside developed campgrounds at certain times of the year because of the high fire danger. Permits for entrance into the wilderness areas are issued here, too. The wilderness permits also serve as fire permits for your trip, so you don't have to have both.

While you're camping you can pick up all the dead and down wood you need for your fire, but if you want to take some home a permit is required, and a small fee is required for each cord. Different forests have differing regulations, but ranger station personnel can answer your questions and will give you a map showing where you can cut.

Northern forests, such as the Klamath, Six Rivers, and Shasta-Trinity, also allow you to cut your own Christmas tree with a permit. Fees for Christmas tree cutting range from $2 to $10.

The wilderness areas within the national forests of the state are preserved in undisturbed condition and access in most cases is limited to travel on foot, horseback, or with stock animals. No mechanized travel is permitted, It's important to follow the "no-trace" camping techniques when in the wilderness in order to give the campers still to come the same kind of experiences we can now enjoy.

The wildernesses range in size from the 500,000 acres of John Muir Wilderness in the central Sierra down to little Hauser Wilderness with its 7,500 acres at the extreme southern end of the Cleveland National Forest, almost in Mexico.

Throughout the book you'll come across references to National Recreation Trails and the Pacific Crest Trail. In 1968 Congress formally established a system of scenic and recreational trails on federal lands. the act designated the Pacific Crest and Appalacian National Scenic Trails as the keystones of the system. The National Recreation Trails form the next level in the system, and there are more than forty-five of them in the state. Each is special in some particular way; perhaps extraordinarily scenic, perhaps historical.

Every forest in the state except Modoc, Six Rivers, Mendocino, and Los Padres has a portion of the Pacific Crest Trail (PCT) running through it offering challenge and beauty. The trail travels through cathedral-like groves of Douglas firs in the far north to doubly fascinating deserts in the south, and includes the wild beauty of the Sierra and the gentler, chaparral-covered foothills.

For this book, each of the forests in the state was visited over an extended period of time. Developed campgrounds as well as primitive ones were used while exploring each forest and enjoying the many special programs available to visitors. The recreation officer on each forest was interviewed along with the recreation specialists on most of the separate districts within each forest.

Fascinating stories came up that aren't included in the chapters, such as the pair of mergansers that took up residence above the fish tank of the Stream Profile Chamber at Lake Tahoe and gorged themselves on the fat trout to the point they could hardly fly away. There was also the story of the family that rebuilt its vacation cabin three times in the avalanche chute above Echo

4

The forest rangers of the California National Forests are responsible for a variety of interpretive programs such as campfires, nature walks, and junior ranger programs for the kids. Here Smokey the Bear talks to a child about fire prevention in the Cleveland National Forest. Jean Hawthorne photo.

Lake and wondered why they had all the bad luck.

Go into the forests of California and enjoy yourself. Swim in the lakes and rivers, go fishing and hiking, slide down a mountain. Hunt for deer or quail. And as you go, keep in mind these lines from the book, *Toward Zero Impact:*

> Let your footprints be obscure;
> Let your voice not overwhelm the still air.
> Let your leavings go out in your pack
> That meadows and forests and mountains
> And all therein may persist.

CLEVELAND
NATIONAL
FOREST

Sacramento

San Francisco

Los Angeles

CLEVELAND NATIONAL FOREST

The Cleveland National Forest is an interesting forest comprised of three non-contiguous land areas. The areas make up the Descanso, Palomar, and Trabuco ranger districts, and are located in San Diego, Orange, and Riverside counties. They offer a wild land of steep-sided mountains covered with chaparral and conifers, and they offer recreational opportunities to a vast urban population from Mexico to the Los Angeles Basin.

A warm, dry mediterranean climate prevails over the Cleveland. Hot in summer but mild in winter, its elevations range from sea level to 6,000 feet. The trails of the Cleveland are usually open year 'round, and hikers can spend time in the out-of-doors when the Sierra trails are deep in snow.

It is by nature a land of fire. Every year, in the fall, hot easterly winds called the "Santa Anas" blow with gale force intensity causing extreme burning conditions. Historically, fires ignited during this time have consumed huge acreage before they're controlled.

Camping

The Cleveland is, to a degree, a "day-use" forest, and people come in to enjoy the cool mountains in the summer heat and to play in the winter's snows. Consequently, there are not very many developed campgrounds—only five or six on each ranger district.

Trabuco Ranger District Camping

Camping on the Trabuco District is permitted in designated campgrounds only, except when traveling in the San Mateo Canyon Wilderness, where wilderness permits are required. Much of the visitor recreation use on or near the Ortega Highway (SR 74), which runs through the San Juan Canyon from San Juan Capistrano to Lake Elsinor. At the head of the canyon, the El Cariso campgrounds are on both sides of the highway in oak woodlands that grow along San Juan Creek. There's a memorial to firefighters on the south side of the highway and a visitor information station in the fire station complex.

Down the hill about half way through the forest, you'll come to the Upper San Juan Campground. Like the El Cariso campgrounds, Upper San Juan is adjacent to the Ortega Highway in a wooded area filled with coast live oaks, cottonwoods, and sycamores. This is a beautiful springtime campground, and birders will find three for four different warblers and both golden and ruby-crowned kinglets in the shrubbery along the creek.

The largest campground on the Trabuco is Blue Jay, which is three miles north of Ortega Highway adjacent to Long Canyon Road. Coast live oaks and sycamores shade campers in this quiet spot, and all the chaparral species surround the campsites.

Tenaja Campground at the southeastern edge of the district can be reached by twelve miles of dirt road from Murrieta on Interstate 15. This is the favorite campground for horsemen who want to go into the San Mateo Canyon Wilderness. Hitching posts are provided for riders who want to go into San Mateo, Tenaja, and Los Almos canyons.

A visitor information kiosk at entrance to Mt. Laguna Recreation Area. George Stratton Photo. (All photos by George Stratton unless otherwise noted.)

Palomar Ranger District Camping

The Palomar District has a concentration of recreation facilities, including Palomar Mountain State Park and both county and private facilities.

Dripping Springs Campground, at the north boundary of the district, is the gateway to the compact, 16,000 acre Agua Tibia Wilderness. Old oaks, both coast live oaks and black oaks, are scattered across the flat where the camp is located. Camp sites are far enough apart, and enough white sage and mountain mohogany have grown to make for privacy and a sense of being almost alone.

Along Highway 79 on the eastern edge of the district Oak Grove Campground hosts large numbers of RV campers in the valley of Temecula Creek. Individual sites are shaded by oaks, sycamores, and occasional alders. Oak Grove Ranger Station is across the street from the camp as is the beginning of the Oak Grove Trail to High Point Lookout.

High on the slopes of Palomar Mountain you'll come to Observatory and Fry Creek campgrounds. Here you can find a campsite next to a wildflower filled meadow, or sheltered under a spreading black oak, or deep in the shade of a grove of Jeffrey pines. Observatory National Recreation Trail starts at the eastern edge of Observatory Campground and continues for two miles to Palomar Observatory.

At Fry Creek, you'll be deep into a dense forest of evergreens and oaks, which not only provide shade for almost all of the sites, but the setting for a loop trail around the campground. Fry Creek itself flows through both campgrounds before joining the San Luis River farther down the mountainside. Campground hosts will greet you at these sites and can answer your questions about fishing, hiking, or visiting hours at the observatory.

East of Temecula Creek, there is a small separate section of Palomar District with picturesque rock formations and a ten-mile long section of the Pacific Crest Trail. You can reach Indian Flats Campground here by driving 1.5 miles north of Warner Springs on Highway 79, and then seven miles north on unpaved FR 9S05 to the sites on the northern slope of Pine Mountain. Scattered oaks provide protection from the elements in this high desert campground.

Descanso District Camping

All but two of the developed campgrounds on the Descanso District are in the Laguna Mountain Recreation Area.

Burnt Rancheria Campground is the highest on the forest at 6000 feet elevation. Both the PCT and Desert View Nature Trail are adjacent to the campground. Jeffrey pines, sugar pines, and the immense-coned Coulter pines, as well as incense cedars and white firs grow all along the plateau.

Laguna Campground is spread out through a forest of old conifers and newly-planted Jeffrey pines next to a huge, green meadow. Little Laguna Lake is within easy walking distance, and the campfire center for the district is here,

Mt Palomar observatory is open to visitors on a daily basis.

too. Both Laguna and Burnt Rancheria get lots of use in the summer as people come up to the pines and oaks to escape the relentless heat of the desert. Reservations are required at some campgrounds.

Also within the district are two other places where families can make reservations to camp by calling Mistix. One of these, Yerba Santa Campground, is wheelchair accessible. It's across the meadow from Laguna Campground and is actually a part of El Prado group camp. The other reservation camp for families is Agua Dulce Walk-in Campground at the southern edge of the Recreation Area near Wooded Hill.

There are two more campgrounds that are not within the recreation area: Cibbetts Flat and Boulder Oaks campgrounds. Cibbets Flat is near the junction of Kitchen Creek and Long Canyon Creek. The stream flows year-round along the edge of the oak-shaded camp. Small trout occasionally can be attracted to worm or fly. Boulder Oaks Campground sits in a savannah of coast live oaks that are home to acorn woodpeckers and red-tailed hawks. The PCT passes through the camp on its way north from Mexico about ten miles to the south. Huge granite boulders are scatttered through the camp sites, offering excellent places to camp. This campground also has equestrian facilities with corrals and rails for stock.

On the Trail

Off-season hiking, winter and spring, is a tremendous draw on the Cleveland National Forest. This is especially true along sections of the Pacific Crest Trail and Noble Canyon National Recreation Trail.

Pacific Crest Trail

Except for a ten-mile section on the Palomar District near Indian Flats, the Pacific Crest Trail is entirely contained within the Descanso District while traveling through the Cleveland. The rest of the time it's on Bureau of Land Management land or nearby Anza-Borrego Desert State Park, although it is still administered by the Forest Service.

The trail enters the Descanso from the north near Pioneer Mail picnic ground in the Laguna Mountain Recreation Area. It passes down the ridgetop to Long Canyon and then southwest to an intersection with I-8. At Boulder Oaks campground, the trail goes on south, dipping briefly into Lake Morena County Park before reaching Hauser Canyon at the southern tip of the forest, five miles at the crow flies from the Mexican border.

The section of the trail on Laguna Mountain is occasionally closed by snow in the dead of winter but otherwise is open and available all year long. The views out over the southern California deserts to the east are unparalleled. In places you'll be looking almost straight down from the pine forested top of the range to the cactus covered desert below. In the distance the Salton Sea shimmers like a mirage.

National Recreation Trails

On the Palomar District the self-guided Inaja Nature Trail is located within the Memorial Picnic Grounds dedicated to fire fighters who lost their lives near here in 1956. The elevation is just over 3,200 feet and the vegetation is all mixed brush—manzanita, whitethorn, ceanothus, and scrub oak. People traveling Highway 78 from Escondido through to Anza-Borrego State Park frequently stop here to enjoy the vistas from points on the trail.

CLEVELAND NATIONAL FOREST

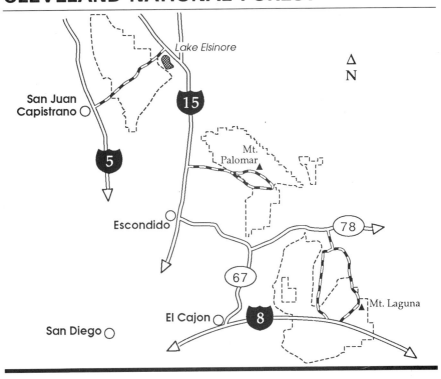

The Observatory Trail is also on the Palomar District, and travels through a forest of mixed conifers from Observatory Campground to the parking lot adjacent to Palomar Observatory. Just over two miles long, the trail climbs gently through the East Mesa Trail in the State Park to the Noble Canyon National Recreation Trail. You'll travel part of the way under Kellogg oaks whose acorns provided the staple food of the Kwaaymii. The people gathered them in the fall just prior to returning to their winter homes in the desert. The elevation is almost all between 4,000 and 5,500 feet. Forest Service volunteers constructed the entire trail within the National Forest.

South of I-8 chaparral dominates and all of the hiking trails will be thickly lined with brush, although one section of the Espinosa Trail is in an oak-riparian woodland. The western end of the Espinosa Trail is in the Pine Creek Wilderness along Espinosa Creek. Winter and spring are the best times to hike this low-altitude trail. The same goes for another entry into Pine Creek Wilderness, the Horsethief Trail, which switchbacks down into the canyon of Pine Valley Creek.

Palomar Ranger District Hiking Trails

At the northern tip of the Palomar District, the Dripping Springs Trail serves as the gateway to Agua Tibia Wilderness. Starting from the Dripping Springs Campground, the trail crosses Arroyo Seco Creek, then starts ascending Agua Tibia Mountain. Low chamise and sage give way to dense stands of unusual twenty-foot high manzanitas and the maroon-trunked desert tree, red shank. As you reach the crest of Agua Tibia Mountain, 6.5 miles from your start, the brush changes to oak woodland and then to a forest of conifers.

From Augua Tibia Mountain, the Magee-Palomar Trail goes south to the edge of Agua Tibia Wilderness through Crosley Saddle and back up to Eagle Crag. Scenic views of Pauma Valley, Eagle Crag, and the San Bernardino Mountains can be observed along the trail, which follows part of the old Crosley Road.

The main east-west connection through the Palomar is along the Cutca Trail, north of Palomar Observatory. It joins the Magee-Palomar Trail in the Agua Tibia Wilderness with the High Point Truck Trail above Oak Grove Campground. From either end of the trail, you'll go down into the southern end of Cutca Valley through some oak woodland. Creeks here are seasonal, and water is scarce. Look for the effects of 6,400-acre Aguanga fire of 1984 which took place to the north of the trail.

South of the observatory, the Barker Valley Trail will take you along seasonal tributaries to the headwaters of the San Luis Rey River. Views of the pot hole lakes and ponds in Mendenhall Valley, the shining observatory domes and towers, and some wildlife prescription burns can be seen from the trails.

Trabuco District Hiking Trails

The Tenaja Trail through the San Mateo Canyon Wilderness is the major developed trail on the Trabuco Ranger District. From Fisherman's Camp at the southwestern edge of the wilderness the trail parallels Blue Water Canyon to Pigeon Spring above Upper San Juan Campground. San Mateo Trail also begins at Fisherman's Camp, but travels southwesterly down San Mateo Canyon almost to the Camp Pendleton Marine Base.

Probably the most spectacular trail in San Mateo Canyon Wilderness is the Morgan Trail from Main Divide Road south to Tenaja Road through the upper part of San Mateo Canyon. Fed by winter's springs and intermittent streams, the San Mateo River has cut a narrow, winding canyon through the sedimentary range. It plunges over a seasonal falls just before it becomes a permanent stream near the southern boundary of the wilderness.

Horsethief and West Horsethief trails pass through the forest east and west from main Divide Road to the north of Ortega Highway. The West Horsethief Trail goes down Trabuco Canyon past Alder Springs and the remains of an old tin mine. Man's search for mineral wealth has left scars and tailings throughout the district.

A long loop hike can be made from Blue Jay Campground off Long Canyon Road using the San Juan and Los Pinos Trails. Going west on San Juan Trail will take you through heavy thickets to the top of the Sugarloaf and then down almost to San Juan Hot Springs and the junction with the Lost Pinos Trail. The Los Pinos Trail climbs the ridge between Hot Springs Canyon and Bell Canyon, with views down into each before reaching the top of Los Pinos Peak outside the campgrounds at your starting place.

Touring, Sightseeing and Special Programs

One of the most active volunteer associations in all the forests of the state is the Laguna Mountain Volunteer Association. This non-profit association is dedicated to assisting the Descanso Ranger District by providing quality recreation experiences and educating visitors to the district and especially to the Laguna Mountain Recreation Area. The members conduct campground

Desert View Picnic Area in Mt Laguna Recreation Area sits right at the edge of the precipice overlooking the Salton Sea and Desert.

activities including nature walks, junior naturalist events, and campfire programs. They staff the visitor information center in the community of Mt. Laguna and maintain all trails within the Recreation Area and in selected locales throughout the District.

The volunteers also assist the Forest Service in the more remote areas of the Descanso by providing foot and mounted patrols in the Pine Creek and Hauser Wildernesses. In addition, the association is the concessionnaire for Laguna and Burnt Ranch campgrounds.

One of the most popular of the interpretive programs at Laguna Mountain is offered jointly by San Diego State University and the Forest Service at the university's observatory off Morris Ranch Road. Called "Star Parties" the night-time programs introduce visitors to the wonders of the firmament on selected summer evenings.

Three short interpretive trails at Mt. Laguna also attract many visitors. Just behind the visitor center you'll spot the Kwaaymii Trail, named for the Native Americans who spent each summer here, coming up from the desert in the springtime to take advantage of the climate, the naturally growing crops, and the plentiful game. Villages located near the laguna meadows were home to several hundred Indians. The half-mile trail introduces you to the Kwaaymii and shows how they lived here on the Forest.

The other two interpretive trails, Desert View Nature Trail and Wooded Hill Nature Trail, have been constructed mostly to take advantage of magnificent viewing points. A trail brochure for the tough Wooded Hill Trail is available at the visitor center. At the top, you'll have a 270 degree panoramic view, and some days, San Diego's Point Loma, sixty-five miles to the west can be seen. On the Desert View Trail, clear days will reveal the Salton Sea far to the east. This trail follows right along the precipitous rim of the mountain.

Automobile Touring

One of the best and most popular tours on the forest takes you through both the Laguna Mountain Recreation Area and the adjacent Cuyamaca Rancho State Park. The tour leaves I-8 at Laguna Junction twenty-seven miles east of El Cajon and goes north on "Sunrise Highway," climbing to the top of the Mt. Laguna Ridge. There's a stunning picnic ground, right at the very edge of the mountaintop called appropriately Desert View, where you can have lunch while enjoying the shimmering views in the distance of Anza-Borrego and Salton Sea.

Stop at the visitor information center in Mt. Laguna where docents from the volunteer association will answer your questions and show you around their museum. Make sure to look at their photo collection, which is gathered in albums displayed in the museum.

The highway will follow the ridge for a few miles and then drop out of the forest and down to Cuyamaca Lake at the edge of the state park. Here you'll turn on to Highway 79 for the southbound leg of your trip through the park and back to the interstate near Descanso.

Another interesting tour begins at the Pala Indian Reservation north of Escondido. Follow Highway 76 up the San Luis Rey River through waterside woodlands to Lake Henshaw, turning north on Highway 7 just before you reach the reservoir. Highway 7 will take you up and up to Crestline where you'll turn to Highway 6 for the last few miles to the top of Palomar Mountain. The observatory and its museum are open to the public almost every day. Just to see the immense telescope is to be awed, and then to realize that the scientists there have seen stars so far away that their light's journey to earth started before there was an earth is to be completely wonderstruck.

On your return trip, check out Palomar Mountain State Park, where the view from Boucher Hill Overlook is incomparable. You'll look down into the Pauma Valley and on to the rounded tops of the Merriam Mountains beyond. Continue on down Highway 6 and back to pala. (Remember—up on Highway 7 and down on Highway 6. Highway 6 is steep!)

Sports

Opportunities for sports on the Cleveland National Forest are different from most of the forests of California because of the terrain. The streams are small and many dry up in the summer and fall. There are few reservoirs, and what there are are subject to severe draw-down. Consequently, fishing is limited to a few spots. hunting is permitted on all three sections of the forest, but is mostly for small game such as rabbits and quail. The thick chaparral cover is too much to mess with for most hunters and the population makes deer hunting a forlorn hope.

However, there is almost endless chances for horseback riders, hikers, and mountain bikers to travel the trails and back roads. Campers and picnickers have limitless choices of places to go and things to do.

While there aren't any downhill skiing facilities on the Cleveland, there is frequently enough snow during January, February, and March for cross-country skiing and lots of room for snow play. As a matter of fact, snow play is one of the most popular activies on the Laguna Mountain Recreation Area. On weekends when snow is present the Forest Service will set up an information station at the Sunrise Highway and I-8 to inform visitors of snow and parking conditions, forest regulations and safety information.

Off Highway Vehicle Travel

Off-highway vehicle travel on the Palomar Ranger District is limited to selected roads on the southern portion of the District. Black Canyon and Orosco Ridge Roads north of Highway 78 are popular, as is the Cedar Creek Road south of Highway 78.

Both Descanso Ranger District and Trabuco Ranger District have special open ORV areas. Corral Canyon Open ORV Area on the Descanso District is an 1,800-acre facility with roads, campgrounds, and "play areas." Additional designated four-wheel and cycle trails extend out from the area to the north and west, effectively enlarging the area to one of the largest in Southern California.

On the Trabuco District, the Wildomar ORV Area can be reached by way of Clinton Keith Road through Slaughterhouse Canyon. From Wildomar campground, you can get to a number of excellent four-wheel routes, including Los Alamos and Tenaja Roads at the edge of San Mateo Canyon Wilderness.

Target Shooting

Target shooting is prohibited on the Trabuco District, but both Palomar and Descanso Districts have set aside specific target shooting areas. Most of all three districts are open to hunting during season.

Areas open to target shooting, "plinking," on the Palomar are pretty much where you'd expect to see them: Away from civilization. The eastern half of the district is practically wide open, while much of the western half is closed. The entire southern section below Highway 78 has been open to target shooting. Of course, regulations change from year to year, so make sure you check in with a ranger before opening fire.

On the Descanso District, less of the forest is open to target shooting, especially near the Laguna Mountain region. A map showing the boundaries of land open to plinking can be obtained from any station on the District.

Mountain Bicycling

Most of the trails and back roads of the Cleveland are open to mountain bicycles, with the exception of the PCT. In many places, however, the land is so steep that mountain bicycles haven't seen a lot of use. Main Divide Road on the Trabuco District has probably the best conditions for mountain biking on the Forest.

From the community of Descanso, cyclists can travel for days on backcountry roads through forest, state park, county, and Indian reservation lands. Ask at the Descanso Ranger Station in Alpine for the best routes.

CLEVELAND NATIONAL FOREST CAMPGROUNDS

	Piped Water	Camp Sites	Trailer Space	Fishing	Boating	Swimming	Store	RV Dump Station	Reservations	Special Attractions
Descanso Ranger District										
Boulder Oaks	•	18	•	•			•			PCT Trailhead
Burnt Rancheria	•	108	•				•			Resorts
Cibbets Flat	•	23		•						
Corral Canyon		14								ORV Area
Laguna	•	105	•				•			Resorts; PCT Trailhead
Agua Dulce	•	6							•	Walk-in
Yerba Santa	•	4	•						•	Wheelchair
Palomar Ranger District										
Dripping Springs	•	26	•							Vail Lake
Fry Creek	•	20								
Indian Flats	•	17								
Oak Grove	•	93	•							
Observatory	•	42	•							
Trabuco Ranger District										
Bluejay	•	51								
El Cariso North	•	24	•							Visitors center
El Cariso South	•	19								Visitors center
Tenaja		5								
Upper San Juan	•	18	•							

(All three ranger districts provide Group Campgrounds.
Contact Ranger Stations on the districts for reservations.)

SAN BERNARDINO
NATIONAL
FOREST

Sacramento

San Francisco

Los Angeles

San Bernardino National Forest

San Bernardino National Forest is the most heavily used forest in southern California. The highest mountain in the southern part of the state tops the San Bernardino Mountain Range. The forest is fragile and it's scenic. In every season people who love the forest's attractions flock to visit it and take part in the fun.

The forest has a tremendous diversity of terrain and habitat. Rocky peaks higher than anywhere else in this part of the state and sheer escarpments that rise vertically from the desert floor. In other places, rolling hills dominate the landscape. There are some huge impoundments of water—Lake Hemet, Big Bear Lake, Lake Arrowhead, and Silverwood Lake—and some boggy meadows and quiet brooks. In many places, barrel cactus and Joshua trees flourish within sight of Jeffrey pines and incense cedars.

There are lots of people living within the forest confines; twenty-four communities with over 35,000 homes. The summer population far exceeds 100,000. Almost all of the land around Lake Arrowhead is privately held, and well over half the shoreline at Big Bear is similarly private. Commercial establishments include ski resorts, campgrounds, resorts, marinas, restaurants, garages, and stores.

Camping

There are twenty-six family campgrounds on the San Bernardino and almost as many group campgrounds. Because fire danger is so great due to the long, dry summers and steep, rough mountain slopes covered with thick vegetation, campfires are restricted to designated sites except by special permit. If you want to camp in a site away from the improved camping places you can stop at any ranger station and pick up the necessary campfire permit.

San Jacinto District Camping

The Boulder Basin Campground is an exceptionally scenic one, overlooking the canyon of Twin Pines Creek. This is the only family campground in the Black Mountain Scenic Area. You'll camp under Jeffrey and lodgepole pines along with white firs. The understory contains some exceptionally large manzanitas, over twenty feet high.

Anglers will enjoy using Dark Canyon, Marion Mountain, and Fern Basin campgrounds. They're all located within a short distance of streams that are regularly planted with catchable-sized trout. Dark Canyon is the lowest at 5,800 feet above sea level, while the other two are up at the 6,400-foot elevation. Tall, widely-spaced conifers guard the campsites at all three of these campgrounds, along with more of the exceptionally large manzanitas. Some of these red-and-green shrubs have trunks on them a foot-and-a-half in diameter.

At the top of Thomas Mountain Ridge across the canyon of the San Jacinto River are a couple of undeveloped campgrounds, Thomas Mountain and Tool Box Spring. Both of these smaller sites can be reached by turning west off Highway 74 just south of Lake Hemet of Forest Road 6S13. Hunters find these camps useful in the season as good headquarters for hunting forays in nearby canyons and creek bottoms. Take your own water to Thomas Mountain, and be prepared to purify the water at Tool Box Spring, and to carry out your own trash.

There is substantial cooperation among the various public agencies that handle camping on the San Jacinto, and if you can't find a camping place in the Forest Service campgrounds, perhaps the state or county sites will suit.

The Idyllwild County Park Campground, a mile west of the community of Idyllwild, has room for much larger RV's—up to thirty feet—than the other camps in the region, as well as hot showers and firewood for sale. The units are well-spaced and sheltered in a mixed forest of ponderosa, Jeffrey and Coulter pines, incense cedars, and Kellogg oaks.

McCall Park, another Riverside County park, is for equestrian camping only. They have fifty-three corrals and can handle up to 125 horses at one time. Two miles of trails within the park connect to many miles of good Forest Service trails. You'll have to bring your own feed.

Hurkey Creek Campground is across the highway from Lake Hemet, and provides for hiking, fishing, and picnicking. Restrooms, showers, and parking for big RV's are other features of the 4,400-foot altitude locality. Some of the oaks in the campground are gigantic, easily covering a fifty-foot diameter circle.

The California State Park system operates two campgrounds in the region: Idyllwild and Stone Creek. Idyllwild, like most state park campgrounds, is fully developed with restrooms, hot showers, and heavy picnic tables with food boxes to frustrate unwanted visitors of the raccoon type. Stone Creek is not as highly developed, but is located in a grove of magnificent pine trees in combination with the huge manzanitas of the San Jacinto.

On Highway 74, twenty-six miles down toward Palm Desert, there's one more USFS campground, Pinyon Flat. Here you'll camp in the high desert surrounded by pinon pines, junipers and sage brush. Look for pinon cones in the fall. By heating them in a foil-lined pan in your oven, you can extract the pine-nuts that were a staple food among high desert-dwelling Native Americans. Across Highway 74 is the dirt road leading to the Santa Rosa Wilderness.

Arrowhead District Campgrounds

Dogwood Campground is the largest and most popular of Arrowhead's four developed camping places. And, it does have dogwoods, their white blooms shining among the dark green foliage in the spring. The campground is near Lake Arrowhead and the community of Rimforest. Huge Jeffrey pines grow all through the camp along with occasional sugar pines. The understory is made up of manzanitas and whitethorn, giving a sense of privacy for campers.

Unique among California's national forests, the Arrowhead District has a campground that's only open on summer week-ends. North Shore's twenty-seven units in one of Lake Arrowhead's side canyons are the closest you can camp to the lake. A trail connects the camp with the PCT and Deep Creek about two miles distant. Deep Creek is the home of large, naturalized brown trout, avidly sought by anglers from all over.

Green Valley and Crab Flats campgrounds are accessed via Green Valley Road off Highway 18 near Arrowbear. Green Valley Campground is past the private property surrounding Green Valley Lake. Sites are under the big pines and firs typical of the San Bernardino crest. Both Crab Flats and Green Valley are near road and trailheads for off-highway vehicles, and enthusiasts use these

Spring skiers get in a last fling at Bear Mountain Ski Resort.

camping places for their headquarters spring through fall.

Big Bear District Campgrounds

Big Bear Ranger District gets lots of use year-round. Its seven campgrounds frequently have plenty of space, if you can get to the mountains during the week. Pineknot, and Serrano campgrounds are all in the Big Bear Lake Basin. Serrano is closest to the water. Located on the north shore of the lake, this camping place is off-limits during the winter and early spring, December 1 to April 1, because of its proximity to the largest bald eagle over-wintering area in southern California. If you're here during January or February, you can take a guided bald eagle tour given by Friends of the Big Bear Valley Preserve. The organization works in concert with The Nature Conservancy and the Forest Service to preserve the eagle's habitat.

Pineknot is located away from the shores of Big Bear on the south side of the basin. It has comfortable campsites in the shelter of the big trees, mostly pines and firs, that grow throughout the camps. This campground is a favorite of families with children. There are tiny creeks for water play, close to civilization at Big Bear Lake Village, and there's just enough room to roam. Serrano Campground has showers, flush toilets, and hookups for RVs.

Hanna Flat Campground is another family favorite. A little farther from the lake, this camp is spread out over a shoulder below Hanna Rocks and

Little Bear Peak. It overlooks the canyon of Holcomb Creek, an easily accessible and good fishing spot. This is the place where Mom or Dad can teach the youngsters how to hook'em. Forest Road 3N14, which connects the campground with the community of Fawnskin on Big Bear Lake's north shore, continues on past the campground and intersects both the PCT and Holcomb Creek within about 1.5 miles. Beyond Holcomb Creek, there's access to both four-wheel drive and motorcycle trails for OHV enthusiasts.

For history buffs, the Holcomb Valley Campground is adjacent to the Holcomb Valley Historic Site. There are remnants of early gold mining relics, and looking for the precious metal is still a popular pastime along the creeks and streams in the area. This is forested land, interspersed with broad meadows.

Cajon District Campgrounds

Although it's only 2.5 miles from Interstate 15 as the crow files, Applewhite Campground is protected from sight and sound of the freeway by Lower Lytle Creek Divide which rises behind the camp. Its chaparral covered slopes form the background against which campers and hikers enjoy themselves. This is the "low country" of the San Bernardino, and the campground is only 3,300 feet. This means plenty of heat in the summer, but good camping conditions the rest of the year.

Remote camping is your other choice on the district and several recommended sites are available, most of them on roads too tough for the family sedan. Four-wheelers will enjoy staying at Paiute Campground. Stone House Crossing campgrounds, on the Middle Fork of Lytle Creek, are for hikers headed into Cucamonga Wilderness.

San Gorgonio District Campgrounds

There are more than 225 family camping units on the San Gorgonio District, all within five or six miles of each other above the Santa Ana River along Highway 38. Barton Flats is the first one you come to on the way up the hill from Redlands and Mentone; Heart Bar, recently completely reconstructed, is the last. In between are San Gorgonio and South Fork campgrounds. All four of them are located in the pines: Barton Flats and San Gorgonio on a branch of Barton Creek, and Heart Bar and South Fork on branches of the Santa Ana River. Grayback Amphitheater is centered in the middle of these camping places and summer interpretive programs are featured during the camping season. The summer programs range from sing-alongs and contests to films and slide shows depicting the natural history of the forest.

These are wonderful family campsites, located on broad, flat savannahs, with tall Jeffrey and sugar pines towering above. You can hike into the San Gorgonio Wilderness from trailheads throughout the region, fish in the Santa Ana River or Jenks Lake, both of which are regularly stocked, or ride horseback on miles of trails beyond Heart Bar equestrian camp.

On The Trail

Hiking and backpacking bring outdoors people to the forest all year long. The Pacific Crest Trail travels almost 200 miles through the forest and there are about thirteen miles of National Recreation trails. More than 400 other trails criss-cross the forest in and outside of the wildernesses.

Pacific Crest Trail

The portion of the Pacific Crest National Trail on the San Bernardino National Forest runs for almost 200 miles from Lookout Mountain at the southern border of the San Jacinto District north through the San Jacinto Wilderness, across I-10 into San Gorgonio and Big Bear districts. It then goes west to Wright Mountain above Wrightwood in the far northwestern portion of the forest.

This segment of the trail passes through a wide variety of ecosystems from desert to alpine. Swollen streams and difficult crossings should be expected in the spring. However, spring is the best time of year to travel the trail. Access points to the trail are on every ranger district and are close enough together most of the time to make short hikes as well as long ones equally possible.

National Recreation Trails

The Camp Creek Trail, 3.6 miles in length, begins near Highway 18 about a mile east of Snow Valley Ski Resort at an elevation of 6,900 feet and drops 2,100 feet through a series of switchbacks to Bear Creek. Along the way you'll pass through pine and oak woodlands, some brush, and lots of wildflowers, especially penstemons, lupines, and vetch. At Bear Creek you stand a chance of seeing a real beaver, although deer and quail are more common. Both brown and rainbow trout inhabit Bear Creek in good numbers.

A thirty-foot waterfall, meadows filled with blooms, and mixed stands of pines, oaks, and firs, are some of the sights along the North Shore Trail. This 5.2 mile hike is on the north side of Lake Arrowhead on the Arrowhead Ranger District. It crosses two streams on its way to several fine viewing points at the higher elevations. About a mile east of Rock Camp Station you can look down Willow Creek Canyon all the way to the shadowy bottoms of Deep Creek.

Fairly light use can be expected on the Sugarloaf Trail, which begins at Green Canyon Creek southeast of Big Bear Lake and winds five miles up to the top of Sugarloaf Mountain. The climb is a steep one, from 7,400 to almost 10,000 feet, but the view from the top is worth it. You'll look out over San Gorgonio Mountain to the south, Big Bear Valley, the Santa Ana River drainage, and the vast Mojave Desert.

Hiking on the San Jacinto District

Special circumstances affect hikers on the San Jacinto Ranger District because of the location of Mt. San Jacinto State Park within the National Forest boundaries. It's in the San Jacinto State and National Forest Wilderness where confusion sometimes arises. If you're going to camp overnight you'll need a permit from the State, if you're staying on the State Wilderness, a permit from the Forest Service if you're going to camp on the National Forest. Day use only permittees may use either.

Day use is only limited on the Devil's Slide Trail on weekends and holidays from Memorial Day through Labor Day weekend. Since the trail is on National Forest land and the number is limited, you cannot get a permit for this trail from the State Parks office.

One of the most remarkable trips to be had in this region is on the Palm Springs Aerial Tramway. This largest double-reversible passenger-carrying tramway travels from the desert within the city of Palm Springs to the eastern edge of Mt. San Jacinto State Park. Park your car at the valley station and

The area around Mt. San Jacinto boasts manzanitas of near-record size.

be whisked to the top in about fifteen minutes and be on the trail among gigantic Jeffrey and sugar pines the minute you step off.

Two of the favorite hikes from the top of the tram go to Mt. San Jacinto, a distance of just under six miles, and to Round Valley, a comfortable 1.7 miles. Or, you can have someone meet you at Idyllwild and make a shuttle trip through one or both wilderness areas.

The Fuller Ridge section of the PCT is another good introduction to the San Jacinto high country. It starts on Black Mountain Road north of the Boulder Basin Campground. It's an easy hike for the first five miles and then climbs steeply to the top of San Jacinto Peak. It travels along the high, timbered ridge above Snow Creek offering spectacular views of the desert near Palm Springs.

A somewhat easier walk is on the Deer Springs Trail. This is the easiest of the moderate trails in the region, with a gradual elevation gain of 1,900 feet to the top of the dome-shaped granite outcrop called Suicide Rock on the north side of Strawberry Valley. It offers a splendid panorama of the valley floor, dense forest, the village of Idyllwild, and the rugged granite cliffs of Lily Rock. The trail begins right in the community of Idyllwild near the County Visitors' Center.

A trail into Santa Rosa Wilderness starts about a mile up Forest Road 7S01 across from Pinyon Flat Campground. Part of the time you'll be walking the cottonwoods and sycamores of Horsethief Creek Canyon, but most of the time you'll be doing desert hiking through chaparral and cactus. This area is so

SAN BERNARDINO NATIONAL FOREST

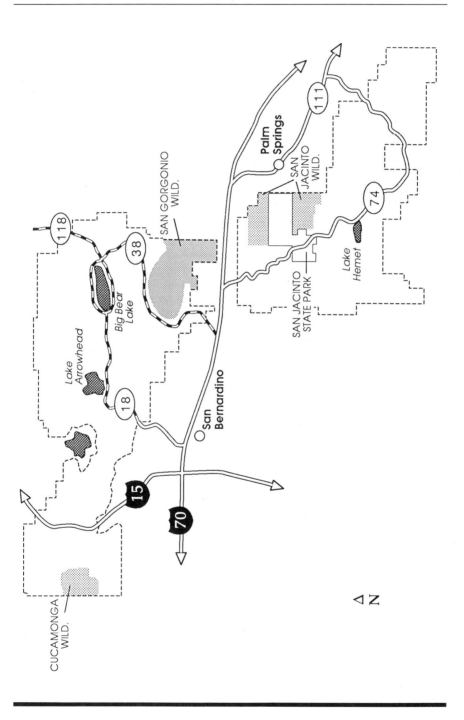

different from the Idyllwild area, you'll have trouble believing they're in the same National Forest. You might, with luck, be able to see the most famous residents of the Santa Rosa—bighorn sheep.

Arrowhead District Hiking

The PCT travels for forty miles on the Arrowhead District, but perhaps the most interesting and scenic is the fifteen-mile section between Holcomb Crossing and the Mojave River Flood Control Dam. You spend the entire trip walking along either Deep Creek or Holcomb Creek, and travel through a wide variety of plant life from cactus to pines and firs. There are hot springs along the way, as well as a granite gorge—Devil's Hole. This makes a great shuttle trip, and if you're going to fish Deep Creek, remember barbless hooks only and a limit of two trout.

The charms of Willow Creek makes the Metate Trail an excellent choice for a half-day—or even a full-day—outing. You pick up the trail just to the east of Rock Camp Station and follow it down Line Creek to Willow Creek. The trail sticks close to the water as it tumbles down the canyon through a thick forest cove. After covering four miles, you'll reach a jeep road (FR 3N34). This is the end of this section of the trail, but intrepid explorers may want to follow an unmarked trail to the PCT at Deep Creek. The lower trail is partially covered with brush, and somewhat more difficult to maneuver than the upper section, so allow plenty of time to make the trip.

Hiking on the Big Bear District

The Pacific Crest Trail section on the Big Bear District is consistently easy, with outstanding scenery, vistas, and varying topography. Portions of the trail can be used for day hiking, overnight hikes, or even short nature walks. Near Onyx Summit at the eastern part of the district the trail makes a wide sweeping turn down into Arrastre Creek and up on to Nelson Ridge. Although you can't actually see it from the trail, about halfway through this stretch you'll be overlooking the "world record Joshua Tree," largest in the world. (the largest lodgepole pine in the world is at the opposite end of Big Bear Lake.) Another interesting section of the PCT goes up into the upper reaches of Holcomb Creek north of the lake.

A tough hike for fishermen is the Siberia Creek Trail, which goes from the Champion Lodgepole Pine down Siberia Creek to Bear Creek. It's seven miles down into Bear Creek, and the lower two-thirds of the trip is quite steep. Fishing can be good for both brown and rainbow trout, although it does get brushy as you descend, making for some tough fishing.

A moderately difficult trail, but well worth the trip, is the Pineknot Trail. The three-mile walk will take you from Aspen Glen picnic area near the south shore of Big Bear Lake up to the top of the ridge to the south at Grand View Point. Views of Big Bear Lake through stands of white fir and Jeffrey pine timber can be enjoyed all the way up . Make a picnic of it, and spend the lunch hour at the top enjoying the almost 360 degree view out over the lake and the surrounding ridges.

The Cougar Crest Trail begins across Highway 38 from Meadows' Edge picnic grounds on the north shore of the lake. The two-mile trail traverses a mixed conifer forest of junipers and pinon pines, and there are some outstanding views of Big Bear Lake before you reach the PCT near the top of Bertha Peak. On a bright, breezy day waves and white-caps on the lake cause it to sparkle, its blue-green surface contrasting with the white sails of catamarans darting across the wind.

Hiking on the Cajon District

The Cajon is generally the lowest altitude section of the San Bernardino, and you may not think of it as a hiking section of the forest. However, a long section of the Pacific Crest Trail goes through the Cajon, and there are a couple of high country trails on the Cucamonga Wilderness where you won't have a lot of competition.

Just south of the community of Wrightwood, the PCT enters the Cajon District on the slopes of Wright Mountain. Then it begins to drop down Blue Ridge and Upper Lytle Creek Divide, crossing and recrossing the jeep road on top of the ridge. It drops down into Lone Pine Canyon, crosses I-15, and heads east into Little Horsethief Canyon. There are several points where you can get on it for short hikes or longer ones. After it comes down from Wright Mountain, most of the way is through think stands of chaparral and occasional junipers and pinons.

A wilderness permit must be obtained for either day hikes or overnight camping before you enter the Cucamonga Wilderness on the Middle Fork or Wilderness Crest trails. The Middle Fork Trail takes the eastern approach to the Cucamonga, coming up through the canyon of the Middle Fork of Lytle Creek. It's a tough hike with a climb of 3,600 feet in about 5.5 miles. From the chaparral at the beginning of the trail, you climb through succesive belts of junipers, pinons, and big cone Douglas firs, sugar and Jeffrey pines, and end up in the cool high country of the lodgepoles and white firs. The Cucamonga herd of bighorn sheep occupies this portion of the wilderness, and the members of your party with real sharp eyes may spot one. You actually almost have to catch them when they're moving to see them, because their coloration is such that they blend perfectly with the background rocks and shrubbery.

The Wilderness Crest Trail travels through the wilderness from north to south traversing the highest peaks in the area. Thunder Mountain, Telegraph Peak, Timber Mountain, and Cucamonga Peak are all approached by this sub-alpine trail as you make your way through the wilderness. You'll zig-zag over crests and saddles and through open stands of firs, pines and some incense cedars. From Telegraph Peak, the view of the desert rivals that from the top of Mt. San Antonio (Old Baldy), highest in the San Gabriel Range.

San Gorgonio District Hiking

The San Gorgonio Wilderness, with magnificent San Gorgonio Mountain, provides most of the hiking opportunities on this District. There are seven trailheads around the perimeter of the wilderness; all of them get you into the high country in a hurry. South Fork Trailhead is used the most because there used to be campsites within a short distance—1.5 miles and 1.8 miles. But they're now closed because of overuse. It's 8.7 miles to top of San Gorgonio Mountain and its Summit Camp. You'll travel through wide open meadows part of the way, and through thick groves of lodgepoles as you go from one part of the wilderness to another.

Aspen Grove and Fish Creek trailheads on the east side of the wilderness start you at the highest points. 7,400 and 8,200 feet respectively. Aspens arre very rare on the San Bernardino, and one of only two known groves on the

Mountain biking near Crab Flats. Gail Van Der Bie photo.

forest are encountered along Fish Creek near Fish Creek Meadows. Both trails are very near the wilderness, and you'll be in it within a very short time after leaving your auto.

From the south side of the Wilderness, the Vivian Creek trailhead leads to a trail built in 1898 to the top of Mt. San Gorgonio from Mill Creek Canyon at Big Falls Picnic Area. There are several campsides along the seven mile trail to the top, and all of them have water. Hikers use this trail and nearby Momyer Creek Trailhead in winter because of their southern exposure. Trails are steep if you travel directly up the mountain, but side trails ease off a bit and lead to camping places and interesting locations among the meadows and granite.

Outside of the wilderness, Wildhorse Creek Trail, should appeal to hikers. The trail begins just west of Heart Bar turn-off from Highway 38 and contours north to a junction with Sugarloaf National Recreation Trail. The way follows the ridge above Wildhorse creek about three miles before dropping down to cross the creek and then follow it up to the remote camping area near Wildhorse Meadows. While on the ridge on the way up you'll be looking out over the canyons and valley of the Santa Ana River and beyond to the crystalline peaks of the San Gorgonio Wilderness.

There is some interesting desert hiking in the far southeastern portions of the San Gorgonio District in the newly added sections of San Gorgonio Wilderness on the drainages of the Whitewater River. Baywood Flat Trail and Millard Canyon Trail, both rated moderately difficult take you into the high desert above the Morongo Indian Reservation. Both can be accessed by using Millard Canyon Road off I-10 east of Banning. These are winter and spring hikes at about the 5,000-foot level.

Touring, Sightseeing, and Special Programs

Automobile touring enthusiasts have plenty of things to see and do on the San Bernardino National Forest. All five ranger districts have special programs to interest visitors, ranging from self-guided nature trails, to lookouts, arboretums and a National Children's Forest.

Highway 18 enters the Forest from the city of San Bernardino below Crestline and travels east along the very crest of the mountain range past the big lakes and out into the Mojave Desert on the northeast. An alternative is to turn south on Highway 38 at Big Bear Lake and loop back into San Bernardino via the Santa Ana River Valley, Metone and Redlands. Either way, you'll be seeing the fascinating things of the Forest.

First stop is at **Baylis Park** picnic area, about a mile before you come to Rimforest. This little park sits right at the edge of the world, and from the picnic sites you can look out over the cities and towns from San Bernardino to the Pacific. In clear weather, the peaks of the San Jacinto Mountains stand against the changing sky to the southeast like sentinels guarding their mysteries against all intruders.

Arrowhead Ranger Station is in Sky Forest, right on the highway. Stop for pamphlets and information explaining the Forest and ask any questions about the Forest. Visitors are welcome, too, at the Strawberry Peak fire lookout just across from the ranger station at Rimforest. A two-mile drive will take you to the top of Strawberry Peak. From the parking area you ascend the fire tower for views in every direction. Besides the cities, towns and peaks to the south and west, you'll see down to the busy, privately-owned shores of Lake Arrowhead and beyond.

Heaps Peak Arboretum, just west of Heaps Peak, was dedicated in 1984, but its story really began almost seventy years before. 1922 witnessed a huge wildfire that left this site completely devastated. In 1928, replanting of the area began, and in 1931 it was called "Heaps Peak Reforestation Project." Tree planting continued until World War II put a stop to it, and in 1955 another fire burned over the area, but not doing as much damage as the '22 burn. In 1982, the Mountain Chapter of the San Bernardino County Museum Association, (now known as Rim of the World Interpretive Association), received permission from the Forest Service to develop the site into an arboretum.

Three-fourths of the way through this 3/4-mile trail, you will come to a grove of fifty-year-old giant sequoias. From the bridge on the path, you can look up into the great trees, already among the largest in the arboretum, and imagine what they'll be like in a thousand years. In addition to the big trees, there are dogwoods, Coulter pines, knobcone pines, currants, bracken, aspen, whitethorn, and much more

Next stop is the **National Children's Forest**. Turn at FR 1N96 at Deer Lick Station for the three-mile drive to this tiny forest located in one of the most scenic areas of the San Bernardino National Forest. The area was burned during the Bear Fire of 1970. The "Trail of the Phoenix" is a handicapped-accessible nature trail through the area that was planted after the fire. The interpretive signs along the trail and in colorful print and braille.

As you approach the dam at the foot of Big Bear Lake you'll have to make a decision on whether to take Highway 38 around the north side or Highway 18 round the south side. On Highway 38 you'll pass the winter bald eagle resting sites near Grout Bay, and the turn-off to Holcomb Valley and its Gold Rush Remnants. On Highway 18, you'll go through the city of Big Bear Lake, the side roads to the ski resorts, and an occasional sighting of rock climbers on the sheer granite heights of Castle Rock.

If you choose to go on Highway 38, stop at the Big Bear District Ranger Station and pick up the pamphlet "Gold Fever Trail Self-Guided Tour." This will take you through the now-peaceful Holcomb Valley where the saga of early miners is still recorded. It's a fascinating tour through mining sites, cabins, a "hangin' tree", arrastres, the remains of Belleville, and a lone grave. Allow about three hours for the drive, which covers about eleven miles of dirt road and nine of state highway.

On the San Gorgonio Ranger District, USFS staff have constructed four self-guided nature trails, all of which are easily reached from the campgrounds in the Barton Flats area. The **Ponderosa Nature Trail** begins at the junction of Highway 38 and the Jenks Lake Road. It's an easy .6-mile walk through tall ponderosas and the manzanita understory. Interpretive signs include information on plants, wildlife, and Forest Service management.

Associated with the Ponderosa Trail is **Whispering Pines Nature Trail**, designed for use by the blind. Interpretive signs are in large print and braille, and a cord stretches the full half-mile of the trail to guide the seeing-impaired. The trail is a wonderful challenge to you to use all of your senses; to smell the duff of the forest floor, and touch the smooth manzanita limbs and sharp-prickly ponderosa cones. Listen for the sounds, too. Trunks of trees groan when the wind moves them; squirrels scold, and dry leaves rustle.

For a nature trail with outstanding views of the Santa Ana River Valley and Barton Flats, take **Hidden Cliffs Nature Trail** from the parking lot at Jenks Lake. Ponderosa and sugar pines keep the trail in the shade for most of the trip.

The longest of the trails is the **Rio Monte Nature Trail** which begins at the Barton Flats Information Center and ends 2.5 miles later at Rio Monte Overlook beyond the campgrounds and the amphitheater. Twenty-five interpretive signs tell the story of Barton Flats and the natural surroundings.

Also on the San Gorgonio District there's the chance to see the highest waterfall on the Forest. Follow Highway 38 to Forest Home Road and drive to its end. The .3-mile walk begins at the end of the pavement and proceeds north across Mill Creek Wash to within 200 yards of the falls on Vivian Creek. Two other falls, Monkeyface Falls and Forest Falls, also can be seen along Forest Home Road. Late winter and early spring are best viewing times, especially in years when there's been a heavier than usual snow fall.

In the western section of the Forest, Highway 138 swings up Cajon Canyon toward Valyermo and Palmdale. About two miles west of Interstate 15, you'll come to **Mormon Rocks.** These formations stand out from the surrounding desert in what are called "hogbacks." Pockmarked and weatherworn, they are a series of naturally cemented sandstone beds tipped up on edge by movement of the earth's tectonic plates. Behind the Forest Service fire station, and across a small footbridge, a well-marked half-mile nature trail winds through manzanita, yucca, chamise, sage, and other high desert plants to a vista providing a view of the Cajon Summit region in one direction and the Upper Lytle Creek Divide and Cucamonga Wilderness in another. To the north, the Mormon Rocks are clearly seen, including the small holes and caves that are home to pack rats, owls, and lizards. The Mormon Trail from Salt Lake City to San Bernardino passed through the canyon below you in the last century.

Each of the ranger districts, except Cajon, on the San Bernardino National Forest has a "handout" called "Where to go from here," and the one printed for the San Jacinto District has quantities of information about touring opportunities. First on its list you'll find the **Idyllwild County Visitors' Center.** This modern building just off the highway north of Idyllwild adjacent to the Riverside County campgrounds offers museum displays interpreting early days on the mountain, as well as short natural history walks.

About eight miles north of Idyllwild, you'll come to **Fuller Mill Creek.** There's a picnic ground here and a well-worn trail beside the whispering waters of the creek. Willows make up much of the understory near the creek, with the huge San Jacinto manzanitas on drier slopes.

Other creeks to walk along near Idyllwild include **Strawberry Creek**, which runs right through town, and the **North Fork of the San Jacinto River** near Dark Canyon campground. From May until late June, an estimated 1,000 flowering dogwoods put on an unmatched display in Dark Canyon. Their white flowers sparkle among evergreen pines and cedars. In the fall, the leaves turn orange-red, and along with willows, poison oak, and sumac, give a touch of fall color in the predominately evergreen forest.

Drive up Strawberry Creek Canyon to **Humber Park** for a staggering view of Lily Rock. With binoculars you can watch the rock climbers trying to get the best of this granite monolith. In the summer, this is the most used entrance point for hikers into the San Jacinto Wilderness via Devil's Slide Trail. Walk back down to Idyllwild on the **Ernie Maxwell Scenic Trail.** This easy 2.5-mile downhill jaunt takes you through a magnificent forest of Jeffrey pines and a continuous panorama of Strawberry Valley and the surrounding mountains, some with lingering snow.

Sometimes a picnic beside the waters of a mountain lake will make your day, and the San Jacinto has two lakes that fit the bill perfectly. **Lake Hemet**, ten miles south of Idyllwild is a favorite spot for both anglers and picnickers. The picnic area is located on the north shore, with Thomas Mountain reflecting on the lake's surface when the water is calm. **Lake Fulmor** is about ten miles northwest of Idyllwild. Much smaller than Lake Hemet and tightly enclosed in the forest, Lake Fulmor gives a wilder, more mountainous feeling. A short nature trail through the forest of pines, manzanitas, and Kellogg oaks helps visitors interpret the local vegetation.

Sports

Winter sports, especially downhill skiing, are one of the largest single attractions on the San Bernardino National Forest. Furthermore, whether it's Nordic or alpine skiing, inner tubing, snowshoeing, or just rolling around in the stuff, it's the fastest growing recreation activity on the Forest.

For skiers **Snow Summit, Snow Valley, Bear Mountain, Snow Forest**, and **Ski Green Valley** ski resorts, reached via Highways 18 or 38 are open at the first sign of snow each winter, sometimes well into April. Because snow-making has become such an art, most of these resorts are able to pile up tons of man-made snow even if the clouds won't cooperate. Consequently, there's good skiing for several months each year.

Snow Summit, Snow Forest, and Bear Mountain are on the slopes above Big Bear Lake, while Snow Valley and Ski Green Valley are between Running Springs and Big Bear. Green Valley (not the same as **Ski** Green Valley) is the favorite of many cross-country skiers with both loop and one-way trails. One ten-mile trail connects Green Valley with Fawnskin on the north shore of Big Bear Lake. The tour in long, but there are few steep sections, and the snow is reliable.

Boating and Water Skiing

Getting out on the water for recreation continues to grow in interest on the Forest. Having the huge impoundments in what is basically an arid environment draws thousands of boaters, water-skiers, and fishermen.

Boaters are out on **Big Bear Lake** and **Lake Arrowhead** just as soon as weather permits in the spring until the snow flies in late autumn. Arrowhead is entirely private, but Big Bear has about 50% of its shoreline on the Forest. **Lake Silverwood** is now under state control, and is open year round for boating and water-skiing.

Over on the San Jacinto District, only **Lake Hemet** permits boating. The launch ramp is on private property at the east end of the lake, and launching from National Forest controlled shore is not permitted.

The smaller lakes on the Forest are usually open for car-toppers and inflatables. **Lake Gregory** permits small electric motors and anglers enjoy both Lake Gregory and Green Valley Lake.

Off Road Motoring

Four-wheeling, three-wheeling, and dirt biking are among the many activities the San Bernardino National Forest has to offer. Licensed, street-legal vehicles are generally permitted on all roads open to the public. In addition, the Forest has an Off-Highway Vehicle Trail System brochure which shows those roads and trails open to "green sticker" or non-street-legal vehicles such as all-terrain three-wheelers and dirt bikes.

Much of the OHV activity is centered on the Arrowhead District, with some spilling over on the Big Bear and Cajon. The major staging area are near **Rock Camp Station, Crab Flats**, and **Cactus Flat**. From all three of these locations, you can get into the back country north, east, and west of the big lakes. There are trails for beginners as well as advanced and expert rides. Check in at any ranger station for your copy of the OHV brochure, which describes legal routes and equipment.

Mountain Biking

Among the fastest growing activities in the mountains is hitting the trail on mountain bicycles. Even some ski resorts are getting in on the act, offering lift rides to the top of the ridge in the off seasons when the snow has melted. You can ride on any road open to motor vehicles on the Forest, and bike riding is permitted, although not encouraged, on trails that are not part of the wilderness system or the PCT where their use is prohibited. These trails were developed for hikers and horses, so bicycles can pose a safety hazard to hikers and especially to equestrians.

Hunting and Fishing

The San Bernardino offers the best trout fishery in Southern California. On the San Jacinto, Lakes Fulmor and Hemet are regularly stocked with catchable sized rainbows, as are Fuller Mill and Strawberry Creeks, and the North Fork San Jacinto River in Dark Canyon.

Lytle Creek on the Cajon District is stocked for "put and take" fishing as is the Santa Ana River above Seven Oaks on the San Gorgonio District. But the best stream fishing is to be found on Deep Creek, Holcomb Creek, and Bear Creek on the Arrowhead and Big bear District.

All of the lakes on the Forest, except Lake Arrowhead, are regularly planted by the California State Department of Fish and Game, and both shore fishermen and boaters stand a chance of hooking some good ones. Both Holcomb and Deep creeks are classified as "wild trout fisheries" and require that you fish with a single barbless hook, use only artificial lures, and keep only two fish.

Most hunters who go into the back country of the San Bernardino are searching for deer or quail. There is a small population of band-tailed pigeons, and upland shooters occasionally bag a few. Bear hunters, too, come to the Forest. In recent years an attempt has been made to establish a wild turkey population to broaden the number of targets for hunters. Ninety birds were released in 1988 in three different areas of the Forest in hopes that they'll naturalize and become a part of the Forest environment.

Much of the Forest is open to hunting during the seasons established by state and county authorities, but those who go for target shooting and "plinking" are restricted to certain areas. Among the favorite plinking and target areas are those on the Cajon District near Lytle Creek, which have become so popular that they are now regulated by a permittee. This is now a "charge area," and a small fee is collected. Any ranger station can give you directions to areas in their part of the Forest where you can target shoot.

SAN BERNARDINO NATIONAL FOREST CAMPGROUNDS

	Piped Water	Camp Sites	Trailer Space	Fishing	Boating	Swimming	Store	RV Dump Station	Reservations	Special Attractions
Arrowhead Ranger District										
Crab Flats		29	22'							
Dogwood		93	22'					•	•	Amphitheather, nature trail
Green Valley		36	22'							
North Shore		27	22'							
Toll Road		10	22'							
Big Bear Ranger District										
Big Pine Flat		19	16'							
Grout Bay		23	16'	•						
Hanna Flat		88	16'							
Holcomb Valley		19	16'							
Horse Springs		17								
Pineknot		52	16'							
Serrano	•	55	50'	•	•		•	•		
Cajon Ranger District										
Applewhite		44	22'	•						
San Gorgonio Ranger District										
Barton Flats		47	21'							
San Gorgonio		60	24'						•	
South Fork		23	16'							
Heart Bar		100	30'							
San Jacinto Ranger District										
Boulder Basin		34								
Dark Canyon		22	22'							
Fern Basin		22	15'							
Pinyon Flat		18	15'							
Marion Mountain		26	15'							
Herkey Creek County Pk		105	40'							
Idyllwild County Park		90	22'							
Idyllwild (State Park)		33	24'							
Stone Creek		50	24'							

ANGELES
NATIONAL
FOREST

Sacramento

San Francisco

Los Angeles

Angeles National Forest

Remarkable and astounding, fascinating and wonderful are adjectives used repeatedly to describe the Angeles National Forest in the "back yard" of the Los Angeles Metropolitan Area. Sixteen million people live within two hours of the Forest, and yet, with all the pressure, it remains an oasis of calm at the edge of cacaphony.

The Forest covers more than 650,000 acres, and is as diverse in appearance and terrain as the diversity represented by the population it serves. Elevations range from 1200 to 10,064 feet. Much of the Forest is covered by dense chaparral which changes to pine and fir-covered slopes as you reach the majestic peaks of the higher elevations. Wildflowers, birds of all kinds, and mammals big and small overspread the landscape throughout the Forest.

Camping

Angeles National Forest has more than 100 developed campground and picnic sites on its five ranger districts. You can choose form a wide variety of camping places—from the cool, secluded forest sites found in the high country, to sunny, streamside locations at the lower elevations. Besides the family campgrounds, there are eight large, group campgrounds that can be reserved for as many as 300 people. At the present time, all family campgrounds are on a first come, first served basis, although plans are being considered that would allow for reservations at some sites.

Arroyo Seco District Camping

Two of the most beautiful campgrounds in southern California, Buckhorn and Chilao, are located along the Angeles Cress Highway on the Arroyo Seco Ranger District. Buckhorn, especially, will remind you of camping in the remote Sierra Nevada. Set in a canyon of tall incense cedars and mixed conifers, a branch of Little Rock Creek runs through it lined with rare ferns. The Burkhart Trail follows the stream down Buckhorn Canyon, where there is fishing and waterplay for those who hike the distance.

At Chilao, a recently rebuilt and upgraded campground, you'll camp on a broad savannah dotted with widely spaced big timber. Ponderosa and sugar pines tower over the campsites.

Hiking trails, including the Silver Moccasin National Recreation Trail, go in several directions from Chilao. The Chilao Visitor Center is among the finest in the country, and you'll enjoy visiting the displays as well as taking advantage of its interpretive programs. There are campfires, guided nature walks, and children's activities planned by the Forest Rangers. The center is also noted for bird observations. Birders will find dozens of varieties in any given season form mountain quail and bandtailed pigeons to warblers, kinglets, and hummers. Grassy meadows and panoramic views of canyons and peaks complete the picture.

Horn Flats campground is located on the Santa Clara Divide Road north of Angeles Crest Highway a mile or so beyond Chilao. Like Sulphur Springs campground, closer to the high desert, it is used by families enjoying the out-of-doors.

All four of these campgrounds are in the middle altitudes, from 5,200 to 6,500 feet, thus the appearance is of broad meadows laced with big pines, cedars, and occasional firs, combined with the yucca and sagebrush of the arid southwest.

There are also a number of trail camps on the Arroyo Seco, such as Little Jimmy and Cooper Canyon, both on the Pacific Crest Trail, and Idlehour and Mt. Lowe above Altadena, that are open to those who want to backpack. Devore and Spruce Grove are on Gabrielino National Recreation Trail above Chantry Flat in the "front country."

Mt. Baldy District Camping

Two major recreation areas are located on the Mt. Baldy Ranger District, Crystal Lake in San Gabriel Canyon, and Mt. Baldy, with Crystal Lake having the most developed camping opportunities. The Crystal Lake Campground high up in the canyon has 176 campsites spread under the pines—Jeffrey, Coulter, and sugar. There's also a visitor center open week-ends the year round, and a small store providing basic food and grocery service, ice and firewood.

Forest Ranger-naturalists lead nature walks and campfire programs during the summer season. There are four self-guided nature trails for which brochures are available at the center.

Halfway up San Gabriel Canyon, you'll come to the Coldbrook campground at the 3,350-foot altitude point. This charming little campground is sheltered in a riparian forest along the banks of the North Fork of San Gabriel River. At one time the location of a private hunting lodge and later a CCC camp, traces of its historical past can be spotted under the native alders and pines, and in the introduced sequoias, cedars and spruce trees.

Over in the Mt. Baldy Village area in San Antonio Canyon, the Manker Flat campground accommodates twenty-two families in an open pine forest up at 6,300 feet. Hikers enjoy this campground, with its trails going into two different wildernesses—Cucamonga and Sheep Mountain—as well as shorter day hikes to San Antonio Falls, Devil's Backbone and Bear Canyon.

Saugus District Camping

The Saugus Ranger district is separated from the rest of the Angeles National Forest by a corridor containing the Antelope Valley Freeway, and has more developed camping places than any of the other four districts on the Forest. Pyramid, Castaic, and Elizabeth Lakes are on—or partially on—the Saugus District, and account for much of its attraction.

The campgrounds away from the lakes are squeezed into the riparian woodlands along the creek bottoms in such places as Bouquet Canyon and Elizabeth Lake Canyon. Most of the campgrounds are small, with many having fewer than ten sites. About half of the campgrounds are kept open all year long in this low-altitude portion of the forest.

Two beckoning campgrounds in Elizabeth Lake Canyon are Cottonwood and Prospect. Their locations are almost identical along the canyon bottom, one at Prospect at 2,100 feet and Cottonwood at 2,600 feet. In both cases, the year-round creek flows through the campgrounds and provides a place for kids to play and sounds of water gurgling around the rocks and boulders to lull campers to sleep at night. At Prospect, the Forest Service has erected

The oldest ranger station in California was built for $75 near the turn of the century.

privacy screens at each site. The ells created make each site's cooking and dining areas quite private.

Campers who want to stay near Pyramid Lake have two choices, basically, north of the lake at Los Alamos (or Hardluck on the Los Padres National Forest), or ten miles south of the lake at Oak Flat campground. Los Alamos is nearest the recreation areas at the lake, and has ninety-three campsites spread out over the flats in lower Hungry Valley. Oak Flat campground is on Old Highway 99 adjacent to the Oak Flat Ranger Station. The oaks are mostly scrub oaks, although some valley live oaks are present with welcome shade. The heat build-up in the summer can be pretty terrific, consequently spring, late fall, and even winter are the most comfortable camping periods here.

Five campgrounds line the road up Bouquet Canyon above the town of Saugus, form Zuni at the lower end to The Falls at the top. Sycamores, willows, black oaks, cottonwoods, and alders provide shade for campers and shelter for countless birds. Flycatchers, both ash-throated and western, are common, as are the canyon wrens and bushtits. Scrub jays will wake you at dawn with their raucaus calls, and appear for a hand-out with little provocation.

Tujunga District Camping

The Tujunga is a large District with only three developed campgrounds, so opportunities for dispersed activities are greater here.

Monte Cristo campground, on the banks of Mill Creek, can be reached just off the Angeles Forest Highway a dozen miles beyond its turn-off from the Angeles Crest Highway. Oaks, cedars, and ponderosa pines are dotted through the camp spots, and you'll stand a good chance of spotting squirrels, cottontail rabbits, and maybe even a raccoon or skunk coming to the water. For sure, you'll be serenaded by coyotes at night as they greet the rising moon.

On the northern boundary of the District, you'll find little Soledad campground. This isolated camping place is great to "disappear" to in the winter or early spring. It's only two miles from access to the Pacific Crest Trail, and hikers use it as a rendezvous point.

Up on top of the Forest on the partly paved road that goes from Mill Creek Summit west to Mt. Gleason and Messenger Peak, you'll find the Messenger Flats campground. The PCT passes Messenger Flats at its edge, and campers here have access to that trail and several others, as well as having some spectacular views. You can see all the way to the Mojave Desert on the north and Big Tujunga Canyon to the south. Don't try to pull a trailer up here but do come up to see the lights of Los Angeles on one of its oh-so-rare clear evenings. It's an unforgettable sight.

Valyermo District Camping

The Valyermo Ranger District contains two important recreation areas—Big Pines and Littlerock Canyon.

Littlerock Recreation Area is one of the major off-highway vehicle areas of the Angeles, and Basin campground has direct access to the off-road vehicle area. Fishing is popular, too, along the shores of Littlerock Reservoir as well as upstream in the many pools of Little Rock Creek. Lakeside and Juniper Grove campgrounds are small units located close to the shore of the reservoir. The altitude here is just 3400 feet, and basic environment is chaparral on the hillsides with oak and sycamore woodlands along the bottoms.

The higher concentration of campgrounds on the Valyermo District occurs near Big Pines, an enticing region of rangy pines and open meadows near the top of the San Gabriels. Table Mountain campground, a mile from the Big Pines Visitor Center, has 115 units on the edge of the ridge where you can see the Mojave Desert and the far-off space-craft landing area at Edwards Air Force Base. Campers here can take advantage of the campfire programs, guided nature walks, and children's activities planned by the forest rangers at Big Pines.

Mountain Oak, Peavine, and Lake campgrounds share proximity to Jackson Lake, a fishing and swimming pond atop the San Andreas earthquake fault. Peavine is a walk-in campground just off Big Pines Highway sheltered by giant Jeffrey pines. Both Lake and Mountain Oak camping places will accommodate trailers to twenty-two feet in length. Like Peavine, Lake is sheltered by huge Jeffrey pines, but has well-constructed paved interior roads and parking spurs. Mountain Oak sites are further apart, and thicker growth of underbrush makes each of the units more widely separate.

High up on the Angeles Crest Highway three miles west of Big Pine, Grassy Hollow campground is right at the tip-top of the mountain range. Western bluebirds, stellar jays, and magnificent mountain quail will be your companions at this pine-dotted meadow.

At the very edge of the Sheep Mountain Wilderness are three more campgrounds reachable only with four-wheel drive vehicles. These three—

ANGELES NATIONAL FOREST

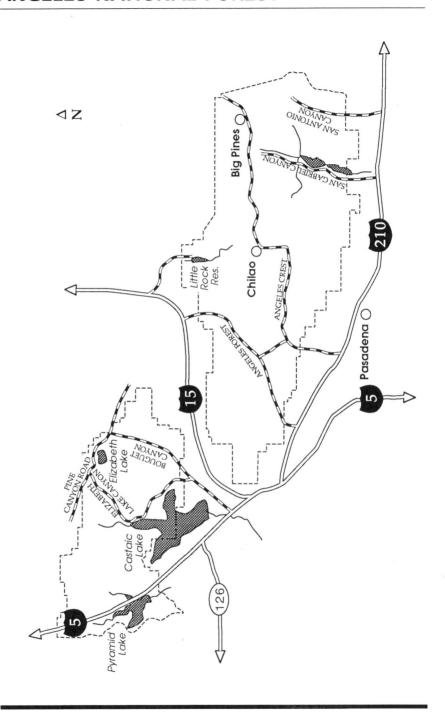

blue Ridge, Guffy, and Lupine—can also be used as staging areas for hikers going into the wilderness or to the Pacific Crest Trail, which passes through on its way southeast into the San Bernardino National Forest.

Between the Big Pines and Littlerock Canyon Recreation Areas are several more attractive campgrounds. Big Rock, Sycamore Flat, and South Fork are all accessible on big Rock Creek out of Valyermo. Halfway up the north slope of Pleasant View Ridge and Mt. Lewis, they're about 4,500 feet elevation. There's yucca and sage, and there's pine and oak in this boundary zone between desert and mountain environments.

On The Trail

While automobile touring and picnicking are the number one recreation activities on the Angeles National Forest hiking is a clear third. One of the best ways to experience the Forest is to go on a hike. The Angeles offers 557 miles of hiking and equestrian trials which include seventy-three miles of National Recreation Trails and 145 miles of the Pacific Crest Trail. The trail within the Forest offer ample choice for all, form beginners to experienced outdoor enthusiasts.

The Pacific Crest Trail

Traveling through the Angeles on the Pacific Crest Trail is one of only two times in its long journey from Mexico to Canada that hikers will be going mostly east-west instead of north-south. The north-bound trail enters the Forest near the little town of Wrightwood at the far eastern edge of the Forest. It them continues in a generally westerly direction for all of its miles on the Angeles until it leaves the Saugus Ranger District in the neighborhood of Liebre Mountain.

Best access points to the PCT are near Wrightwood and Big Pines, along the Angeles Crest Highway, at Mill Creek Summit, near Soledad campground, and all along the northern edge of the Saugus District wherever one of the roads enters the forest.

The spring is far and away the best time of the year to hike the PCT on the Angeles. There's much more available water, and temperatures are comfortable for walking and camping. Many of the hikes in the succeeding paragraphs are either portions of the PCT or direct connections with it, and day hikes are the most popular way of utilizing the PCT on the Angeles.

Some special features of this segment of the trail are Mt. Baden-Powell, named for the founder of the Boy Scouts of America, bands of bighorn sheep which are occasionally seen in the area from Mt. Baden-Powell to Mt. Pacifico, and the Angeles Crest itself with altitudes well above 8,000 feet. Ancient limber pines, over 2,000 years old, occur near timberline on Mt. Baden-Powell to Mt. Burnham and Throop Peak.

National Recreation Trails

Of the four National Recreation Trails on the Angeles, Gabrielino and West Fork are the best for wintertime hiking, while the Silver Moccasin and High Deserts Trails are better at other times of the year. Indeed, the upper reaches of both the High Desert and the Silver Moccasin are sometimes closed in the winter because of heavy snow and avalanche danger.

The Gabrielino Trail is in the Angeles "front country" behind the cities of Pasadena and Altadena. It's close to civilization and gets heavy use all year round. There are four trail camps along the twenty-eight-mile route. Biggest attractions of this hike are Big Santa Anita Canyon and Sturtevant Falls.

The West Fork National Bicycle Trail is one of the few paved National Trails in California, and with grades of less than two percent on its 6.8-mile length, it's understandable that it gets heavy bicycle use. There's a good parking lot with restrooms where the trail intersects Highway 39 in San Gabriel Canyon just above the ORV Staging Area near the reservoirs. The river is regularly stocked with trout, and fishermen can almost always be found in the alder and ash trees that make up the woodlands along the water.

The High Desert Trail is on the Valyermo District overlooking the Mojave Desert to the north. The trail is about seventy miles northeast of Los Angeles. It passes through two geological zones as it climbs to the PCT at 7,500 feet. There are grand vistas of the Angeles Crest country, a wide range of desert flora and fauna, two waterfalls, and a number of year round streams and springs. Devil's Punchbowl County Park offers a natural history museum and trail at the northern-most extension of the trail.

The Silver Moccasin Trail is about fifty-three miles long, with the lower 15.5 miles designated as National Recreation Trail, and the balance a part of the PCT. It's a Scouting trail, and if you follow is all the way you'll be walking in the footsteps of thousands of Scouts who have done it ahead of you, earning their Silver Moccasin Badge in the process. The trail rises out of the West Fork of the San Gabriel River, climbing up to 6,000 feet at Three Points where it ties in with the PCT. Most vegetation along the first part is of chaparral varieties, with riparian woodlands in San Gabriel Canyon, and pine and fir trees scattered throughout the higher elevations.

Other Hiking Trails of the Angeles

The Chilao Visitor Center and adjacent campground is the starting point for several interesting and beautiful walks. Go from Chilao to Mt. Hillyer via Horse Flats and enjoy the yuccas blooming along the lower portion of the trail during spring. As you gain elevation, you'll leave the dry chaparral and enter wondrous stands of Jeffrey pines and incense cedars. The one-way distance is only three miles and a picnic atop Mt. Hillyer is a great reward for making the hike.

In the same general area, the walk from Eagles Roost to Littlerock Canyon, which also has a three-mile one-way distance, traverses an almost ornamental forested area of the high country. Lush forests of pines, firs, and cedars, and tiny waterfalls are only part of the reward for making the trip. This is an excellent place to enjoy a primitive area and true solitude.

Down in the Mt. Baldy area, the trail past San Antonio Falls to Mt. San Antonio (Mt. Baldy) is the easiest and shortest hike to the top of the highest peak in the San Gabriels, even though it's a thirteen-mile round trip. The trail follows a dirt road past spectacular San Antonio Falls to Mt. Baldy Notch, and then up the Devil's Backbone Trail to the top. As you gain elevation, you'll climb through the pine forest to true sub-alpine terrain. Pick a clear day if you can. The views are unequaled out over most of Southern California.

San Gabriel Wilderness

The San Gabriel Wilderness was first set aside as a primitive area back in 1932 to preserve its wilderness character, and, with passage of the National Wilderness Preservation System Act in 1964, became a member of the first group of wilderness areas nationwide. It offers a unique opportunity for solitude within an hour's drive of some nine million people. Within the Wilderness, the Bear Creek Trail is an eleven-mile rough country challenge to the experienced hiker; you can walk it from either end and have someone meet you. You can also get into this wilderness from the Angeles Crest Highway on the Mt. Waterman or Devil's Canyon Trails.

Sheep Mountain Wilderness

Larger by almost 25 percent than the San Gabriel, the Sheep Mountain Wilderness' 44,000 acres range in altitude from 2,400 feet to well over 10,000 feet. It is truly one of the nation's unique wild areas. Most of the remaining range of the east fork herd of Nelson bighorn sheep is within this wilderness. Its very rugged terrain provides a variety of opportunities for outdoor activities such as hiking, camping, and fishing. You'll need a permit if you go into the wilderness from the east fork entrance but otherwise none is needed. Although as always throughout the Angeles, fire permits are required from May 15 until the winter rainy season sets in and the fire season is over.

Cucamonga Wilderness

Much of the Cucamonga Wilderness is on the San Bernardino National Forest to the east of the Angeles, but a major entry point is through Ice House Canyon in the Mt. Baldy Recreation Area. You can get to Cucamonga Peak and the middle fork of Lyttle Creek from this western entry point.

From the top of Ice House Saddle, you can go north along the 3 T's Trail to the summits of Thunder, Timber, and Telegraph mountains and down again via Baldy Notch. More high country lies to the south of the saddle along Bighorn Peak and Ontario Peak trails.

Touring, Sightseeing and Special Programs

Auto touring is the number one recreational pursuit on the Angeles, and two highways provide excellent routes in three of the four adjacent ranger districts. Baldy Road and San Gabriel Canyon Road will take you deep into the Mt. Baldy Ranger District. In addition some loops are eminently possible on the Saugus District. Angeles Crest Highway—California State Highway 2—goes from La Canada-Flintridge to Wrightwood, following the crest of the range for almost its entire length. The other highway is the Angeles Forest Highway and crosses the forest from north to south from the Soledad Canyon near Palmdale to Tujunga-Sunland. Both highways tie into side roads that can lead to adventures off the beaten track.

The Angeles National Forest has constructed some of the most effective visitor centers in the state. Of special interest is the visitor information center at Chilao on the Arroyo Seco District. This interestingly-domed structure offers an introduction to the forest through a variety of exhibits, trails and activities. A combination of outdoor nature trails leading from the building plus more than 20 indoor exhibits introduce visitors to themes of national forest management, history of the San Gabriels, forest wildlife, and recreational opportunities in the high country.

During the summer months, you can join a forest naturalist on a nature walk, participate in children's activity, or attend an evening campfire program at the Chilao amphitheater. Adjacent to the visitor center is the oldest ranger station building in California built with federal funds—$75 in 1900. It was

The Chilao Visitor Center holds fascinating displays.

once located on the west fork of the San Gabriel River, but changes in roads and traffic patterns made it obsolete. Abandoned, it was almost destroyed by the vicissitudes of time until rescued and moved to this location.

The drive to Mt. Wilson Skyline Park and the Mt. Wilson Observatory and communications tower "forest" probably has seen a million visitors over the years. At the end of the road you come to a museum, viewing gallery for the Mt. Wilson Planetariun's 100-inch telescope, and a picnic grounds. A sandwich shop is open daily, and snacks are reasonably priced.

Over on the Mt. Baldy District, the Mt. Baldy Road offers many scenic vistas and photographic points. San Antonio Falls overlook can be reached by walking a half mile on a paved roadway located 100 yards north of the Manker Flats campground. The cascading falls are fed by three springs in Mt. Baldy Bowl. In the same general area sightseeing chairlift rides to Mt. Baldy Notch and Desert View are available at Mt. Baldy Ski Area.

Stop in the Schoolhouse visitor center at Mt. Baldy Village. It's open Friday through Sunday and has all the information you'll need about the region.

For panoramic views, the Glendora Ridge Road offers a breathtaking alternative route on your return trip. You'll be able to catch glimpses of the Sheep Mountain Wilderness, rugged San Gabriel Canyon, and the vast metropolitan area below.

An interesting drive on the Saugus Ranger District leaves from the city of Saugus up Bouquet Canyon Road. As soon as the road enters the forest, you will come to Los Cantiles day-use area. This is a reservations-only group site and is accessible to handicapped persons using wheel-chairs. The waterside trees grow thickly on both sides of the road as you follow it up the canyon of Bouquet Creek.

Just past Bouquet Reservoir, which is closed to use, you will want to turn left on Spunky Canyon Road. At the top of the pass. stop and look at the "Penny Pines Plantation" inaugurated in memory of firefighters who have lost their lives fighting wildfires on the Angeles. The Jupiter Mountain Trail leaves from the plantation, and you'll be able to see down into Green Valley and Francis-quito Canyon, a charming rural community neatly fenced and cross-fenced into a checkerboard pattern.

At the bottom to the canyon, turn right to Andrade Corner, and on to Elizabeth Lake. This thirty-five-acre lake has twelve picnic units with grills, and a paved boat launching ramp. The lake is regularly stocked each winter, and fishermen enjoy the sport from small boats and from the shore. Also in the area are Lake Hughes, and some smaller private ponds in a commercial campground.

Your return trip will be down Elizabeth Lake Canyon past Cottonwood and Prospect campgrounds to Castaic Lake. Just as you arrive near the dam that forms this immense impoundment, pull into the visitor center operated by the State of California. It gives the history of the California Water Project from the far northern reaches of the state to the Mexican border. A bonus is the fantastic view from the outdooor platform out over the blue lake waters to the brown hills beyond. White sails and waterskiers' roostertails criss-cross the gigantic reservoir.

The San Gabriel Mountains are one of the most faulted and fractured land masses in the world and strong evidence of this faulting can been seen in the vicinity of Big Pines on the Valyermo District. Stop in at the visitor center in its temporary location in Big Pines and ask for their self-guided auto tour, "Earthquake Fault Tour." This brochure will tell you how to find earthquake fault features in the Big Pines region. The exact mileage, highway designa-tion, and direction of travel from the center are indicated in the narrative for each feature.

The permanent visitor center at Big Pines was destroyed by fire recently, and a new center is still in the planning stage at publication time. Even so, the rangers offer regular interpretive programs in the summer camping period and are there to answer your questions all year long. Five short nature trails— one leaving directly behind the visitor center—provide a mountain of infor-mation about the plants, trees, birds, mammals, and the mountains themselves.

Sports

Target shooting is a major sport in all of the Southern California National Forests. Eleven sites have been set aside in the Angeles for recreational shooters. All other portions of the forest have been closed to this type of shooting. There are just too many people in the forest.

Target shooting material is restricted to commercial target systems and biodegradeable paper to help facilitate clean-up of the areas. "Trash" targets are prohibited, and you will be fined if you use them. The Forest Service has banned alchoholic beverages at shooting areas.

Southern California has been called the "Off-Highway Vehicle Capital" of the country. The Forest Service provides three major off-highway staging areas and several off-road trails which provide a variety of terrain for all skill levels: Rowher Flat, in the Saugus District, San Gabriel Canyon, eleven miles north of Azusa, and Littlerock Reservoir, in the Valyermo District.

Winter in the Angeles not only provides magnificent snowcovered scenery, but offers a large variety of recreational activities including nordic skiing, snow camping, hiking and downhill skiing. There are downhill areas at Mt. Baldy, Mountain High—both East and West—Ski Sunrise, Kratka Ridge, and Mt. Waterman. The Mountain High areas also feature night skiing.

Cross-country ski trails are located in the Big Pines Recreation Area and Charlton-Chilao Recreation Areas, especially. Favorite spots in the Big Pine are East Blue Ridge, Table Mountain, and Grassy Hollow.

Sledding, tobaggoning, and tubing can be enjoyed, although there are no maintained or supervised areas.

The two great big reservoirs on the Saugus Ranger District, Castaic Lake and Pyramid Lake provide the only big opportunities for boating on the Angeles. Water-skiing, jet skiing, fishing, swimming and boating are offered at Pyramid, while Cataic Lake has facilities for fishing, swimming, boating and boat rentals. There are no public campgrounds at either lake.

Elizabeth Lake has a paved boat launch, and sail boats, non-motorized watercraft and boats with ten horsepower or less are permitted. All three lakes have picnic facilities.

Mountain bicycling is without a doubt the fastest growing sport in Angeles National Forest.

ANGELES NATIONAL FOREST CAMPGROUNDS

	Piped Water	Camp Sites	Trailer Space	Fishing	Boating	Swimming	Store	RV Dump Station	Reservations	Special Attractions
Arroyo Seco Ranger District										
Buckhorn	•	40	•							
Chilao	•	110	•				•			Vis. & int. center
Horse Flats	•	25	•							
Millard	•	5								
Mt. Pacifico		10								
Valley Forge	•	17								
West Fork	•	7								
Mt. Baldy Ranger District										
Coldbrook	•	14	•	•						
Crystal Lake	•	232	•	•			•	•		Vis. & int. center
Manker Flats	•	21	•	•			•			Vis. & int. center
Saugus Ranger District										
Atmore Meadows		8								
Big Oak	•	9								
Bouquet	•	5								

ANGELES NATIONAL FOREST CAMPGROUNDS

	Piped Water	Camp Sites	Trailer Space	Fishing	Boating	Swimming	Store	RV Dump Station	Reservations	Special Attractions
Saugus Ranger District										
Cienaga		17	•							
Cottonwood	•	27	•	•						
Hollow Tree		5								
Los Alamos	•	93	•	•	•	•	•			Pyramid Lake
Lower Shake		5								
Oak Flat	•	23	•	•						
Prospect	•	22		•						
Sawmill Mountain		10								
South Portal		11								
Spunky	•	10	•							
Streamside	•	9								
The Falls	•	14								
Upper Shake		18	•							
Warm Springs	•	12	•	•						
Zuni	•	10								
Tujunga Ranger District										
Live Oak	•	10								
Messenger Flats	•	10								
Monte Cristo	•	19	•	•						
Round Top		4								
Soledad	•	6	•							
Vogel Flats	•	18		•						
Valyermo Ranger District										
Apple Tree	•	8		•						
Basin	•	24	•	•						
Big Rock	•	8	•	•						
Blue Ridge		8	•							
Cabin Flat		12								
Grassy Hollow	•	15	•							
Guffy		6								
Joshua Tree	•	11	•	•		•				
Juniper Grove	•	7		•		•				
Lake	•	8	•	•		•				
Lakeside	•	6	•	•		•				
Little Cedars		3		•						
Little Sycamore		8		•						
Lupine	•	11								
Mescal	•	9								
Mountain Oak	•	17	•	•		•				

ANGELES NATIONAL FOREST CAMPGROUNDS

Valyermo Ranger District	Piped Water	Camp Sites	Trailer Space	Fishing	Boating	Swimming	Store	RV Dump Station	Reservations	Special Attractions
Peavine	•	4		•	•					
South Fork	•	21	•							
Sulphur Springs	•	10								
Sycamore Flats	•	11	•							
Table Mountain	•	115	•			•				Inter. programs

LOS PADRES
NATIONAL
FOREST

Sacramento

San Francisco

Los Angeles

Los Padres National Forest

Named for the Franciscan missionaries who first brought European culture to California, the Los Padres National Forest includes most of the mountainous land along the central coast and is some of the most rugged land in the state. Popular with Bay Area residents, it's a place where people can go in the Sierra "off season" to hike and enjoy the wilderness.

The California condor, an endangered species, once could sometimes be seen over the southern portion of the forest. None of the birds remain alive in the wild, but attempts to insure their survival go on. Two sanctuaries have been established for them on the Los Padres.

Camping on the Los Padres

There are more than eighty designated campgrounds accessible by automobile on the Los Padres, and of these about forty-five qualify as "improved," with piped water, picnic tables, and fire rings. Many primitive campgrounds are available for use free-of-charge.

Monterey Ranger District

The campgrounds that most people coming to the Monterey District encounter first are those along Highway 1. Kirk Creek and Plaskett Creek campgrounds are immediately adjacent to the highway, yet far enough from the actual traffic that its noise is inconsequential. Kirk Creek Campground is on an open bluff with lots of chamise and lupine overlooking the blue Pacific. Although many people use this coastal camping place as only an overnight stop on the way north or south, it really makes great headquarters camp for exploring the forest and the adjacent sites. Such places as Mission San Antonio de Paudua, Cone Peak, Jade Cove, and Salmon Creek Falls can be visited.

Plaskett Creek campground, also on a bluff on the rugged Big Sur Coast, has more trees than Kirk Creek. Cypress, pines, and alders shelter the site in this green campground.

Bottchers Gap Campground, one of the departure points for backpackers heading into the Ventana Wilderness, can also be reached from Highway 1, fifteen miles north of Big Sur off Palo Colorado Road. Covered by oak and smooth-trunked madrones, this saddle provides an excellent view of the Ventana Double Cone, highest peak of the region.

The California State Park System has campgrounds at Andrew Molera and Big Sur State Parks, as well as an environmental campground at Julia Pheiffer Burns State Park. In addition to these public camping spots, there are several commercial campgrounds as well.

A warning: In summer, all of these campgrounds are very busy, and if you aren't prepared with reservations at the state parks or commercial sites, you'll have to check quite early in the day to make sure you have a place for the night at one of the Forest Service campgrounds.

Several campgrounds are accessible from the east side of the Monterey District. Among them are White Oaks on the north, Arroyo Seco west of Greenfield, and Memorial Park at the edge of the southern portion of Ventana Wilderness. White Oaks is up the steep Jamesburg-Tassajara Road at 4,000 feet. Its seven campsites are widely spread under a canopy of coast live oaks and blue oaks. The pungent odor of bay leaves emanates from laurels at the edge of camp. Long-eared owls, great horned owls, and band-tailed pigeons are among the large birds you can spot here.

Arroyo Seco Campground is just downstream from the junction of Arroyo Seco, Santa Lucia, and Tassajara creeks. Fishing and swimming in the stream attract picnickers as well as campers from the hot valleys below. Huge oaks are scattered across the wide campgrounds, and there's access to bass fishing—but no swimming—on the nearby Abbott Lakes.

Santa Lucia Ranger District

Highway 41 cuts across the Coast Range from Atascadero to Highway 1 just north of Morro Bay. At the top of the ridge among the huge trunks and limbs of coast live oaks, Cerro Alto Campground offers an alternative to the sometimes fog-shrouded coastal camps.

The Figueroa Mountain Recreation Area lies thirty minutes north of Los Olivos off Highway 154 and can be reached by Figueroa Mountain Road or Happy Canyon Road. Both roads are paved, but Happy Canyon is not recommended for trailers and is occasionally closed in winter because of slides. Most of this recreation area is covered by heavy chaparral, although large big-cone Douglas firs, ponderosa and Jeffrey pines occur at higher elevations, and blue oaks and digger pines occur throughout the lower elevations.

Camping is especially interesting in the springtime, a season of fantastic wildflower displays. Purple shooting stars, filaree, lupine, chocolate lilies, and Indian paintbrush are some of the blooms you can see. Figueroa campground, set in an impressive stand of pines and large manzanitas, is open all year-round and offers a good view of the valley below. At night you can see the lights of Santa Barbara glowing over the southern horizon.

Davy Brown Campground is for fishermen who try their luck on Davy Brown Creek from early spring until late May or June. It's close to a number of hiking trails, and the creek usually flows all summer long. Upstream a couple of miles is Nira campground, right at the edge of San Rafael Wilderness. Manzana Creek flows beside the campground, its pools holding small trout and sometimes small children. This camping place is a jumping off spot for hikers and backpackers going into the wilderness. Equestrians also make use of Nira because the wilderness here is well-suited for horseback riding.

Accessible from the oil field country on the east side of the forest, Aliso Park and Bates Canyon campgrounds are a relief from the stark countryside below them. Far cooler in the summer than the Cuyama Valley they overlook, the campgrounds also serve as home base for deer hunters in the fall who like to come into the back side of the forest to avoid the more crowded western portion.

Santa Barbara Ranger District

The Santa Ynez River is the longest stretch of free-flowing river in southern California, and the recreation facilities in Santa Ynez Recreation Area provide a great place to enjoy the river. There are five family campgrounds in the canyon: Fremont, Paradise, Los Prietos, Upper Oso, and Santa Ynez. Immense, twisted oaks and peppery bay laurels cover the broad flat along the river, and campsites are clustered on the flat. Santa Ynez is day use only.

The Los Prietos Ranger Station near the camping places has information

A wheelchair access trail in the Los Padres National Forest. Jean Hawthorne photo.

on the fascinating hiking trails in the region, and rangers can tell you when the state "fish truck" has brought catchable trout to plant in the river. The Aliso Canyon Nature Tail, which begins from Sage Hill group camp, provides an introduction to the natural history of the area.

The other major camping area on the Santa Barbara District is the Pendola or Upper Santa Ynez Recreation Area. There are four reduced service campgrounds here, but only Middle Santa Ynez has piped water. Again, the Santa Ynez River is the main attraction, and shady oak-covered campgrounds can be accessed by auto via the East Camino Cielo Road above Santa Barbara.

Ojai Ranger District

Highway 33 transects the Ojai Ranger District from the city of Ojai north to the district boundary on Pine Mountain. The highway provides access to six of the developed family campgrounds on the District. Wheeler Gorge Campground is right off the highway, seven miles north of Ojai. The north fork of the Ventura River runs through the campground and offers a refreshing place to dangle your feet or a fishing line. A nature trail—self-guided loop—starts at the north end of the campground. The campsites are in the riparian woodlands on the canyon bottom, and trails going out and up from the camps soon take you into the heavy chaparral of the mountainsides. Creosote bush, palo colorado, and the ever-present sage predominate.

On up Highway 33, about two miles past the Rose Valley turn-off, you'll come to Beaver Campground. This small streamside camping area offers swimming, fishing, and hiking. Oaks and sycamores shelter your campsite. The chaparral takes over once you get out of the canyon bottom.

The other campground that's close to Highway 33 is at Cherry Creek on the south side of Sespe Creek Canyon near Pine Mountain Inn. This spot is near the beginning of the Ortega OHV Trail, and off-highway vehicle enthusiasts frequently use it.

The Rose Valley Recreation Area can be reached by turning off Highway 33 at the marked road intersection about thirteen miles north of Ojai. Rose Valley Campground is for those who can bring their own water, such as self-contained RV's. It's on an open flat about a half-mile downstream from Rose Valley Falls. There are three man-made ponds in the area which are open to fishing during the fishing season. They're well-stocked with trout on a regular basis until the water reaches seventy-two degrees, usually about the end of July.

Lion and Middle Lion campgrounds are located in the Rose Valley area at the end of Rose Valley Road where it hits Sespe Creek and Lion Canyon. Middle Lion is nicely shaded by large cottonwoods along the creek bank. Lion Campground has far less shade, but the swimming and fishing opportunities make up for it. Several large swimming holes in Sespe Creek are at the edge of the campground. Two major trails—Piedra Blanca National Recreation Trail and Sespe Creek Trail—have trailheads at Lion Campground. Widely spaced sycamores and palo colorado trees provide shade in the sandy, desert environment. Not all camping places have water, so check carefully on the charts or with ranger stations.

Blue Point Campground is six miles north of Lake Piru at the southeastern edge of the forest. Piru Creek, which flows through the campground, is actually the boundary between Los Padres and Angeles National Forests. The campground is in a riparian woodland, with oaks and sycamores predominating. To get to the campsites, you'll have to cross the privately operated Lake Piru. However, you do not have to pay the fee required for the lake. You simply specify that you're headed for Blue Point and a day pass will be issued at no charge.

Mt. Pinos Ranger District

There are parts of the Mt. Pinos Ranger District that are almost like the Sierra Nevada, and you'll find yourself camping in sites that are more than 7,000 feet above sea level. You'll notice this especially up on the Mt. Pinos Road, where McGill, Mt. Pinos, and Chula Vista campgrounds are located. Granite boulders, huge Jeffrey pines, whitehorn and manzanita combine to give a sub-alpine look to the surroundings.

McGill is the major camping spot on the mountain and it's here that District ranger-naturalists put on evening campfire programs during the summer camping season. Close at hand you'll find the Mt. Pinos Botanical Area at the summit where you'll be able to see the plant community growing in this special environment. Also at the summit is one of the specially marked "Primary Condor Observation Points." This region is the major winter recreation area on the forest, with marked and groomed cross-country ski trails.

At the northern edge of the district, Camp Alto Campground perches near the tip top of Cerro Noroeste, high in the Sierra-like mountains overlooking the San Joaquin Valley to the north. You can get away from the intense heat of the lower altitudes up here in the cool pine forest.

LOS PADRES NATIONAL FOREST

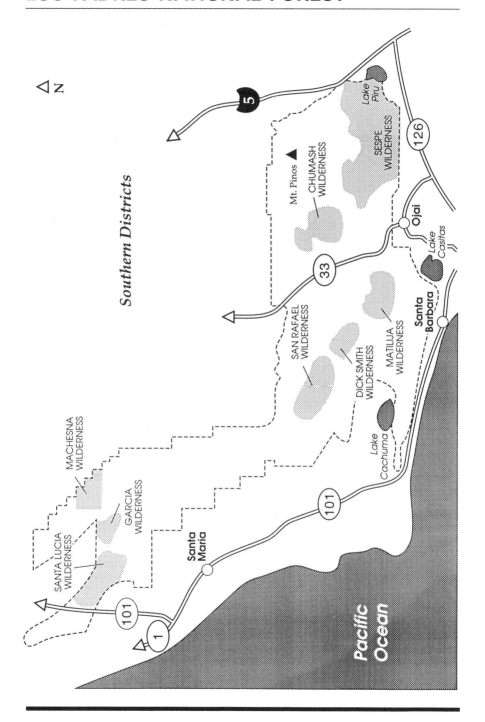

Southern Districts

N

SESPE WILDERNESS

Lake Piru

126

CHUMASH WILDERNESS

Mt. Pinos

5

Ojai

Lake Casitas

33

MATILIJA WILDERNESS

Santa Barbara

SAN RAFAEL WILDERNESS

DICK SMITH WILDERNESS

Lake Cachuma

MACHESNA WILDERNESS

GARCIA WILDERNESS

101

Santa Maria

SANTA LUCIA WILDERNESS

101

1

Pacific Ocean

On The Trail

Nearly 1,200 miles of trails criss-cross the Los Padres National Forest. Recreation opportunities for you are there if you want to hike, backpack, ride a horse, bicycle, motorcycle, all-terrain vehicle, or four-wheeler. Naturally, these trails vary in length and difficulty, from leisurely two-hour day trips to week-long excursions into the wilderness back country.

National Recreation Trails

Piedra Blanca National Recreation Trail travels from Lion Campground on the Ojai Ranger District to Reyes Creek Campground on the Mt. Pinos District. Trail elevations range from 3,000 to 7,500 feet and some gradients are steep. As with all southern California forest landscapes, chaparral predominates. However, there are stands of oaks, grassy meadows, numerous wildflowers species, and mixed conifer forests at higher altitudes. The Chumash Indians inhabited these hills and canyons and their pictographs or cave paintings can be spotted very close to the trail. Rangers can tell you where to look.

The Santa Cruz and Aliso National recreation trails are in the Santa Ynez Recreation Area east of Lake Cachuma. The Aliso portion of the trail is a self-guided nature tail which begins behind the Sage Hill group camp. It follows Aliso Creek and them climbs to the top of the ridge above Upper Oso campground. At this point the Santa Cruz portion of the trail heads north toward Nineteen Oaks. You rise and dip through oaks, sycamores, pines, and firs, as well as the ever-present chaparral species—here mostly manzanita and creosote bush. Every once in a while you'll come to a ridgetop with wide, sweeping views. Above Nineteen Oaks you look back down on the canyon of the Santa Ynez River and La Cumbre Peak beyond. Near Happy Hollow on Little Pine Mountain you'll come to the top of the divide between the Santa Ynez River drainage and that of Santa Cruz Creek. The view ahead of you is into the San Rafael Wilderness with Santa Cruz and San Rafael Peaks in the distance.

Monterey District Hiking Trails

Practically all of the hiking trails on the Monterey District are within the boundaries of Ventana Wilderness, or access trails that end up there. At this writing permits are not required, but you should check with rangers for current conditions and/or fire restrictions.

There are several trailheads around the perimeter of the wilderness. Most popular is at Big Sur Station leading to the Pine Ridge Trail. This is the least likely of all the routes to travel in search of solitude, but it is beautiful. Because it's open to the Pacific's cool, marine air, there's a favorable climate for coast redwoods. As you climb higher, the redwoods, delicate sorrels, and fronds of shade-seeking ferns keep to the canyon bottoms, and oaks, madrones, and bay laurels occupy the hillsides. As the slopes warm up and dry out, chaparral becomes a thick carpet. You first hit the Big Sur River at Barlow Flat, and then cross it at Sykes Hot Springs.

The Cone Peak Trail at the southern entrance to the wilderness can be reached off Nacimiento-Ferguson Road. You can make a short, steep loop around Cone Peak itself, and get a look at the Santa Lucia or bristlecone fir. This rare species was first described here by the botanists Thomas Coulter and David Douglas. The spire-shaped trees is found only in the Santa Lucia Mountains in Monterey and San Luis Obispo counties. It occurs above the redwood belt in rocky soils from 2,000 to 5,000 feet.

LOS PADRES NATIONAL FOREST

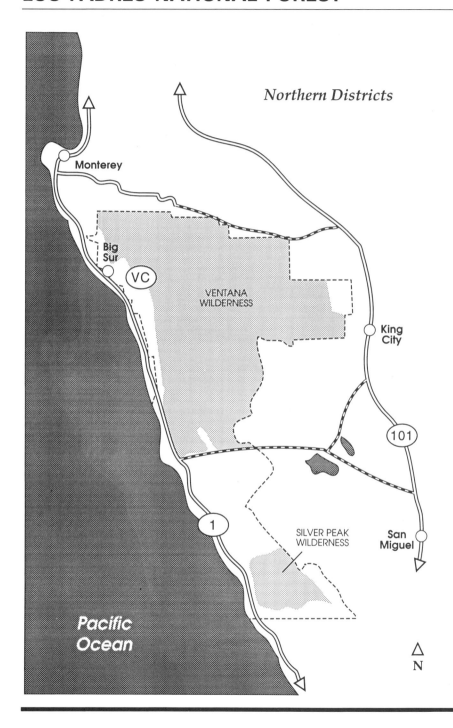

Northern Districts

Monterey

Big Sur

VC

VENTANA WILDERNESS

King City

101

1

SILVER PEAK WILDERNESS

San Miguel

Pacific Ocean

N

To reach the top of Ventana Double Cone you have to take the Skinner Ridge Trail out of Bottcher's Gap Campground. Your total climb will be 3000 feet in 15 miles. There are several campsites along the trail. This hike, too, starts out in the redwoods and ends in chaparral.

Santa Lucia District Hiking Trails

A short, but absorbing, trail leads from Cerro Alto Campground about a mile to the top of Cerro Alto Peak. From the top you get an edge-of-the-world view out over Morro Bay and the Pacific Ocean.

Another short trip is the Lopez Canyon Trail into the Santa Lucia Wilderness. This streamside trail through Lopez Canyon provides a look at a wide variety of vegetation. Side trails head for the top of Lopez Mountain, Black Butte and the eastern ridge above Salinas River Valley.

From Davy Brown and Nira campgrounds in Figueroa Mountain Recreation Area, trails lead into the rugged San Rafael Wilderness. One of the most engrossing of these trails is the high ridgetop Mission Pine Springs Trail, which actually begins at Cachuma Saddle and follows the ridge from Cachuma Mountain east to McKinley Mountain and on over the top of San Rafael Mountain to Mission Pine Springs. The campground here is surrounded by giant salt-and-pepper granite boulders and tall pines. For a real adventure, you can continue along the ridge and finally cross into the Dick Smith Wilderness, or cut south at Mission Pine Basin to the Santa Cruz National Recreation Trail.

From Nira campground, the Manzana Creek Trail will take you to the region known as "Hurricane Deck." Large sandstone cliffs with many wind-blown pothole caves greet the traveler along trails with treacherous footing. Some of the caves contain Chumash pictographs in this unique wind-formed area.

Santa Barbara District Hiking Trails

The Santa Barbara "front country," the ridges and canyons that rise up from the back yards of the cities along the coast, contain a trail in every canyon, or so it seems. The Santa Ynez Mountains, rising from sea level to 4,000 feet, form a backdrop to Santa Barbara that make up a part of the city's attraction. They disclose that the stream-cut canyons form natural paths to the top.

Among the many trails are the Rattlesnake Canyon, Romero, and San Ysidro trails. The Rattlesnake Canyon trail is considered one of the prettiest of these front country trails. It begins on Los Canoas Avenue in Santa Barbara, and follows a creek for three miles past grey and tan sedimentary rock formations and clear pools. It joins the west fork of Cold Springs Trail at the top.

By taking Romero Trail a little over four miles to East Camino Cielo, you pick up another trail to Blue Canyon and on into the Pendola-Upper Santa Ynez Recreation Area. As a matter of fact, you could continue hiking all the way into the Dick Smith and San Rafael wildernesses by starting in Santa Barbara.

From the Los Prietos Ranger Station on the Santa Ynez River, the Snyder Trail makes for a comfortable day hike. It goes six miles up to East Camino Cielo. Just before you reach the top, you can take a fork west to Wellhouse Falls. Enjoy a picnic lunch and watch the sunlight sparkle in the falls.

From the end of Paradise Road at the back of the Santa Ynez Canyon, you can hike on either of the graded roads that lead up to Gibraltar Reservoir. These easy walks lead you under the shade of sycamores and cottonwoods lining the river.

Ojai District Hiking Trails

Most popular back country trail on the Ojai, besides the Piedra Blanca Trail, is the Sespe Hot Springs Trail. The Hot Springs are located about seventeen miles from Lion Campground, and the trail crosses and recrosses Sespe Creek all the way to the mouth of Hot Springs Canyon. This high desert hike takes you through groves of sycamores, palo verde, and cottonwoods along the river. Yuccas are sprinkled above you on the chaparral slopes, their astounding creamy blooms visible in late spring.

For hiking closer to home, try Santa Paula Canyon. Located behind Ferndale Ranch off Highway 150, it's about three miles to Big Cone Camp and another .5 mile to Cross Camp. There are waterfalls on two branches of the stream, and you can bushwhack up the righthand branch along the flanks of Santa Paula Peak to Cienega and Bluff Camps.

From the city of Ojai itself, you can make your way into the "Ojai Front Country." A favorite loop is to make your way up Gridley Trail past Gridley Springs camp to the Nordhoff Ridge fire road. On the road, you go west to the top of Nordhoff Peak and then down the Pratt Trail to the Stewart Canyon picnic area. Take water and a picnic lunch to enjoy the top-of-the-world view out over Ojai and Lake Casitas to the west. Bright green citrus groves contrast most of the year with the grey-tan rock and dried grasses of nearby slopes. The sharply defined canyon of the Ventura River divides the scene in the near distance.

Mt. Pinos District Hiking Trails

Hiking on parts of the Mt. Pinos District is much like hiking in the Sierra Nevada. The walk from Campo Alto on Cerro Noroeste to Chula Vista on Mt. Pinos is almost all above 8,000 feet among granite boulders, manzanita, and whitehorn shrubs, and widely spaced pines. It's enough to make you think you're on the Sierra or Sequoia National Forests.

Two side trips can be arranged from the Pinos-Noroeste Trail. One goes from that trail down to Three Falls on Lockwood Creek through Sheep Camp and Lily Meadows, a drop of about 3,000 feet, so a one-way trip is recommended. A similar one-way trip is the Mt. Pinos Trail which leaves from the McGill Campground and winds its way north down the mountain to civilization near Pinon Pines. This 2.5-mile trip is very popular, and you're apt to have company. The fragrant smelling duff of the forest floor rises around you as you wind down the pine-clad shoulder.

Probably the least hiked of all these trails is in the Painted Rock and Lion Canyon Scenic Area. This unusual area is located on the east side of the San Rafael Wilderness in the far western portion of the Mt. Pinos District, along the Sierra Madre Ridge between Pine Corral and Montgomery Potrero. You get to it by going through the little town of New Cuyama on Highway 166 north of the forest. Both areas carry unique and fanciful rock formations created by wind and water erosion.

Touring, Sightseeing, and Special Programs

Automobile touring is the number one recreational activity on the Los Padres National Forest, but here the statistics may be a little misleading, because 18 miles of California's first designated Scenic Highway, State Highway 1, passes through the Monterey District on the Big Sur Coast. Millions of people pass this way each year to see some of the most spectacular coastline California has to offer.

The only alternative route available from the Big Sur to Salinas Valley makes a wondrous sidetrip adventure. The Nacimiento-Ferguson Road traverses the Santa Lucia Mountains for twenty-nine miles from Kirk Creek to the community of Jolon and its mission, San Antonio de Padua. The 18th Century mission welcomes visitors. This is a steep, narrow, and winding road—not for motorhomes or trailers. An interesting side trip is up Cone Peak Canyon. Here a short, but steep walk will take you to see the rare Santa Lucia firs.

Wildflower fanciers will want to drive the Happy Canyon Road—Figueroa Mountain road from Solvang. This loop will take you through some of the brightest wildflower areas of the coastal hills. Purple shooting stars, Indian paintbrush, California poppies, lupine, dodder vine, owl's clover and monkeyflower turn the spring-green hills into a kaleidescope of color.

In the same area, the San Marcos Pass Road takes you the "back way" from Solvang to Santa Barbara. You'll drive past Lake Cachuma and the turn-off to the Santa Ynez Recreation Area before climbing to the top of the pass. On a clear day—and there are lots of them in Santa Barbara—you look down over the coast, the city clustered against the mountains, and the Channel Islands across a piece of the great Pacific Ocean.

Highway 33 divides the Forest in half, going from Ojai on the south to the Cuyama Valley north of the Forest. You'll drive through Wheeler Gorge, named for an early-day entrepreneur who advertised his health resort throughout southern California. Beyond Beaver Campground, you'll pass through Sespe Gorge and follow up the river to Pine Mountain and down to Ozena. Below Ozena, you'll come to the Ballinger Canyon OHV area and pass out of the forest along the dry bed of the Cuyama River.

It's possible to make a big loop out of the Highway 33 trip by turning off the highway at Ozena and traveling east on a county road. This will take you through high desert at first and then up to the region around Mt. Pinos west of Frazier Park. From there you can scoot down I-5 to Highway 126 and back to your beginning point in Ojai or Ventura.

The beaches on the Monterey District deserve special attention. Pfeiffer Beach, 2.5 miles from Big Sur, has huge wave sculptured rocks and a wild crashing surf. People don't swim here, but surf casting for fish, gathering driftwood, and marveling at the blowholes in the rock are fun. Sand Dollar Beach, across from the Plaskett Creek campground, is the largest public beach on the southern Big Sur Coast. It's accessible by a trail and steps down the cliff to a point where you can picnic, sunbathe, beach comb, or cast for fish.

Most unusual of the Monterey District beaches is Jade Cove, a half-mile south of Sand Dollar Beach. From the parking area at the top, you can see the green cliffs giving the cove its name. At the bottom, jade is found as deposits in the cliff face, and as pebbles on the rocky beach. The cliff deposits may not be disturbed, but you're welcome to collect from the beach. Occasionally, you'll see skin-divers working the deposits from the surf off-shore. The "Monterey jade" found here is mostly gray-green in color and of only mediocre quality, but for a rockhound, its worth adding to your collection.

To the south of the Monterey District, traveling down highway 101, you can stop at the top of Cuesta Pass and take a right turn to the Cuesta Ridge Botanical Area. The serpentine soils and stunted Sergeant cypress trees are an interest-holding phenomenon.

Besides the campfire programs at McGill campground on the Mt. Pinos District, volunteers from the Los Padres Interpretive Association present campfire programs during the summer season at Santa Ynez Recreation Area. And, up on the Monterey District, the State Park Rangers and members of the Big Sur Natural History Association put on similar programs in the adjacent Big Sur State Park.

Sports

Winter sports are relatively limited over most of the forest. The big exception is up on Mt. Pinos, where cross-country skiers and snow play afficionados get their chance. There are groomed Nordic ski trails in the area of the campgrounds on the mountain, and lots of places for tubing and sledding. Parking is sometimes a problem on weekends, and the numbers of people may make you wish you had come on Thursday.

LOS PADRES NATIONAL FOREST CAMPGROUNDS

	Piped Water	Camp Sites	Trailer Space	Fishing	Boating	Swimming	Store	RV Dump Station	Reservations	Special Attractions
Monterey Ranger District										
Alder Creek		5								
Arroyo Seco	•	51	•	•		•				
Bottchers Gap	•	8								
China Camp		8								
Escondido		9	•							
Kirk Creek	•	33	•	•		•				
Memorial Park		8	•	•		•				
Nacimiento		8	•	•						
Plaskett Creek	•	44	•	•		•				
Prewitt Ridge		3								
Sycamore Flats		4								
White Oaks		8		•						
Santa Lucia Ranger District										
American Canyon		14	•							
Agua Escondido	•	3								
Barrel Spring		5								
Bates Canyon	•	6	•							
Brookshire Spring		2								
Cerro Alto	•	26	•							
Colson		10	•							
Davy Brown		13	•	•						
Figueroa	•	33	•							
Friis		3	•				•			
Hi Mountain		11	•							
Horseshoe Spring		3	•							
La Panza		16	•							
Miranda Pine Spring		3								
Navajo		3								

LOS PADRES NATIONAL FOREST CAMPGROUNDS

	Piped Water	Camp Sites	Trailer Space	Fishing	Boating	Swimming	Store	RV Dump Station	Reservations	Special Attractions
Navajo		3								
Queen Bee		3								
Stoney Creek		12								
Santa Barbara Ranger District										
Cachuma		5								
Fremont	•	15	•		•					
Juncal		6		•						
Los Prietos	•	38	•							
Middle Santa Ynez		6		•						
Paradise	•	15	•						•	
P-Bar Flat		3		•						
Sage Hill	•	62	•	•	•				•	
Santa Ynez	•	34	•	•	•					
Upper Oso	•	28	•	•	•					
Ojai Ranger District										
Blue Point		26	•	•	•					
Lions Canyon	•	22	•	•	•					
Middle Lion		11	•	•	•					
Rose Valley Falls		9	•	•	•					
Wheeler Gorge	•	68	•	•	•		•		•	
Beaver		7	•	•	•					
Mt. Pinos Ranger District										
Aliso Park		10	•							
Ballinger		5	•							
Caballo		6	•		•					
Campo Alto		17	•		•					
Half Moon		10	•							
Hard Luck		4	•		•					
McGill		78	•							
Mt. Pinos		19	•							
Ozena		12	•		•					
Pine Mountain		8								
Pine Spring		8		•						
Reyes Creek	•	30	•	•	•					
Reyes Peak		7								
Toad Spring		7			•					
Twin Pines		5			•					
Valle Vista		7								

SEQUOIA NATIONAL FOREST

Sacramento

San Francisco

Los Angeles

Sequoia National Forest

Sequoia National Forest is the southern end of the Sierra Nevada and extends from the Kings River on the north to the Kern River on the south; it's eastern border is the Sierra crest, the west the San Joaquin Valley.

Elevations range from 1,000 feet in the foothill region to peaks over 12,000 feet in the rugged high country, providing visitors with some of the most spectacular views of mountain landscape in the entire west, but the outstanding feature of Sequoia National Forest is the monarch of the plant kingdom, the giant sequoia (*Sequoiadendron giganteum*). The big trees tower more than 270 feet above the ground and reach diameters of over thirty feet.

The forest offers year-round recreation in the form of camping, picnicking, riding, hiking, hunting, white-water rafting, and kayaking, sightseeing, touring, winter sports, nature study, and trout fishing in high country streams of the Golden Trout Wilderness.

Camping

There are forty-six campgrounds on the forest, most of them small, intimate sites. You can plan an itinerary to visit camps along the big Kern River, or hidden away in a creekside woodland.

Cannell Meadow District Campgrounds

The Kern River corridor is by far the busiest area of the forest. Not only are there many established campgrounds, there is also dispersed camping on every river flat in between the campgrounds. Places called Halfway, Thunderbird, Chico Flat, Spring Hill, and Ant Canyon, are just as full of campers on busy summer weekends as the developed campgrounds at Headquarters, Camp 3, Hospital Flat, Fairview, Limestone, and Goldledge. There are a total of 250 developed campsites between Kernville and Limestone, yet on a busy weekend there may be as many as 500 camping groups in the area.

They're all there to enjoy the Kern crashing over boulders, or flowing smoothly through placid pools. The campsites are only a couple of hours from Bakersfield and the rest of the San Joaquin Valley.

The developed campgrounds along the Kern are in what amounts to a high desert ecological area. Cottonwoods, alders, oaks, and sycamore dominate the upper story, along with some digger and ponderosa pines. The understory consists of chaparral species such as chamise, buckthorn, whitethorn, silktassel, and manzanita. Fire danger is extreme during much of the camping season, and fire restrictions are usually in force.

The Cannell Meadow District includes the Kern Plateau, another important camping area beyond the Upper Kern. The diversity of this area provides a wide range of camping facilities. Four developed campgrounds serve as headquarters for exploring the back country. **Horse Meadow** Campground, on Salmon Creek, is the only developed campground in the southern part of the Plateau. Surrounded by sharp granite peaks almost 10,000 feet high, you'll camp in a bowl under towering Jeffrey pines at 7,600 feet elevation. Troy Meadow and Fish Creek campgrounds, both a little over 50 miles northeast of Kernville via the Sherman Pass Road, are close to the edge of South Sierra and Dome Land wildernesses. Both serve as wilderness take-off points. Fish Creek, itself, flows through both camps providing creekside homes for numerous warblers and bushtits, while violet-green swallows skim the surface of the water for insects. All three of these campgrounds give access to the well-developed off-highway vehicle trails of the Kern Plateau.

Lake Isabella has thirteen campgrounds around its perimeter. These COE sites are good camping places for boaters and fishermen who use Lake Isabella for their recreation.

Greenhorn District Camping

Sequoia National Forest has five camping spots on the Greenhorn District, and three of them are in the neighborhood of the Kern River Canyon or the sparsely timbered desert mountains to the south.

Perched under the shadows of Ball Mountain at the edge of the Kern River at the 2,200-foot level, Hobo Campground is a favorite of rafters using the Lower Kern runs. To the west of Lake Isabella, high in the Greenhorn Mountains, three more forest campgrounds and one Kern County campground, welcome travelers. The county campground, at Greenhorn Summit, is above 6,000 feet elevation near the community of Alta Sierra on the pine-covered mountain ridge. Cedar Creek Campground west of the summit and a little lower has access to both Cedar and Slick Rock creeks in their wooded canyons. Deer hunters like to use Alder Creek and Evans Flat in the fall season. Evans Flat, on the west slope of Woodward Peak, also attracts birders who come to see the hawks that gather near the peak.

Hot Springs District Camping

Popular for the many summer home tracts centered around California Hot Springs, Hot Springs Ranger District also has the southernmost grove of giant sequoias, the Deer Mill Grove. Three campgrounds along the Western Divide Highway, Holey Meadow, Redwood Meadow, and Long Meadow, sit adjacent to broad, green fields where brown and white Hereford cattle graze and deer slip down to the edges at sundown. At Redwood Meadow, location of the interpretive "Trail of a Hundred Giants," there is a camp host on weekends. The individual camp units are widely separated under red and white firs with clumps of manzanita and whitethorn between each camping place.

Other campgrounds on Hot Springs District at Panorama, White River, and Frog Meadow, are more difficult to get to over winding dirt roads. Don't take your trailer. All three are deep in the forest and long walks in the shade of tall conifers bring campers back again and again to enjoy the silence interrupted only by the wind softly whispering among the branches. Only Lower Peppermint Campground, accessible from Forest Road 22S82, north of Johnsondale, has room for trailers in this part of the forest.

Tule River District Camping

Two exquisite campgrounds are features of the Tule River District's camping possibilities. Both Quaking Aspen and the hidden Coy Flat campgrounds have the kind of beauty that photographers like to show when they take pictures of camping places.

You can reach Coy Flat two miles south of Camp Nelson on a narrow gravel road. It sits in a grove of firs and incense cedars amidst branches of the Middle

The world famous Sequoias of Sequoia National Forest. Jerry Gelock photo.

Fork Tule River. A steep hiking trail will take you up Bear Creek to Belknap Camp Grove of big trees.

Quaking Aspen Campground sits in a high meadow where the Western Divide Highway meets Highway 190. At 7,000 feet elevation you'll be high in the red fir belt, and some of the specimens at Quaking Aspen are more than 18 feet in diameter. You'll see white-headed woodpeckers and northern flickers here, as well as red-tailed and cooper's hawks.

Camp Wishon Campground, in the northern portion of the district, is a popular campground. Giving access to the North Fork Tule River and the Golden Trout Wilderness, this old camping place among the oaks and ponderosas has been attracting campers for generations.

Peppermint Campground, south of Ponderosa Lodge, is on a dirt road about two miles below the Western Divide Highway on the banks of Peppermint Creek. From your campsite climb the ridge beyond the camp for a view across the chasm of the Kern to the Kern Plateau beyond. Belknap Campground, near Camp Nelson, is on a twisting, narrow road adjacent to two groves of giant sequoias. This is an angler's camp for getting to the Tule River's south fork.

Hume Lake District Camping

Next to the Upper Kern Recreation Area and Lake Isabella, the Hume Lake Ranger District is the most visited region of the forest. Hume Lake itself is one major attraction, as is the Kings River and the entrance to Kings Canyon National Park and Sequoia National Park to the south. The Grant Grove portion of the national park is almost completely surrounded by Hume Lake District and attracts hundreds of thousands of visitors annually.

Hume Lake covers eighty-seven acres and the campground sits back from the lake among huge pines and gnarled, twisted black oaks. Boats on the lake are limited to twelve feet. Electric trolling motors are permitted. Small sailboats, up to sixteen feet can be used, too.

Other camping places on the Hume Lake District are Princess Campground at Indian Basin, and Stony Creek near the entrance to Sequoia National Park. Princess Campground is off Highway 180 between Grant Grove and Cedar Grove. Stony Creek attracts campers because of its close access to Sequoia National Park and because of its striking setting across the canyon from Chimney Rock and Big Baldy high on the western rim.

Big Meadow Campground is the closest to the Jennie Lakes Wilderness tucked away in the southeast corner of the District. The camps are in an uncrowded, meadow-dotted, forest-covered landscape. The Big Meadow Trailhead for Weaver Lake and points south and east is .25 mile away.

On The Trail

Hiking on Sequoia National Forest is great, especially in the wilderness areas, and there are five of them. Some areas, the lower altitude sections of Greenhorn and Cannell Meadows ranger districts offer some of the finest off-season hiking in the Sierra. The trails are free of snow much of the year, and you can get into the back country while the high sections of the forest are still winter-bound.

SEQUOIA NATIONAL FOREST

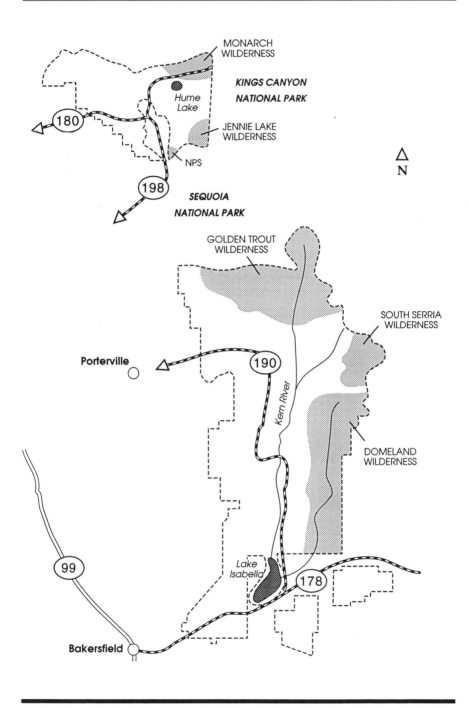

MONARCH WILDERNESS

KINGS CANYON NATIONAL PARK

Hume Lake

JENNIE LAKE WILDERNESS

180

NPS

198

SEQUOIA NATIONAL PARK

N

GOLDEN TROUT WILDERNESS

SOUTH SERRIA WILDERNESS

Porterville

190

Kern River

DOMELAND WILDERNESS

99

Lake Isabella

178

Bakersfield

National Recreation and Pacific Crest Trails

There are three National Recreation Trails on the forest and a seventy-five-mile section of the Pacific Crest Trail. The **Cannell Meadow National Recreation Trail** begins about two miles north of Kernville at an elevation of 2,800 feet and ends nine miles later in Pine Flat at 7,280 feet. The sharp elevational change carries the trail through a variety of flora and fauna. At lower elevations are sage, ceanothus, pinon pine, digger pine, and live oak. Grouse, squirrels, and rabbits will be your companions on the trail. Above 6,000 feet are mainly Jeffrey and lodgepole pines and grassy meadows. Deer and bears thrive in this climate. The rare Piute cypress can be seen along this trail at about 4,800 feet.

Jackass Creek Trail is only three miles and winds along Jackass Creek through a red fir forest and wide open meadows. The forest is cool and refreshing during the hot days of summer, and the meadows are filled with wildflowers until August. Brodiaea, Indian paintbrush, blazing star, and Douglas iris bloom in the short summer's heat.

Longest of the National Recreation Trails on the Sequoia is **Summit Trail** which travels from the edge of Sequoia National Park south along the crest of the Western Divide, partially in the Golden Trout Wilderness and partially in the forest of Tule River and Hot Springs ranger districts. Easiest access to the trail is at Quaking Aspen Campground where the trail crosses Highway 190. The trail runs north and south with elevations between 7,000 and 9,000 feet. Grades along the trail are generally gentle, except in the Slate Mountain area. Scenery visible from the trail includes parts of the Golden Trout Wilderness, the Mineral King region of Sequoia National Park and Peppermint Basin.

The **Pacific Crest Trail** enters Sequoia National Forest along its eastern edge in the South Sierra Wilderness. It hits civilization at Kennedy Meadows and then continues south. At one point it leaves the forest and travels over a long section of BLM land before reentering the forest near Walker Pass. From the pass, the trail goes southwest to Burning Moscow Springs and finally out of the forest at its very southernmost point, Geringer Grade.

Sequoia Forest Trails

The twenty-three-mile-long Rincon Trail follows the Rincon Fault along the east side of the Kern River Canyon, undulating along the fault, rarely dropping below 5,000 feet, and not getting above 6,000 feet. It passes in and out of drainages, going through flats of Jeffrey and digger pines, cedar and chaparral.

One trail that is a good day hike for families, with a picnic lunch on the summit, is the **Sunday Peak Trail.** It begins at the Girl Scout Camp parking area on Forest Highway 90 north of Greenhorn Summit. It climbs through mixed conifer forest on a moderate grade to the summit of Sunday Peak, a trip under two miles. The chaparral and interspersed pines of the Upper Kern River Canyon will be below you. Looking east across the canyon you'll see the pine and fir covered Kern Plateau. Here and there the bright green of a meadow will interrupt the somber darkness of the forest. Against the horizon the bare peaks of the Sierra crest stand sentinel.

Probably the most interesting hiking on the forest is in the Tule River District, and one of the most adventurous of these is the **Lewis Camp Trail.** This trail leaves from Lewis Camp trailhead eight miles north of Quaking Aspen, and travels east to Trout Meadows in Golden Trout Wilderness, then north to Kern

Ranger Station in Sequoia National Park. The eighteen miles of the trip offer fishing for golden trout on the Big Kern River, Little and Big Kern lakes, as well as campsites among speckled granite boulders at the edge of wide emerald meadows of the high Sierra.

A short trail leading to a spectacular view is the **Needles Trail,** which travels easterly from the Needles Road four miles from the Western Divide Highway to the Needles Fire Lookout. The trail is on the north slope of Needles Ridge and offers a view of the Lloyd Meadows and western half of the Golden Trout Wilderness. The "Needles" is a series of massive granite monolith rock formations rising out of the North Fork of the Kern River near its junction with the Little Kern. From the fire lookout at the top, you can see almost straight down into the Kern Canyon. An occasional flash of light hits your eye as the sun reflects from the river's surface 3,000 feet below.

Hume Lake District Hiking Trails

The lakes, meadows, forests and streams beyond Big Meadow and Horse Corral Meadows are criss-crossed with trails leading to spots in the wilderness on the crest of the ridge at the eastern edge of the forest. Take Sunset Meadow Road, Forest Road 13S14, south from Big Meadow Road. You'll hit the Rowell Meadow Trail which will take you to trout fishing in Jennie Lakes Wilderness.

Just past the Kennedy Grove of big trees north of Big Meadows Road there's a trailhead from where you can hike into the remote Monarch Wilderness along the steep slopes of Kings River Canyon. It winds along the side of the canyon about nine miles, finally joining Highway 180 as it enters Kings Canyon National Park.

Wilderness on the Sequoia

There are five wilderness areas within Sequoia National Forest. Golden Trout Wilderness is the most visited of all Sequoia Wildernesses and requires a wilderness permit in order to stay overnight. The other four do not require permits yet because the level of use doesn't call for limitation.

Golden Trout Wilderness in both Sequoia and Inyo national forests, includes 305,484 acres of lakes, meadows, forests, peaks, streams, and plateaus. The back country is ideal for camping, hiking and exploring and is accessible from several points on Sequoia National Forest. Camp Wishon, White Meadows, Loggy Meadows, and Lloyd Meadows are the most usable trailheads on the southwestern side of the wilderness.

South Sierra Wilderness borders Golden Trout Wilderness on its northern boundary and Dome Land Wilderness on the south, and is all within the South Fork of the Kern River watershed, which has been given Wild and Scenic River designation. Fragile meadowlands, diversity of flora and fauna between forested ridges, rolling hills, and craggy, steep peaks describe this wilderness. A relatively gentle terrain area of about 25,000 acres on the Sequoia is ideally suited to family-oriented recreation. The more adventurous can frequent the more than 38,000 acres along the Sierra crest on the Inyo Forest which completes this new wilderness.

Dome Land Wilderness is noted for its many granite domes and unique geological formations. Church Dome is one of its most outstanding scenic points. The semi-arid and arid country has elevations from 3,000 to 9,730 feet. The South Fork of the Kern River and its tributaries attract many anglers to this unusual place. The spring and fall fishing in these lower altitudes is especially good when the weather conditions are just right for camping, hiking and fishing.

The Monarch and Jennie Lake wildernesses are in the Hume Lake District, and are much smaller than Golden Trout. Jennie Lakes, for instance, has only a little over 10,000 acres. It is easily accessed by trail from the Big Meadows Road southeast of Grant Grove. Hikers and some fishermen are attracted here because it isn't particularly well-known, and you can have long periods of solitude to enjoy the wild surroundings.

The same is true of Monarch Wilderness, which is shared with neighboring Sierra National Forest. Dramatic, spectacular, multicolored geologic, rugged, rocky formations of the Monarch can be accessed by trail from either Highway 180 or from Kennedy Meadows northeast of Quail Flat along Generals' Highway.

Touring, Sightseeing, and Special Programs

The Trail of a Hundred Giants, at Redwood Meadow Campground on the Western Divide Highway, provides excellent interpretation about life among the giant sequoias. Trail markers along the way point out the environmental necessities for the big trees' success, and the other trees, plants, and life associated with them.

There are several other things to see and do that are fun to search out for yourself. One is to drive the Sherman Pass Road, Forest Road 22S05. This scenic road leaves the Kern River Highway at the Johnsondale Bridge and climbs northeast to the Kern Plateau. Climbing steeply, it passes through succeeding life zones in classic manner with the typical trees of each zone appearing as if planted by textbook authors. At 6,000 feet the ponderosas and black oaks give way to Jeffrey pines and white firs. At 8,500 feet the Jeffreys are replaced with lodgepoles and red firs.

At the top of Sherman Pass you come to Sherman Pass Vista. From here look out to the north all the way to the mammoth heights of Mt. Whitney and the glistening peaks of the Great Western Divide in Sequoia National Park.

Once you reach the Kern Plateau, stop at the visitor information center at Blackrock Ranger Station (closed Tuesdays and Wednesdays). Attendants can fill you in on a number of places to visit. One of these may be Bald Mountain Lookout. About five miles south of Blackrock Station, a short, one-mile road, Forest Road 22S77, turns east and climbs swiftly almost to the top of Bald Mountain. The short hike up to the lookout will reward you with electrifying views out over Dome Land and South Sierra wildernesses, the Kern Plateau, the Whitney Range, and the Great Western Divide. It's an incomparable 360 degree view. You'll be able to count the domes and related formations in the Dome Land and watch the shadows move across the land as the setting sun moves down the sky.

Surrounding the lookout is Bald Mountain Botanical Area, which consists of 440 acres, recognized by the scientific community as a most unusual botanical and geological island in the midst of the Kern Plateau. Over 100 species of plants have been recorded on the rocky summit, and one sensitive plant species, the Bald Mountain potentilla, occurs nowhere else.

Birders will love Bald Mountain, especially for the raptors, including Cooper's, sharp-shinned, and red-tailed hawks. You stand a better chance of seeing a blue grouse here than almost anywhere else in the wild; their drumming sound is a frequent counterpoint to the wind soughing in the trees.

Searching out all the different groves of *Sequoiadendron giganteum* in the forest

Cross-country skiing on the Quaker Meadow Trail in the Tule Ranger District. Jerry Gelock photo.

would be an exercise in futility for most of us. However, a "Giant Sequoia Grove" plan is underway by the national forest. They have identified 38 groves, but some are very close together and may be combined. There aren't any road signs telling you to "turn here for the Big Trees," and except for the Trail of a Hundred Giants, there aren't any interpretive trails leading through the groves. To find them yourself with the aid of your maps and the friendly services of a forest officer can be a great adventure. The groves of Hume Lake Ranger District are numerous and probably easiest to find.

One fascinating drive starts in the Kern River Canyon and ends at Camp Nelson. You will pass through Johnsondale, formerly a mill town. The mill pond is still there, and about four miles before you come into town, you'll see the stunning **South Creek Falls**

Beyond Johnsondale, the road climbs to the Western Divide Highway at Holey Meadow. Continuing north on this highway will bring you to the Trail of a Hundred Giants at Redwood Meadow campground, and the turn-off for **Dome Rock**. Park at the end of the short spur and walk out on to the rock. Stand at the edge where it juts out over the Kern River Canyon. To the north you can see The Needles, a similar granite outcropping. Quaking Aspen campground and Ranger Station are near the junction of the Western Divide Highway and Highway 190 which leads down slope to Camp Nelson and Pierpoint Springs.

Hume Lake Ranger District

Hume Lake was formed by a multiple arch dam constructed in 1908. It provided water for the longest lumber flume ever built. The Hume-Bennett Lumber Company built the dam and floated lumber by flume to Sanger through the Kings Canyon, a distance of fifty-nine miles. The eighty-seven-acre lake is the center of recreation activities in the Hume Lake Recreation Area.

Converse Basin, the area from which much of the timber for the Hume Lake mill was cut is the site of the **Chicago Stump**. In the late 1800s an immense giant sequoia was selected for display at the Columbian Exposition in Chicago just to prove how large the sequoias really were. The feat to remove the giant and display it is still an unique engineering story. You can see the stump of the tree in Converse Basin. The **Boole Tree**, the largest tree in any National Forest is growing just north of Converse Mountain on a 2.75-mile loop trail. It stands all by itself, the only remaining old growth sequoia in Converse Basin.

You don't just "see" a sequoia like the Boole Tree, you *experience* it. Until the loggers came the Converse Basin Grove was the world's largest, but saws and drills and dynamite reduced all but this lonely sentinel. Great stumps and monstrous chunks of the almost decay-proof trunks scattered over the landscape are all that remains.

Sports

Snow comes each winter in the Sierra in amounts and depths unknown to most of the country. It piles up as the winter weeks go by, sparkling in the sun, bending branches as the weight piles up. There is one small ski resort at **Shirley Meadow** on Greenhorn Summit. It features one chair-lift, a rope-tow, and seven downhill runs. There are rentals and a warming hut.

Cross-country skiing and snowmobiling are more widely enjoyed. In the Tule River Ranger District, Highway 190 and the Western Divide Highway are plowed each winter as far as 2.5 miles east of Quaking Aspen Campground. At this point separate areas have been established for Nordic skiers and for snowmobilers. In most of the forest, both use the same trails.

At Hume Lake there is a much-used XC area, with miles of trails over unplowed Forest Service roads and trails.

Boating and Waterskiing

Traditional boating and water-skiing is as big on the Sequoia National Forest as river rafting is. Because of the tremendous demand quotas and permits have had to be inaugurated on the Kern River.

Unique among California's great rivers, the Kern flows north-south instead of east-west for more than 100 of its 165 miles. With an average gradient of thirty feet per mile, the Kern is one of the steepest and wildest white-water rides not only in California, but in all of North America.

The **Lower Kern Run** begins ten miles southwest of Kernville off Highway 155, south of the Lake Isabella Main Dam. There are three usual put-in spots, BLM South, Keyesville Bridge, and Sandy Flat. Typical take-out is Democrat Beach, eighteen miles downstream from BLM South. There are all classes of runs from Class II through Class V+ (easy to expert).

The **Upper Kern Runs** begin between the Johnsondale Bridge and Riverkern Beach. This twenty-one-mile stretch of river has four non-contiguous raftable runs with varying degrees of difficulty. **Limestone Run** is farthest upstream. The put-in is just below Johnsondale Bridge and the take-out is Fairview Dam. This is a Class III or IV run depending upon the amount of the flow.

Fairview Run begins at the north end of Road's End Resort below Fairview Dam. This Class III and IV run has take-outs at Chamise Flat, Calkins Flat, and Salmon Creek. **Goldledge Run** begins ten miles north of Kernville just upstream from Goldledge campground and ends at Riverkern Beach. This 11-mile run has Class III, IV, and V sections. The bottom run on the Upper Kern is the **Camp 3 Run**, and is the easiest to maneuver. Begins downstream from Camp 3 Campground and runs for 4.5 miles through Class II, III, and IV runs, and takes out at Riverside Park.

Wildest of all whitewater runs on the Wild and Scenic Kern River is the **Forks Run**, considered by many to be one of the most demanding runs in North America. It combines a wilderness experience with whitewater rafting, and is classified Class V all the way. Put-in is at Forks of the Kern some forty-five miles north of Kernville at the end of a two-mile trail. For most boaters, getting equipment down the two-mile trail to the Forks put-in will require the use of pack horses or mules. For details on renting animals contact Golden Trout Wilderness Pack Trains (see chart).

Sequoia National Forest regulations require permits for all rafters, canoists and kayakers boating the Kern River from May 15 to September 15, between 7 a.m. and 4 p.m. Group size is limited to fifteen. The permits are available free of charge through both the Greenhorn and Cannell ranger district offices. Reservations for permits are accepted beginning March 1 each year.

Off Road Motoring

The Kern Plateau provides recreational opportunities for off-highway enthusiasts of all ability. The Kern River borders the area on the west. The terrain varies from the high, rocky trails near Sherman Peak to the open country of Monache Meadows. Challenging rocky side-hill type trails can be found in Rattlesnake and Bonita creek drainages, and enjoyable forest trails can be experienced on the Jackass, Albanita, and Osa Meadow trails.

You'll need a valid OHV "Greensticker," and you'll have to keep in mind that cross-country travel is strictly *prohibited*. However, there certainly are enough trails to keep many, motorcyclists busy.

The **Rattlesnake Creek Trail** begins about two miles east of Paloma Meadows just off the Sherman Pass Road and at the end of Mohagany Creek Trail. It has a variety of conditions ranging from steep, gradual hill climbs to creek bottom riding. It connects with Rattlesnake and Beach trails near Bonita Creek. The **Rattlesnake Trail**, itself parallels Rattlesnake Creek for eight miles and has no connections at its lower end, but it's really great for more advanced cyclists.

At the Cannell Meadow Ranger Station in Kernville, or at Blackrock Information Station, you can get a free map of the Kern Plateau Off-Highway Vehicle Area, which has a complete list of the trials, where they go, and what kind of experience is necessary to undertake any particular trail. In other parts of the forest, off-highway use is available, inasmuch as there are many miles of logging roads.

Fishing and Hunting

When you talk of fishing in the Sequoia National Forest, the talk immediately turns to golden trout, and little else. To be sure, there are miles and miles of streams with rainbow, brook and brown trout planted in them, but it is the goldens that most of the many fishermen come for, even though it takes quite a bit of physical effort to get to them.

The Kern River watershed is unique in that golden trout evolved here and nowhere else. Of these golden trout, one subspecies, the little Kern golden trout, is listed as "threatened" under the Endangered Species Act.

Hunters enter the forest with regularity to try for deer. The packers all have special places where they take clients to try for that big buck. The Kern Plateau, the Greenhorn Mountains, and the wildernesses, especially in the northern part of the forest, all produce their share of the deer harvest each year.

Resorts, Lodges and Hotels

There are a number of resorts and lodges on private enclaves within the forest at Riverkern, Calkins Flat and Fairview along the Kern River Canyon; Pine Flat near California Hot Springs; at Ponderosa and Camp Nelson on the Tule River District; and at Montecito-Sequoia and Stony Creek on the Hume Lake District.

In addition, some lodges operate as permittees on National Forest land, such as Pierpoint Springs Resort.

SEQUOIA NATIONAL FOREST CAMPGROUNDS

	Piped Water	Camp Sites	Trailer Space	Fishing	Boating	Swimming	Store	RV Dump Station	Reservations	Special Attractions
Cannell Meadow Ranger District										
Boulder Gulch	•	78	•	•	•	•	•		•	Lake Isabella
Camp 3	•	52	•	•		•				rafting
Camp 9	•	109	•	•	•	•	•		•	Lake Isabella
Fairview	•	55	•	•		•	•		•	rafting
Fish Creek	•	40	•	•						
French Gulch Group	•	1	•	•	•	•	•		•	Lake Isabella
Goldledge	•	37	•	•		•			•	rafting
Headquarters	•	44	•	•		•			•	rafting
Horse Meadow	•	41	•	•						
Hospital Flat	•	40	•	•		•		•		
Hungry Gulch	•	78	•	•	•	•	•		•	Lake Isabella
Kennedy Meadows	•	38	•	•						PCT Trailhead
Limestone		22	•	•		•			•	rafting
Live Oak North	•	60	•	•	•	•	•		•	Lake Isabella
Live Oak South	•	90	•	•	•	•	•		•	Lake Isabella
Main Dam	•	80	•	•	•	•	•		•	Lake Isabella
Paradise Cove	•	138	•	•	•	•	•		•	Lake Isabella
Pioneer Point	•	78	•	•	•	•	•		•	Lake Isabella
Tillie Creek	•	159	•	•	•	•	•		•	Lake Isabella
Tillie Creek Group	•	4	•	•	•	•	•		•	Lake Isabella
Troy Meadow	•	73	•	•						
Greenhorn Ranger District										
Alder Creek		8		•						
Breckenridge	•	8								
Cedar Creek	•	11		•						
Evans Flat		12								
Greenhorn Summit	•	91	•							country park
Hobo	•	25		•					•	rafting
Hot Springs Ranger District										
Frog Meadow		10								
Holey Meadow	•	10							•	
Leavis Flat	•	9	•	•					•	
Long Meadow		6		•						
Lower Peppermint	•	17	•	•					•	
Panorama		10								
Redwood Meadow	•	15		•					•	trail of 100 giants
White River	•	12	•	•					•	

SEQUOIA NATIONAL FOREST CAMPGROUNDS

	Piped Water	Camp Sites	Trailer Space	Fishing	Boating	Swimming	Store	RV Dump Station	Reservations	Special Attractions
Hume Lake Ranger District										
Aspen Hollow Group	•	71	•	•						
Big Meadows		25	•	•					•	
Buck Rock		5	•							
Camp 4		5		•						
Camp 4½		5		•						
Cove Group	•	1				•			•	
Eshom Creek	•	34	•	•						
Fir Group	•	1				•			•	
Hume Lake	•	74	•	•	•	•	•		•	Hume Lake
Landslide		9		•						
Logger Flat Group	•	1	•						•	
Mill Flat		5		•						
Princess	•	90	•	•					•	
Stony Creek	•	49	•	•					•	
Tenmile		10		•						
Tule River Ranger District										
Belknap	•	15		•					•	
Coy Flat	•	20	•						•	
Peppermint		19								
Quaking Aspen	•	32	•						•	
Quaking Aspen Group	•	7	•	•					•	
Wishon	•	33	•	•					•	

SIERRA
NATIONAL
FOREST

Sacramento

San Francisco

Los Angeles

Sierra National Forest

Wilderness and water are two key elements in the environment of the Sierra National Forest. There are eleven major reservoirs on the forest, and five major wilderness areas. There are nine major rivers on the forest, five are already designated (Nov. '87) as Wild and Scenic Rivers, and the other four are recommended.

With Yosemite National Park on its northern boundary and Sequoia-Kings Canyon National Park on its south, the forest has an abundance of visitors. Its magnificently diverse topography makes possible a wide variety of recreational opportunities.

Each of the four ranger districts on the forest, Kings River, Pineridge, Minarets and Mariposa, has something special to offer visitors, from giant sequoia groves to competitive sailing to wilderness camping and fishing to historic interpretive trails.

Camping

There are sixty campgrounds on the forest with more than 1,300 developed sites, plus, of course, the almost unlimited chances for dispersed camping in the less-used parts of the forest. There are private campgrounds at Shaver Lake and Bass Lake, but for the most part, camping on the Sierra is on Forest Service land.

Kings River Ranger District

Most of the developed campgrounds on this district, as in the other three, center around the recreation areas. In this case Dinkey Creek, the Courtwright and Wishon area, and along the Kings River at the southern end of the forest. **Dinkey Creek** Campground, at an elevation of 5,700 feet nears the upper limits of the ponderosa pine forest, and a few lodgepoles and red firs intrude. The understory has manzanitas and pungent mountain misery. Birders can spot the bright red, yellow, and black western tanager, as well as the orange-hued Bullock's Oriole. Eight warblers have been seen on the Sierra National Forest, and sharp-eyed visitors at Dinkey Creek can spot at least three: Wilson's, Yellow-rumped, and Nashville.

There are four campgrounds located on the shores of the rock-bound reservoirs, Courtwright and Wishon, **Lily Pad** at Wishon, and **Marmot, Trapper Springs**, and **Voyage Rock** campgrounds at Courtwright. Voyager Rock Campground is located on the east side of the reservoir on the Dusy Off-Highway Vehicle Route and can only be reached with a four-wheel drive vehicle. Clumps of lodgepole and western white pines are scattered across the granite at Lily Pad, interspersed with chinquapin and huckleberry oak. Peaks of the John Muir Trail glow pink and orange each evening at sundown.

Down in the southwestern part of the forest, along the Kings River, Pine Flat Reservoir has two Forest Service camps available, both at **Sycamore Flat**. Chaparral hillsides rise on both sides of the river bottom where sycamores and digger pines shelter the camping places. East of the reservoir on what the Forest Service calls the "Upper Kings River" are four more primitive campgrounds: **Kirch Flat, Mill Flat, Camp 4**, and **Camp 4 1/2**. Road access is difficult past Kirch Flat, where huge granite boulders force the river to twist and dodge its way down the canyon, and provide camp units with some protection. This rugged section of the Wild and Scenic Kings River is popular with experienced river rafters, and Pine Flat Reservoir is a favorite of water skiers and bass fishermen.

Pineridge Ranger District
There are two Forest Service campgrounds in the Shaver Lake area, **Dorabelle** and **Swanson Meadow**. At some time in the past giant sequoias were planted here on the shores of the reservoir, and several camp units contain them along with Jeffrey pines. A big, green meadow fills the center of Dorabelle, with green towhees, rosy finches, and hummingbirds. Under the trees at the edges, Stellar jays gather to scold intruders. There is also a big private campground here operated by the Southern California Edison Company, **Camp Edison**. Camp Edison accepts reservations, while the Forest Service campgrounds remain first-come, first-served.

The Huntington Lake Area offers fishing, hiking, swimming, sailing, and immeasurable mountain scenery. Highway 168 first dips down to the eastern end of the lake, just at the entrance to **Rancheria** campground. Here, under towering Jeffrey pines and red firs, you'll share the forest with golden-mantled ground squirrels, chickarees, and lodgepole chipmunks. Just at dusk, western pipistrelles and California Myotis bats gather overhead to feast on their winged dinners.

Along the north shore of the lake, you'll come to **Deer Creek, College, Catavee, Kinnickinick**, and **Billy Creek** campgrounds. Arrow-straight lodgepole pines dominate, along with Jeffrey and western white pines. The high tree canopy filters the sunlight into dappled patterns on the forest floor and understory. Be aware that many campers like to come to Huntington in the summer, and reservations are a must for all of the campgrounds around the lake.

A number of developed as well as dispersed camping areas are above Huntingon Lake in the Florence and Edison Lake Area. This magnificent high country region is surrounded by the towering, glittering peaks of the Ansel Adams and John Muir wildernesses. All of the campgrounds are at elevations from 6,500 to 7,500 feet, in an area of steep-sided canyons and plunging alpine streams. The area is generally accessible from June through September. However, access is via Kaiser Pass Road, a one-laned, winding road that is not recommended for trailers or large motor homes.

Minarets Ranger District
To get into the dozen or more campgrounds on the Minarets District, take either the Beasore Road from Bass Lake, or Minarets Road from the towns of North Fork and South Fork on the western edge of the forest. You'll soon find yourself away from most forest visitors among the rolling chaparral, grass, and woodland covered hills. Small campgrounds at **Fish Creek, Rock Creek**, and **Sweetwater**, squeeze into side canyons where early season anglers and late season deer hunters take advantage of the shade of ponderosas and incense cedars.

Largest of all the "front country" camping places is at **Mammoth Pool**. Boat ramp and swimming beaches make the campground at the edge of this long, narrow reservoir a favorite with boating families. At 3,500 feet eleva-

Campers at Kirch Flat Campground. Jean Hawthorne photo.

tion this steep-walled lake can get tropical on July and August afternoons, so it's nice to be able to cool off with a plunge into the water.

In the "backcountry" near the entrance to Ansel Adams Wilderness, **Glover Meadow** and **Granite Creek** campgrounds are favorites for hikers and fishermen headed for the high lakes and peaks along the Sierra crest, or those who like to camp in quieter, more remote sites.

You can reach **Upper Chiquito** Campground via Beasore Road, where the Chiquito Pass Trail comes down from Yosemite National Park. Your campsite along the melodic creek is nestled in a grove of lodgepole pines. Above you, western junipers dot the sunlit mountainsides.

Mariposa Ranger District

Major tourist attraction on the Mariposa district is Bass Lake. At about 3,400 feet altitude, the lake is open year round. There are many private resorts and vacation home tracts around the lake, and camp sites are often full.

Lupine Campground, one of five Forest Service camping sites around the lake is halfway down the west side. It has recently been reconstructed and has everything from high density four- or two-party sites to walk-ins. The camp units wind up the hillside overlooking the lake under cover of immense black oaks and towering pines. The other Bass Lake campgrounds, **Denver Church, Forsk, Spring Cove**, and **Wishon Point** line up down the west side of this busy impoundment. Summer homes, marinas, and resorts insure plenty of activities for you. Reservations are a must.

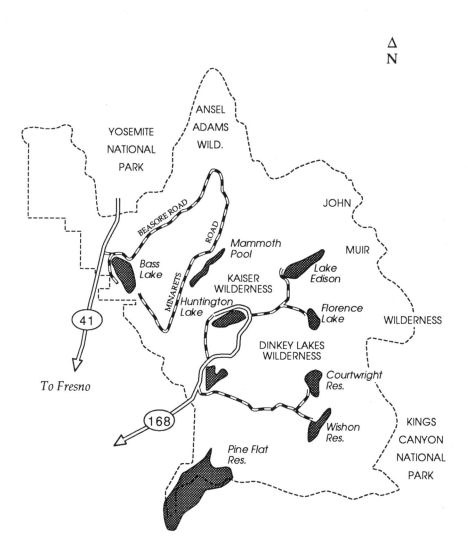

There are a number of smaller and less developed campgrounds away from Bass Lake. **Big Sandy** and **Little Sandy** campgrounds are five and six miles east of Fish Camp on Big Creek almost at the 6,000-foot level. The creek always has trout, and each pool in the stream holds a fighter. Just a couple of miles further, **Fresno Dome** Campground, at an elevation of 6,400 feet puts you into lodgepole and red fir country. You see signs of deer and bears here, and may get a coyote serenade while you sleep. Nearby Fresno Dome offers extraordinary views from the top of the Willow Creek and Beasore Creek drainages, and all the way to the ridges and peaks of Ansel Adams Wilderness.

Summerdale Campground, just outside the south entrance station of Yosemite National Park, can serve as your headquarters while you tour the giant sequoias in the Mariposa Grove just inside the Park.

On The Trail

The **Pacific Crest Trail** traverses the eastern section of Sierra National Forest traveling through the John Muir Wilderness. On the north, it enters the forest just south of Devil's Postpile National Monument and continues south to the junction of Piute Creek and the San Joaquin River just at the edge of Kings Canyon National Park. On the way it crosses Silver and Seldon Passes and comes close to Lake Thomas A. Edison and Blayney Meadows. Many of the packers on the Sierra Forest will drop food packages for long distance hikers. For the list ask at the Kings River or Pine Ridge Ranger District offices for the information sheet, "Food Drop Information."

National Recreation Trails

There are four National Recreation Trails on the Sierra National Forest. Northernmost of these is **Shadow of the Giants** National Recreation Trail, which is a one-mile self-guiding interpretive walk into a grove of majestic sequoias located at Nelder Grove.

The **Black Point Trail** is northwest of Huntington Lake. This short trail climbs steeply through stands of red fir, eventually reaching a view point amid Sierra juniper and Jeffrey pines. You'll get unparalleled views of Huntington and Shaver lakes, the Kaiser Crest, San Joaquin Canyon, and the San Joaquin Valley. Black Point itself is at 8,111 feet elevation.

East of Huntington Lake, the **Rancheria Falls Trail** rises gently for a mile-long walk through red fir stands and an understory of whitethorn, ceanothus, gooseberry, manzanita, and chinquapiin. At the end of the trail, you'll be rewarded with the sight of the never-failing Rancheria Falls. Take a picnic, and save time to play in the icy-clear stream below the falls.

The southernmost trail at the lowest altitude of the group is the **Kings River Trail**. It begins at Garnet Dike Campground and follows the Kings River upstream three miles to Spring Creek. A less well-developed extension of the trail continues another two miles to Garlic Falls. This area is within the newly-designated Kings River Special Management Area.

Day Hikes on the Kings River District

Two of the many possibilities for day hikes on the southern part of the forest are the **Dinkey Creek-McKinley Grove Trail** and the **Woodchuck Lake Trail**. The first starts near the pack station at Dinkey Creek and follows the stream southwesterly for about six miles to the McKinley Grove of big trees. It's a great picnic spot among the giants, and a nice kind of hike for kids, especially if you can spot a car at the grove and drive back.

The trail into "Woodchuck Country" begins on the far side of the Wishon Lake dam at the Coolidge Meadows trailhead. Cross Woodchuck Creek after climbing about a mile along the eastern shore of Wishon, then go upstream, keeping to the left at each branching of the trail, to Woodchuck Lake, about a five mile walk. Sometimes the fishing can be very good for handsome rainbows, and an occasional giant brown.

Day Hikes on the Pine Ridge Ranger District

The **Coarsegrass Meadow Trail** starts where Home Camp Creek crosses the road on the northwest shore of Huntington Lake. The four-mile climb from the lake passes through stands of red firs and Jeffrey and lodgepole pines along the stream to the flowery meadow at the end. An extension of another two miles will take you to Aspen Meadow.

Day Hikes on Minarets Ranger District

To get a taste of the Ansel Adams Wilderness, the **Jackass Lakes** make a wonderful one-day destination. Turn off the Beasore Road near Clover Meadow Ranger Station—where you need to pick up your wilderness permit—at Norris Creek turn-off. Drive about two rough miles up this road to the Norris Creek trailhead. The Jackass Lakes lie in a basin under Madera Peak at the head-waters of Norris Creek. Your trail is going to climb about 1,500 feet in 2.5 miles bringing you out into a vast, green alpine meadow and the glacier blue lakes of the basin.

A similar hike takes you from the trailhead above Upper Chiquito Campground to **Chiquito Lake**. You'll follow Chiquito Creek right up to the boundary of Yosemite National Park. Strong hikers can make the walk in an hour, but you'll see more if you stop and soak your feet in the stream, or try to count how many different wildflowers bloom in the meadows.

Day Hikes on the Mariposa Ranger District

From the Fresno Dome Campground drive east about 1.5 miles to the trailhead on the right side of the road for **Fresno Dome**. It's less than a mile to the top, and the views are remarkable northwest across the edge of Yosemite to the lonely Chowcilla Mountains, south over the valley of Willow Creek to Bass Lake, and northeast to the rocky spires of Yosemite's Boundary Peaks region.

About a quarter of a mile beyond the Fresno Dome trailhead, a rough road turns left (north) to **Iron Lakes**. This three-mile trip *can* be made in a four-wheel drive vehicle, but it's a very nice walk to a group of three lakes and a pond. At more than 8,000 feet elevation, you'll be near the timberline where clumps of whitebark pines and wind-twisted hemlocks form hiding places for pine martens and day beds for mule deer that spend their summers on the alpine slopes.

Wilderness Opportunities

The Sierra National Forest now contains about 528,000 acres of designated wilderness. Almost 227,000 acres were added as a result of the California Wilderness Act of 1984.

The Sierra's five wildernesses are the Ansel Adams, Dinkey Lakes, John Muir, Kaiser, and Monarch.

The dam across the North Fork Kings River forms Lake Wishon.

Ansel Adams Wilderness, located in both Sierra and Inyo National Forests, is characterized by spectacular alpine scenery with barren granite peaks, steep-walled gorges, and rock outcroppings. The 30,000-acre **Dinkey Lakes Wilderness** was created by the Wilderness Act of 1984. It lies on the west slope of the Sierra between Huntington Lake and Courtwright Reservoir. Most of the wilderness is above 8,000 feet in the clear air scented only by wildflowers and junipers. The **John Muir Wilderness** extends along the crest of the Sierra from Mammoth Lakes southeastward for a distance of about thirty miles, then forks around the boundary of Kings Canyon National Park. This is a land of snow-capped mountain peaks with hundreds of sparkling lakes and streams and lush, green meadows. The Pacific Crest Trail traverses the wilderness from north to south.

The wilderness closest to civilization on the Sierra Forest is **Kaiser Wilderness**, which is located immediately north of Huntington Lake. Eighteen small lakes dot the northern half of the wilderness, and campers and fishermen make these spots their headquarters because of water access. Least visited of all the Sierra National Forest wildernesses is the **Monarch Wilderness**. It is extremely rugged and difficult to traverse.

Touring, Sightseeing, and Special Programs

Auto touring on the Sierra will acquaint you with the forest in a hurry because of the differing ecosystems you pass through on each route, from transitional pine and chaparral covered foothills to sub-alpine Hudsonian zone meadows. Both Beasore and Minaret roads will take you deep into the back country. On Minarets Road at Mile High Vista you can see the top ski lift tower at Mammoth Mountain on the other side of the Sierra Nevada, as well as spectacular views of the rock-rimmed Chiquito Basin and the crags of the Upper San Joaquin.

Another favorite drive takes you from Shaver Lake to Courtwright and Wishon Reservoirs by way of McKinley Grove of Big Trees. At all three places, there are picnic grounds, and the entire trip is over paved roads. The LeConte Divide Overloook on Courtwright Road offers a superb view of the high country. Granite domes, rugged peaks and patches of never-melting snow on the northern slopes will meet your eye. Wishon Village, operating on a Forest Service permit, has gasoline, a restaurant, lodge, store, and boat rentals. Driving time from Shaver Lake to Wishon is about an hour and fifteen minutes. You'll want to add an additional thirty minutes or so for the trip to Courtwright

The Forest Service has designated the 100-mile Sierra Heritage drive as a Scenic Byway. The five-hour drive travels through distinctive alpine country which bears the stamp of heavy glacial activity.

Paved, but steep, winding, and narrow, the 22-mile trip to Florence Lake or to Lake Edison captures a different vista at every twist in the road. One of the attractions on the road to Edison is Mono Hot Springs. Here hot natural mineral springs have been captured and brought into a bath house where you may soak away the cares of the world. Plan to lunch on the deck of their restaurant and relax in the sun. Both Florence and Edison Lakes have stores where you can get supplies, and a restaurant at Edison also caters to the inner man or woman.

One of the shorter trips from Huntington Lake is to Mushroom Rock. Drive toward the west end of the Lake about six miles, and turn right at the Black Point/Mushroom Rock sign. This is a graded dirt road with some logging traffic so drive slowly and cautiously. At about the three mile mark, turn left at the Mushroom Rock sign. It's a quarter of a mile to the parking lot, from where a level trail leads to a vista point, the result of wind erosion. The tree cover gives way to an exposed granite shelf, from where you look down into the shadows of Big Creek Canyon and beyond to the rounded spire of Musick Mountain.

Interpretive Programs

Guided nature walks, campfire programs, and a "Junior Ranger Program" are all offered at Huntington Lake during the summer season. Visitor programs center at the Eastwood Visitor Center at the east end of Huntington Lake. The visitor center has a small display of natural phenomena, and sells books, pamphlets, posters, and magazines pertaining to the Sierra National Forest under the management of the "Three Forests Interpretive Association." Outside the visitor center, the Ward Tunnel discharges millions of gallons of water into Huntington Lake. An interpretive gazebo explains how the snow melt is gathered into lakes and reservoirs and transported to the thirsty lands below.

Among the nature walks offered at Huntington are two "regulars" to the "Indian Pools" to examine the flora and fauna of Big Creek, and the "Indian Site Walk" to an archaeological site near China Peak. Evening campfires are on Friday and Saturday nights at Billy Creek and Rancheria campground amphitheaters.

At both Dinkey Creek and Dorabelle campgrounds, students from West Valley College lead nature walks during the summer season as a part of their training. Schedules and subjects change from time to time, so it's best to check at the campgrounds to find out what's going on and when.

A fine Forest Service Interpretive Trail is **Way of the Mono Interpretive Trail** at Bass Lake. Crane Valley Dam which impounds Bass Lake was built in 1900, but there were people living here before that. Prior to the mid-nineteenth century, it was the home of a group of Native Americans known as the Western Mono, or Monache. They were a Shoshonean-speaking group who had migrated to the western side of the Sierra from the Great Basin, settling along the Sierra Foothills from Yosemite south to the Kaweah River. This trail, with eight illustrated stops tells how they used their natural surroundings in their daily lives.

Sports

The **Sierra Summit** ski area is one of the State's major ski resorts, and the slopes of China Peak resound with the happy shrieks of skiers all winter long. Cross country skiers throng to Tamarack Winter Sports Area, half-way between Shaver Lake and Huntington along Highway 168. About fifteen miles of marked trails are patrolled by volunteer ski patrol. There are more than thirty-five miles of snowmobile trails in the same area—although not the same as the XC trails. In the same general area is the fifteen-mile Coyote Trail for Nordic skiers only. This system, too, has the benefit of the volunteer patrol.

The "Sierra Snowmobile Club" is in the process of building more than 100 miles of trails for their sport in this area. Plans call for some, but not all, of the trails to be groomed each winter. Stop at the Pineridge Ranger District Office at Shaver Lake to get details on these and other trails.

A huge snowmobile area east of the town of North Fork can be accessed either near Peckinpaugh Meadows or off Minarets Road near Fish Creek. This area has miles of Forest roads left unplowed, and snowmobilers can go for hours without retracing their tracks.

Boating and Water Skiing

Huntington Lake is perfectly placed on the surface of the earth as far as fresh-water sailers are concerned, and huge sailing regattas are held here each summer. The winds and other conditions are just about perfect for catamarans and other small boats to skip across the water as fast as the breezes will carry them. Hardly a week-end goes by without some kind of competition on the lake.

Down at Shaver Lake and over at Bass Lake, the speedboats and water-skiers hold center stage. Marinas and launch ramps dot the shores of all three of these big reservoirs, and rental boats are available at all of them, also.

Other lakes on the Sierra National Forest have boats on them, but mostly for fishing. Mammoth Pool is unusual in one respect in that all boating activities are closed down for a time in the late spring in order that migrating herds of deer can swim across the lake without interference. All of the high altitude reservoirs, Edison, Florence, Courtwright, and Wishon have 15 mph speed limits.

Whitewater rafting enthusiasts can enjoy their sport on the Kings River at the south end of the forest, or on the Merced River at the north end. The Kings River run from Garnet Dike to Kirch Flat passes through several rapids classed III and IV.

Off-Road Motoring

"High Country Vehicle Adventures" is what the Kings River Ranger District calls the off-highway vehicle routes in their region. The routes are well-named, from the relatively easy 3.5 mile **Brewer OHV Route** to the very strenuous thirty-mile, two-day minimum **Dusy OHV Route**. The Ranger District has prepared a separate information sheet for each of the routes on the District. They are available from any ranger station in the Forest.

Be forewarned: The Dusy OHV Route is a **doozy**! Experienced drivers figure that 1 1/2 mph is top speed to negotiate Thompson Hill, one of the nastiest stretches of road on any of the OHV routes on the forest. This trail spends most of its time in the very high altitudes, sometimes approaching 10,000 feet altitude before arriving at Kaiser Pass.

Other ranger districts on the forest also offer good OHV routes, particularly the Minarets District. Jackass Rock to Jackass Meadow is one of the favorite short runs, as is the trail to Junction and Bare Island Lakes from Fresno Dome. Both are short trips with easy access to interesting country.

Fishing and Hunting

Fishing is a major sport on the Sierra National Forest, and its streams and lakes support several species of game fish, among them black bass, bluegills, crappie and trout.

The many streams of the Sierra contain rainbow, golden, brown, and brook trout. These fish may be caught with flies, lures, and bait.

Hunters come to the forest in large numbers during the deer season, and the experienced ones do very well. The annual harvest is large during both the early season bow-and-arrow hunt, and during the regular rifle season. Packers take hunters deep into the back country away from roads and civilization. A bright October morning spent on a stand deep in the John Muir Wilderness has all kinds of possibilities for your trophy buck.

Resorts, Lodges, and Hotels

Commercial lodging facilities operating with Forest Service permits range from lakeside resorts to a dude ranch along the John Muir Trail. In addition, several enclaves of private property within the forest also have commercial lodging.

At Bass Lake, the north shore has several resorts that are popular with visitors, as well as membership RV campgrounds. **Ducey's Lodge**, and **The Pines Chalets** both attract vacationers, as does **Bass Lake Recreational Resort** for RV'ers. Back in the high country at Lake Thomas A. Edison, **Vermillion Valley Resort** welcomes you with a restaurant, gasoline, groceries, boat rental, lodging, and a ferry across the lake for hikers and back-packers.

The **Mono Hot Springs Resort** has been in business for more than fifty years and affords both sleeping and house-keeping accomodations as well as a restaurant and general store, and of course hot mineral baths. **Muir Trail Ranch** is across Florence Lake and four more miles into the back country at Blayney Meadows. Like Mono Hot Springs, Muir Trail Ranch has been in business a long time—the first permanent structure on the ranch was built in 1895-6, and still serves the resort as office and store.

Several resorts dot the shores of Huntington Lake, including **Will-O-the-Wisp Store**, **Lakeview Cottages**, and **Cedar Crest Resort**. Cedar Crest is the largest of the facilities and includes a restaurant with indoor and outdoor dining, cabins, hotel rooms, tent cabins, and RV spaces. Lakeview Cottage resort has been here for many, many years and offers both sleeping and housekeeping accomodations. Families have been returning to Lakeview for year after year to enjoy their vacations at the lake.

Sierra Summit ski resort stays open for the summer season, too, and offers full service resort accomodations, including restaurant and a heated outdoor swimming pool.

At Mammoth Pool, **Wagner's Mammoth Pool Resort**, located near the reservoir at Logan Meadow, has cabins, trailer court, and campground facilities, as well as groceries and gasoline. The **Jones Store** on Beasore Road at Beasore Meadows has meals, gasoline, and cabins in a rustic high country setting.

SIERRA NATIONAL FOREST CAMPGROUNDS

Kings River Ranger District	Piped Water	Camp Sites	Trailer Space	Fishing	Boating	Swimming	Store	RV Dump Station	Reservations	Special Attractions
Black Rock		7		•						
Buck Meadow		10	•	•						
Dinkey Creek	•	158	•	•			•			
Garnet Dike		3	•	•						Rafting
Gigantea		7	•							
Kirch Flat		26	•	•						Rafting
Lily Pad		16	•	•						
Sawmill Flat		15	•	•						
Sycamore I	•	12	•	•	•	•				Pine flat
Sycamore II	•	20	•	•	•	•				Pine flat
Voyager Rock		14		•						
Trapper Springs	•	30	•	•	•					
Mariposa Ranger District										
Big Sandy		14	•	•						
Chilkoot		12		•						
Denver Church	•	38	•	•	•	•	•		•	Bass Lake
Forks	•	33	•	•	•	•	•		•	Bass Lake
Fresno Dome		9	•	•						
Greys Mountain		8		•						
Indian Flat	•	14	•	•						
Jerseydale	•	10	•							
Kelty Meadow		10		•						
Little Sandy		8	•	•						
Lupine	•	113	•	•	•	•	•		•	Bass Lake
Nelder Grove		10	•							Big trees
Soquel		14		•						
Spring Cove	•	68	•	•	•	•	•		•	Bass Lake
Summerdale	•	30	•	•						
Summit Camp	•	10								

SIERRA NATIONAL FOREST CAMPGROUNDS

	Piped Water	Camp Sites	Trailer Space	Fishing	Boating	Swimming	Store	RV Dump Station	Reservations	Special Attractions
Wishon Point	•	72	•	•	•	•	•		•	Bass Lake
Minarets Ranger District										
China Bar		6		•						
Clover Meadow		7	•	•						
Fish Creek		7		•						
Gaggs Camp		20		•						
Granite Creek		20		•						
Lower Chiquito		7		•						
Mammoth Pool	•	47	•	•	•	•				Mammoth Pool
Placer	•	7		•						
Rock Creek	•	19	•	•						
Soda Springs		16	•	•						
Sweet Water		10	•	•						
Upper Chiquito		20		•						
Pine Ridge Ranger District										
Badger Flat		10	•							
Billy Creek	•	45	•	•	•	•	•		•	Huntington Lake
Billy Creek, Lower	•	13	•	•	•	•	•		•	Huntington Lake
Bolsillo	•	4								
Catavee	•	26	•	•	•	•	•		•	Huntington Lake
College	•	11	•	•	•	•	•		•	Huntington Lake
Deer Creek	•	32	•	•	•	•	•		•	Huntington Lake
Dorabelle	•	67	•	•	•	•				Shaver Lake
Florence Lake		14		•	•	•	•			Florence Lake
Jackass Meadow		15		•						
Kinnikinnick	•	32	•	•	•	•	•		•	Huntington Lake
Mono Diversion		16		•						
Mono Hot Springs	•	31		•			•			
Portal Forebay	•	9		•						
Rancheria	•	150	•	•	•	•	•		•	Huntington Lake
Sample Meadow		16	•	•						
Swanson Meadow		12	•	•						
Vermillion	•	30		•	•	•	•			Vermillion Lake
Ward Lake		17		•		•				

INYO
NATIONAL
FOREST

Sacramento

San Francisco

Los Angeles

89

Inyo National Forest

The Inyo is a resplendent, majestic forest, but it is also high desert, alpine peaks, sparkling lakes, boiling hot springs, endless salt flats, living volcanoes, huge calderas of volcanoes past, vast wilderness and ski slopes. Unpolished pack stations and comfortable resorts, campgrounds and summer homes, jeep trails and National Recreational Trails all vie for visitors' attention.

From Mono Lake and Toiyabe National Forest on the north, this long, skinny forest extends down the east side of the Sierra Nevada and the west side of the Great Basin all the way to the Mojave Desert, about 165 miles.

Summer and winter, this is one of the most-visited national forests in the state. But the forest is so huge that anyone who wants solitude can find it. There are more than 1,150 miles of maintained trails, and thousands of square miles to roam without any company except hawks and eagles overhead.

Camping

Campgrounds on the Inyo are as varied as the forest itself. On the four ranger districts from north to south, Mono Lake, Mammoth, White Mountain, and Mt. Whitney, there are seventy-one developed family campgrounds, and fourteen group campgrounds. They range in size from the five campsites at First Falls walk-in on Big Pine Creek to the 148 sites at Oh! Ridge.

Mono Lake Ranger District

Up at 7,800 feet in the Crestview area, a couple of little-used camping places hide in a mixed conifer forest. Deadman Creek, Glass Creek, and Hartley Springs are off the beaten track and less busy than their June Lake and Mammoth counterparts. Here on the slopes of a craggy volcanic dome, Deadman campers have the many tiny branches of the creek to explore.

A series of popular campgrounds adjoins the lakes and stream on the June Lake Loop. From Oh! Ridge Campground, campers get a view across cobalt-blue June Lake to 11,600-foot San Joaquin Mountain guarding the Ansel Adams Wilderness. The amphitheater here is the setting for interpretive programs presented by interpretive rangers.

Other campgrounds along the loop are Gull Lake, Reversed Creek, and Silver Lake. At Reversed Creek, the campsites are along the shimmering creekside. From Silver Lake, trails lead over rugged Agnew and Gem passes to the Ansel Adams Wilderness.

Highway 120 comes down Lee Vining Canyon from Tioga Pass and Yosemite. A V-shaped gouge in the escarpment packed with aspens, willows, giant granite boulders, and some huge lodgepole pines, it holds two lakes with Forest Service campgrounds along the highway, Two more small camping places are on the side road to Saddlebag Lake. Both Tioga Lake and Ellery Lake campgrounds are close enough to Mono Lake to take advantage of the programs there and still be up in the mountainside forest.

Mammoth Ranger District

Year-round, this is the busiest part of the Inyo. Fifteen campgrounds on the district have space for almost 750 families. They are in three general locations: near "downtown" Mammoth Lakes, in the lakes basin west of the town, and over Minaret Summit in the Agnew Meadow-Red's meadow area.

From New Shady Rest, Old Shady Rest, and Pine Glen campgrounds, the Inyo National Forest Information Center and Ranger Station in Mammoth Lakes is easily reached on foot, and campers can enjoy the interpretive programs centered here with ease. The campgrounds are set on a sandy flat among stands of Jeffrey pines interspersed with granite ridges intruding between camping sites. Sherwin Creek campground is a little further away, about three miles down a dirt road, but still in a more developed part of the district.

There are five campgrounds in the Mammoth Lakes Basin southwest of the village. Highest of these at 9,000 feet is at Lake George. The largest is the first one you come to, Twin Lakes Campground. It lies near the edge of the uppermost of the Twin Lakes, its sites sheltered under substantial Jeffrey and lodgepole pines. Manzanita and whitethorn grow between the sites, and each has a view of the sparkling lake and the distant ridge tops. Coldwater Campground also serves as the trailhead for hikers and riders going on over Duck Pass into John Muir Wilderness.

The road over Minaret Summit and down into the valley of the San Joaquin River is so narrow and heavily used that it's closed to all but shuttle buses, administrative traffic, people camping in the valley, and resort and pack station clients.

The five campgrounds in the valley are Agnew Meadows, Soda Springs, Pumice Flat, Minaret Falls, and Red's Meadow. There is also a campground in Devil's Postpile National Monument, under the direction of the National Park Service. People with large motorhomes or pulling trailers would be better advised to camp on the other side of the hill.

All of these campgrounds are in a glacier-carved hanging valley whose flat bottom and steep sides resulted from an unstoppable prehistoric river of ice scraping away the land. Broad meadows, a meandering stream, and encroaching pines delineate the sites along the San Joaquin.

White Mountain Ranger District

Except for waterless Grandview Campground just before the entrance to the Ancient Bristlecone Pine Forest, all of the developed campgrounds on the White Mountain Ranger District are along the drainages of four streams coming down into the Owens Valley from the Sierra: Big Pine, Bishop, Rock, and McGee Creek drainages.

These are the campgrounds in creek drainages high up among the peaks of the Sierra. It's bright granite country, with stunted trees—whitebark pines, western junipers—and clumps of willows and aspens clinging to the water courses. The campgrounds are mostly in mixed conifer forests along the creek bottoms. Sage Flat, Upper Sage Flat, and Big Pine Creek campgrounds all give access to the alpine lakes huddled in the shadow of the Palisades. Climbers headed for Palisade Glacier and its surrounding peaks make base camp here.

In the Bishop Creek drainage, there are ten campgrounds from 7500 feet all the way up to 9,500 feet altitude. Four Jeffrey is the largest and most developed of these camping places with 104 sites spread out over a grassy granite flat. Even at the highest campground, hikers still have almost 3000 feet to climb to reach the top of Bishop or Piute passes. This is high country! Stop

Fishermen on Lake George above the community of Mammoth Lake.

at the entrance station along the road on the way to these campgrounds to pick up your camping permit.

The Rock Creek campgrounds also require a camping permit. Stop at the entrance station on the Rock Creek Lake Road near highway 395 at Tom's Place. The Rock Creek Lake campground is the favorite here. It's a big campground located in a grove of pines right above the sparkling water of Rock Creek Lake. It's frequently filled on summer weekends, so late arrivals should be prepared with alternate camping plans, such as a stop at East Fork campgrounds on the way up the hill. It, too, is an attractive site in the canyon of Rock Creek. Red Mountain and Round Valley Peak, both well over 11,000 feet, look down on your camp site, and the fishing lakes along Hilton Creek are above you on the ridge to the west. Another creekside camping place is Big Meadow, just downstream from East Fork. Mono Pass into the John Muir Wilderness and Sierra National Forest is at the head of Rock Creek Canyon. At 11,800 feet, this is one of the highest passes across the range. From the top you look south along the very crest to Mt. Mills, Mt. Abbot, and Bear Creek Spire, all approaching the mystic 14,000-foot mark.

The McGee Creek Campground, sheltered under immense lodgepole pines along ice-cold McGee Creek, serves those going over McGee Pass into the Tully Hole and Silver Divide country of John Muir Wilderness.

Mt. Whitney Ranger District

The campgrounds on the Mt. Whitney Ranger District serve both as temporary stopping places for people heading over the crest into Sequoia-Kings Canyon National Parks or the John Muir or Golden Trout wildernesses, and for those who come camping just for the sake of camping in the high alpine country among the granite, the lakes and creeks, and magnificent trees.

Busiest of all is at Whitney Portal where those lucky enough to have permits to try for the top of Mt. Whitney establish their base camps, as well as those folk who like to camp in the shadow of the highest part of the Sierra. At Lone Pine campground, further down the hill, you'll find campsites situated along Lone Pine Creek where you can sit for an evening and watch the sunset turn the Inyo Mountains across the Owens Valley into succeeding values of rose, violet, and purple before the blackness of night settles in.

On the Independence Creek drainage, you'll come to Gray's Meadow Campground at the 6,000-foot mark. This picturesque site just above the sagebrush and pinon covered lands of the range sits at the confluence of Lime Canyon and the main Onion Valley section of Independence Creek. Higher up, you'll come to Onion Valley campground, right under the almost straight-up trail to Kearsarge Pass.

On The Trail

The most spectacular and ethereal hiking in California lies on the Inyo National Forest and adjacent national parks and national forests. Ansel Adams, John Muir, Hoover, Golden Trout, and South Sierra wildernesses are all part of the Inyo, and both Yosemite and Sequoia-Kings Canyon national parks share common boundaries with the forest.

Many of the trails in the wilderness and park backcountry are high above timberline, with only scattered groves of whitebarked pines and occasional hemlocks and lodgepoles hugging the grounds against the winds and snows of winter. Broad meadows with tiny lakes at their centers cover glacially scoured plateaus under the peaks. Alpine wildflowers bloom furiously in the brief spring and summer. Thunderheads roll up on the horizon and lightning crackles all around leaving hardly any time to count the seconds before the ultimate crash of thunder.

Pacific Crest Trail

From the north, the Pacific Crest Trail enters the Inyo over Donohue Pass at the southern boundary of Yosemite National Park. It follows the crest of the range on the Inyo through Ansel Adams Wilderness to Devil's Postpile National Monument, then into the John Muir Wilderness and back across the top into Sierra National Forest at Silver Pass. At this point it passes through the Golden Trout and South Sierra wildernesses and into Sequoia National Forest.

To get to the PCT from the Inyo is simply a matter of turning off at any of the roads leading west from Highway 395, parking at the end, and walking uphill to the trail. However, complications arise. So many people want to do just that, that hordes of hikers were crushing the forest, literally ''loving the wilderness to death.'' Consequently, quotas for all of the wildernesses have been established (except South Sierra—so far.).

Because the PCT is in wilderness, national park, or national monument territory during most of its entire run down the Inyo, wilderness permits are required for all except day hikers between July 1 and September 15. Preservation of the wilderness cannot occur without some degree of management, and by limiting entries the Forest Service can protect the backcountry and better provide a quality wilderness experience.

Approximately half the daily quota is available by advanced reservation. Requests are only accepted by mail with postmark dates of March 1 through May 31, and they're processed in order of postmark date. Permits may be applied for on a first-come, first-served basis on the date of entry, and half the permits are given out in this manner. As you might expect, demand is highest on Friday, Saturday, and holidays. Chances of obtaining a permit for the particular trail you want to travel are much better if you'll plan a mid-week starting date. It's best to keep your party size below six, and have a couple of alternate trips in mind

Mt. Whitney Trail

The entire daily quota for the Mt. Whitney Trail is reservable and the quota period is in effect May 22 through October 15. There is a non-refundable fee of $3 for each person in your party, and these permits go early! Consequently, you should contact the Mt. Whitney Ranger District office for current information and an application form, (619) 876-6200.

The distance from Whitney Portal to the top of Mt. Whitney isn't much, just over seven miles, there isn't any rock climbing with ropes to contend with, but you will reach almost 15,000 feet when you get to the top of the world and look out. The air is thin, and the strongest in your party will pant and heave his chest long before the mission is complete.

Day Hikes on the Inyo

Virtually every trail you try will have incomparable views. Virtually every trail you try will be steep, because you are on the east side of the crest and it does rise sharply to the highest points in the lower 48. Bearing this in mind, there are some walks that are easier than others, and some that are a downright cinch.

From Lake George in the Mammoth Lake Basin, you can walk to TJ and Barrett lakes from the far end of the campground. The trail climbs the volcanic edge of a watershed, and levels off to the two benches holding the lakes. It's a short, but steep hike through pines and aspens at first and then out on to high mountain meadows.

The trail to Mammoth Pass and McCloud Lake takes off from the parking lot at Horseshoe Lake, also in the Mammoth Lakes Basin. McCloud is an easy half-mile trip, and you can stroll all the way around it under the crest of the range. The pass is to the right through a lodgepole forest all the way to Red's Meadow. There you can stoke up for the trip home, or loop up to Red Cones or Crater Meadow.

At Saddlebag Lake, near the top of Tioga Pass, you can walk into the Twenty Lakes Basin and Hoover Wilderness. The remains of old mines are scattered across the nearly flat region. Tiny tarns surrounded with boulders overgrown with mountain heather, and a couple of good-sized lakes come into view at almost every corner. The shattered rock under foot rings almost bell-like as you walk across it.

Hiking in the White Mountains

The White Mountains are a typical Great Basin range, characterized by a great rock mass of uninterrupted material that has been thrust upward 10,000 to 14,000 feet. The range has steep sides that drop 9,700 feet in seven miles along the western slope. It is here in the White Mountains that bristlecone pine trees have survived more than forty centuries, exceeding the oldest giant sequoia by 1,500 years.

Two self-guided nature trails provide you access to forest slopes at Schulman Grove. Discovery Trail describes Professor Schulman's quest for old trees. Along Methuselah Walk you can see 4,000-year-old trees and learn about the bristlecone pine environment. Patriarch Grove is eleven miles beyond Schulman Grove on a dirt road and is where photographers go to capture images of these ancient wonders. Another self-guided trail leads past Patriarch Tree, the largest known bristlecone. There are picnic tables, an outdoor display, and toilets at the grove.

Outside the Ancient Bristlecone Pine Forest, hikers head for White Mountain Peak and Boundary Peak. White Mountain Peak is the third highest in California at 14,246 feet, only about 250 feet lower than Mt. Whitney across the valley. To get to it, hikers have a strenuous fifteen mile round-trip from the nearest parking areas. Begin your trip below the White Mountain Research Station at the locked gate about twenty-two miles from Highway 168 or three miles from Patriarch Grove. Only University of California authorized motorized traffic is permitted beyond the gate. The research lab is not open to the public, and hikers should be careful to stay on the trails so as not to damage the study plots and to protect fragile alpine tundra.

Boundary Peak's popularity is due to being the highest point in the state of Nevada. Located at the northern end of the White Mountains near the California/Nevada border, the summit rises to 13,140 feet. It and its neighbors constitute an impressive granite massif with grand views form their summits. Most hikers begin on the Nevada side from Highway 264 in Fish Lake Valley, about twenty-seven miles north of Oasis Junction. It takes five or six hours to reach the top on this strenuous route.

Touring, Sightseeing, and Special Programs

Inyo National Forest's interpretive programs are rivalled only by those in the Lake Tahoe Basin Management Unit and the Stanislaus National Forest. The Mammonth Ranger District and the Mono Lake Ranger District offer the most varied programs.

Mammoth Ranger District

There is so much activity in the Mammoth Lakes region that it almost needs a chapter in this guide by itself. And to learn about what's going on, there's no better way than to stop at the visitor center at Mammoth District Ranger Station on Highway 203.

In the visitor center, a number of displays will help you get a picture of the place you're visiting, both geographically and historically. For more on the history, you can take guided walks, such as the one called "Dwellers of the Great Basin," which will fill you in on the Paiutes who used to live here. You'll travel to one of their encampment sites with an obsidian workshop, mortar holes, a rock hunting blind, and a cave with pictographs still intact from pre-contact times.

INYO NATIONAL FOREST

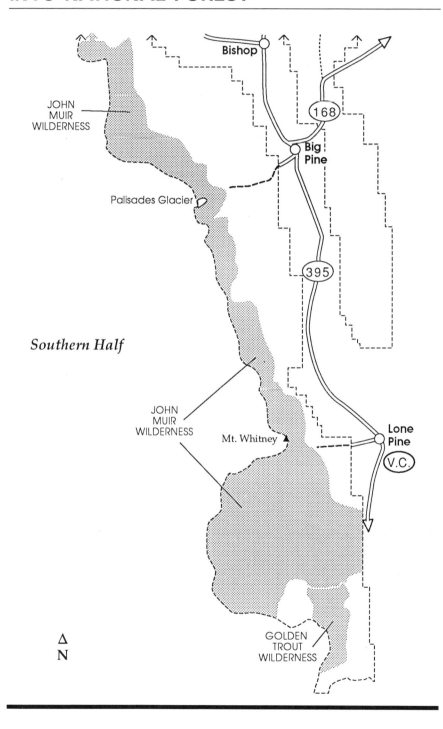

JOHN
MUIR
WILDERNESS

Bishop

168

Big
Pine

Palisades Glacier

395

Southern Half

JOHN
MUIR
WILDERNESS

Mt. Whitney

Lone
Pine

V.C.

Δ
N

GOLDEN
TROUT
WILDERNESS

INYO NATIONAL FOREST

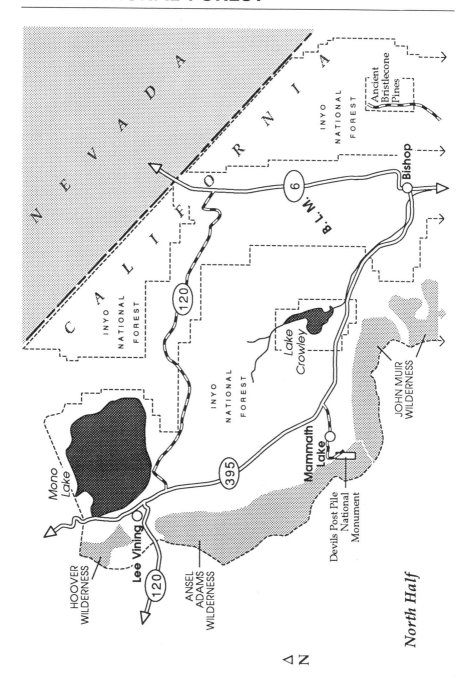

Another history walk is called "Mammoth City," where you'll learn about the hard luck associated with almost all of the mining ventures in the region. Maybe one of the rangers will tell you about the "Lost Cement Mine" and the three unfortunate brothers who died with the secret of the cement-like rock, reddish in color, filled with gold.

Visiting Devil's Postpile National Monument is another great way to learn about the geology of the eastern Sierra. If you go in the day time, you'll have to take the shuttle bus that leaves from Mammoth Mountain Ski Resort. Once over the top, the bus stops at various locations in the valley of the San Joaquin River where the Monument is located. Every one of the stops has something fascinating to see. There is a nature trail at the very first stop near Agnew Meadows that is worth getting off the bus for. It's only about a mile in length, perhaps less, but introduces you to the flowers and trees of the area. You'll wander through a dense forest of Jeffrey and lodgepole pines and red firs for much of the trip, coming into a meadow part way through.

At Monument headquarters, ranger-led walks traverse the short trail to the Postpile itself, by way of the soda springs. The immense basalt columns, the result of extremely rapid cooling of the lava flow and subsequent cracking, look as if they were deliberately created by the hand of man.

Rainbow Falls, on the San Joaquin River, can be reached from the shuttle bus stop at the trailhead just before arriving at Red's Meadow. The easy walk down to the falls crosses the Pacific Crest Trail part way. The river drops 101 feet over an andesite and rhyodacite cliff. The sun strikes the falls at exactly the right angle in the afternoons to create a magnificent rainbow in the gorge through which the river falls.

Mono Lake Ranger District

The major attraction on this district is the lake itself—Mono Lake. Mono Basin is an area of extraordinary contrasts. Perennial snowfields and glaciers at 13,000 feet overlook a dry, sagebrush-covered desert below.

The lake is a sublime body of water covering sixty square miles; thirteen miles east-west by eight miles north-south. And, it's an ancient lake (over 700,000 years old), making it one of the oldest in North America. Because it has no outlet, salts and minerals have washed into it and when evaporation takes the water from the lake, the salts and minerals have been left behind. The lake is about two-and-a-half times as salty and more that eighty times as alkaline as seawater.

The natural history of this area is described and explained in a one-mile self-guided nature trail at South Tufa. This spectacular and easily accessible tufa area is the best place to visit if you have time for only one stop. One hopes that you'll have enough time to go with one of the ranger-naturalists on a walk at the South Tufa Area. The tufa (too-fah) are miraculous examples of what nature can do with a few basic elements. The weirdly shaped spires and knobs are formed when fresh water springs carrying calcium well up through the lake water which is rich in carbonates. The mixture produces calcium carbonate, a white limestone deposit that builds the tufa structures around the springs.

Environmental concerns have led to an ongoing battle between the City of Los Angles and environmentalists bound to save the lake. The environmentalists have joined under the banner of The Mono Lake Committee that have recently won many of the battles. In what they call a landmark decision, the

California Supreme Court announced that Mono Lake must be protected if reasonably possible, and in related cases, a superior court judge ordered the city to release water down Rush Creek into the lake. It isn't enough to stabilize the lake, according to the committee, but they hail it as another victory. For more information about this complex and controversial issue, write: City of Los Angeles, Dept. of Water and Power, 300 Mandich, Bishop, CA 93514, or the Mono Lake Committee, P.O. Box 29, Lee Vining, CA 93514.

Along the June Lake Loop at the Oh! Ridge campground, the Forest Service has regular interpretive programs all summer long, most of them centered around Mono Lake.

One of the most interesting of the basin programs is the auto tour of Mono Craters. You'll become acquainted with local history, geology and flora on this two-hour auto tour. There are eight stops and no hiking is involved. At each of the stops, the leader will fill you in on the important information discoverable there. The tour is given each summer Saturday afternoon.

White Mountain Ranger District

High on the wind-swept, rock-strewn slopes of the White Mountains, northeast of Big Pine, are the oldest living things in the world, the amazing bristlecone pines. The Ancient Bristlecone Pine Forest is home to these short, squat patriarchs, some of which have endured the hardships of mountain winters and summers for more than 4000 years. What most people who come here to see these trees don't recognize is that they grow in other places, too. In fact in all six of the contiguous southwestern states, groves of this wonder survive.

Mt. Whitney Ranger District

Although plans for interpretive programs on the Mt. Whitney Ranger District have been under consideration, they were not yet implemented at publication time. The district ranger station in Lone Pine will be able to tell you more about it. Meanwhile, be sure to visit the Interagency Visitor Center south of Lone Pine. This information center and bookstore is managed by Inyo National Forest, but has the cooperation of nine governmental agencies, including the National Park Service and the Bureau of Land Management.

Sports

Boating And Water Skiing

In the southern half of the forest, on the White Mountain and Mt. Whitney ranger districts, there are not as many boat launching ramps as there are to the north. South Lake at the headwaters of Bishop Creek, Lake Sabrina, and Rock Creek Lake being the only places with ramps. In the Mammoth Lakes Basin and the June Lake Loop almost every lake has a ramp. In the far northern reaches of the forest, both Saddlebag and Lundy Lakes have unimproved ramps. At other lakes, including Mono Lake, you'll have to carry your cartopper or tow-boat to the water's edge to launch. Water sports are extremely popular along the June Lake Loop, with each lake having its devotees.

Off Road Motoring

Whenever talk turns to off-highway vehicles on the National Forest it needs to be noted that in most areas, vehicle use is allowed on existing roads only.

Visitors should check with the ranger stations for current information.

Off-highway enthusiasts have literally thousands of miles of roads and trails on the Inyo, mostly of the "Desert Rat" variety. South of Mono Lake in the Bald Mountain and Sagehen Peak areas, you can drive through deep canyons, across sand flats, and next to intermittant streams and desert springs.

Further south, east of Crowley Lake, Jeepers travel the roads of Casa Diablo and the Banner Range. Abandoned mines, old mining ghost towns and shanties litter the desert, and exploring them is one of the big sports of the off-road enthusiasts.

Fishing and Hunting

Fishing, both lake and stream, attracts thousands of visitors to the Inyo each year. Opening Day at Crowley Lake has a carnival atmosphere, with thousands of fishermen in hundreds of boats catching hundreds of fish. Rainbow, cutthroat and brown trout make up the majority of the catch.

Some special places to fish are these: The Owens River, especially in the Gorge below Crowley Lake; the lakes of Mammoth Lakes Basin; Hot Creek, a California Wild Trout Stream where catch-and-release with a strictly enforced zero limit is the norm; the San Joaquin River in the Reds Meadow-Agnew Meadows area, for anglers who are willing to walk a little way.

Hunters enter the Inyo in large numbers in the Fall season to search for that big buck. And, many of them find him, although the percentage is smaller than the forests of the far northern part of the state simply because of the numbers. Probably the most successful are those who have themselves packed into the back country with one of the many commercial packers who are permittees on the Forest.

There are fourteen packers with permits to operate on the Inyo, from Frontier Pack Train at June Lake south to Kennedy Meadows Pack Train on the border of Golden Trout Wilderness. All of them are licensed under California Guide Law and operate under both National Forest and National Park Service permits.

Resorts, Lodges and Hotels

Largest and most famous of eastern Sierra lodges are in the Mammoth Lakes region, led by Mammoth Mountain Inn. The inn has hotel rooms and cottages. It's well-known as one of the largest ski resorts in the world. However, its summer and fall offerings are not as well known, with all kinds of activities from camera classes to fly-fishing expeditions.

Another year round lodge at Mammoth is Tamarack Lodge Resort at Twin Lakes in Mammoth Lakes Basin. Like the Inn, Tamarack Lodge has both hotel-type accommodations in the main lodge and housekeeping cabins clustered on the shore of the upper lake. The restaurant is locally famous and features such exotic cuisine as blackened salmon, eggplant Parmigiana, and colorful pasta dishes. In the winter, the road is plowed as far as the lodge, and cross-country skiers are a major clientele, while hikers and mountain bikers enjoy the summer.

On Lake Mamie, Wildyrie Ridge opens in the spring and stays open through September each year. It's a complete family resort, with a cafe and general store as well as housekeeping cabins and lodge rooms. Also in the basin at Lake George is Woods Lodge. Like Wildyrie, Woods Lodge opens each spring, usually in June, and remains open through the season, closing down in early

October. This is the highest lodge in the Basin. It's twenty-four cabins overlook the 9,000-foot-high Lake George under shining Crystal Crag.

Cabins, restaurant, soda fountain, and groceries are available in a glorious pine and fir forest at Red's Meadow Resort near Devil's Postpile National Monument. The resort operates the pack stations at Red's Meadow and Agnew Meadows, and provides day rides as well as full pack trips.

Outside of the Mammoth region, there are Forest Service permittees operating at such places as Rock Creek, Bishop Creek, Big Pine Creek, the June Lake Loop, and in the Tioga Pass area.

Meals, lodging and well-stocked general stores are available at Rock Creek Lodge and Rock Creek Lake Resort. At South Lake, Parchers Rainbow Village has cabins, boats, a cafe and store for visitors to the Bishop Creek area.

A unique experience is to stay in the teepees at the McGee Creek Pack Station. Nestled in the aspen and cottonwood trees along McGee Creek, they are authentic Sioux design. Bathrooms with hot showers, barbecues, firepits, and picnic tables are included.

INYO NATIONAL FOREST CAMPGROUNDS

North to South	Piped Water	Camp Sites	Trailer Space	Fishing	Boating	Swimming	Store	RV Dump Station	Reservations	Special Attractions
Lundy Canyon	•	50	•	•	•	•	•			Co. Park, launch
Saddlebag	•	22	•	•	•	•				Launch
Sawmill		12	•	•	•	•				
Tioga Lake	•	13	•	•	•					
Junction		10	•	•						
Ellery Lake	•	12	•	•	•	•				
Big Bend	•	18	•	•						
Rush Creek				•						
Silver Lake	•	65	•	•	•	•	•			Launch
Reversed Creek	•	17	•	•	•	•	•			Launch
Gull Lake	•	10	•	•	•	•	•			Launch
Oh! Ridge	•	148	•	•	•	•	•			Amphitheater
Hartley Springs		20	•	•						
Glass Creek		50	•	•						
Big Springs		24	•							
Lower Deadman		30	•	•						
New Shady Rest	•	95	•	•	•	•	•	•		Visitors center
Old Shady Rest	•	51	•				•			Visitors center
Pine Glen	•	11	•				•			Visitors center
Sherwin Creek	•	87	•	•						

INYO NATIONAL FOREST CAMPGROUNDS

	Piped Water	Camp Sites	Trailer Space	Fishing	Boating	Swimming	Store	RV Dump Station	Reservations	Special Attractions
Agnew Meadows	•	22	•	•						PCT Trailhead
Pumice Flat	•	17	•	•						
Minaret Falls	•	28	•	•						
Reds Meadow	•	56	•	•			•			
Devils Postpile	•	23	•	•						Nat'l Mon (NPS)
Twin Lakes	•	94	•	•	•	•				Launch
Lake George	•	16	•	•	•	•				Launch
Lake Mary	•	48	•	•	•	•				Launch
Coldwater	•	77	•	•						
Convict Lake	•	88	•	•	•	•	•		•	Launch
McGee Creek	•	28	•	•						
Tuff	•	34	•							
Lower Rock Creek		5		•						
Big Meadow	•	11	•	•						
Palisade	•	5		•						
East Fork	•	133	•	•						
Pine Grove	•	11	•	•						
Rock Creek Lake	•	28	•	•				•		
Upper Pine Grove	•	8	•							
Mosquito Flat	•	13		•						
Mosquito Flat Walk-in		10		•						
Big Trees	•	9	•	•						
Four Jeffrey	•	106	•	•				•		
Forks	•	8	•	•						
Intake 2	•	15	•	•						
Bishop Park	•	21	•	•	•	•				Launch
Sabrina		18	•	•	•	•				Launch
North Lake	•	11		•						
Mountain Glen Walk-in		5		•						
Table Mtn Walk-in		5		•						
Willow Camp		7	•	•						
Grandview		26	•							Near Ancient Bristlecone pines
Big Pine Creek	•	30	•	•						
Lower Grays Meadow	•	17	•	•						
Grays Meadow	•	35	•	•						
Onion Valley	•	29		•						
Lone Pine Creek	•	43	•	•						
Whitney Portal	•	44		•						
Tuttle Creek	•	85	•	•						BLM
Diaz Lake	•	150	•	•	•	•	•			Co. Park, launch

*STANISLAUS
NATIONAL
FOREST*

Sacramento

San Francisco

Los Angeles

Stanislaus National Forest

The Stanislaus National Forest covers the western slope of the Sierra Nevada from its highest peaks and ridges down to the sun-baked hills of the Mother Lode, and spans the distance from the Merced River on the south to the Mokelumne River on the north.

The most important feature of the forest and the one which gave it its name is the Stanislaus River. The river takes its name from the fearless Miwok leader, Estanislao, who, in the early 1800s led his band against Mexican troops in the marshes along the lower reaches of the San Joaquin Valley.

The high country of the forest is a mountain wilderness of unsurpassed natural beauty. It abounds with hundreds of blue-green lakes set in the shadow of towering, snow-clad peaks, and countless crystal-clear steams.

Camping

Between Sierra Village and Long Barn a signed road leads north to **Lyons Reservoir**. A campground and boat launch ramp mark this little lake as a likely fishing spot. There's plenty of room for families with children, and in the evening rising trout give fly fishermen plenty of action.

The largest campgrounds on the forest, **Pinecrest**, and **Meadowview**, are on the Mistix reservation system, and in July and August, reservations are essential, even in the middle of the week. The campsites in Meadowview are adjacent not only to a moist, green meadow, but also to an interpretive walk, "Shadow of the Miwok." Both of these campgrounds are near the boating, fishing, and swimming at Pinecrest Lake.

Going up Highway 108 from Pinecrest, the next point of interest is **Herring Creek Road** which intersects Highway 108 about two miles beyond Strawberry. There's only one established campground, **Herring Creek Reservoir** Campground, but "dispersed" camping is possible all along the road. Fiddler's Green, along Herring Creek, in Hammill Canyon, and Bloomer Lake all give you enchanting campsites where you'll find the solitude impossible to come by in the city. At night, away from the lights of the campfires, you can watch the stars and planets set beyond the ridge to the west, so complete is the solitude. Be sure that the forest rules regarding fires, artifacts, vegetation, and pets are followed, so that the next guy finds just as enchanting a campground as you did.

Stop for a time at **Mill Creek** Campground, an undeveloped site, and explore a bit. Cross the creek to the northern or uphill side at the lower end of the campground near the remains of the original highway bridge and walk carefully downstream a couple hundred feet. You'll come to a group of large flat boulders pockmarked with acorn grinding holes made by Sierra Miwok women. This was a major campground for the Miwoks in the summer when they climbed into the Sierra to escape the savage heat of their foothill home.

After Mill Creek, the next stop is **Niagara Creek**. This small campground is away from the highway noise in a grove of Jeffrey pines alongside the creek. From this campground you can explore south to Eagle and Long Valley creeks, and almost adjacent to the camp is the "Trail of the Ancient Dwarfs," where trees grow in soil that has inhibited their growth.

A Columbia Community College ecology class stops along a forest road to hear instructor point out reasons for the growth of the spectacular sugar pines.

Back on 108 you reach the Clark Fork Road on your left. This paved road follows the Clark Fork River, a major tributary of the Stanislaus, upstream about ten miles to Iceberg Meadow at the boundary of Carson-Iceberg Wilderness. At the confluence of Clark Fork and Arnot Creek, you'll find **Clark Fork** Campground, shaded by giant red firs and pines. Manzanita and whitehorn among boulders make each individual camp site seem to be the only one around. There's easy access to the river for the kids to splash and explore streamside trails, and the fishing is easy—especially on the days the "fish truck" comes. Mule deer and an occasional black bear visit the canyon, and coyotes serenade at night.

Bears are a different story. While not as common nor as troublesome as they can be in the heavily-visited national parks, they nevertheless can be a problem.

Back on Highway 108 you turn east again into the long, level canyon along the upper Middle Fork of the Stanislaus. This popular destination is among the most beautiful spots in the mountains. It's no wonder that people return here year after year for their vacations. **Boulder Flat** and **Brightman Flat** campgrounds are the first two you come to. Each sits on a boulder and tree-studded bluff above the river with spaces big enough for RV's. A volunteer camp host at Brightman Flat collects camping fees and serves as an information center for campers. He can tell you which camp sites are open, where to find groceries or a telephone, where the trout are biting and when they'll be planted, and what's the best place to have a picnic.

Dardanelle Campground, next on the list, is directly across the highway from Dardanelle Resort. The campground was recently upgraded and now sports paved parking spaces at each site, new tables and fireplaces. The camp sits at the confluence of Eagle Creek and the Middle Fork and is probably the most attractive camp in the valley.

The sites to the right as you enter the campground are special places. Early in the morning, or better still, in the evening, you can sit in your camp and look out over Eagle Creek at the cottonwoods and alders on the far shore. It's like being in an aviary. Water ouzels hop from boulder to boulder in the stream, stopping to dive into the swift water for caddis larvae and other underwater creatures. Warblers and flycatchers are everywhere, and big northern flickers search through the leaves and needles under the trees.

Beyond Dardanelle you pass **Pigeon Flat** and **Eureka Valley** campgrounds. It's here at Pigeon Flat that the short, quarter-mile trail to "Columns of the Giants" begins. The campground is a walk-in site with camping places on a bench overlooking the river and the basalt scree fallen from the columns high on the bank opposite. Eureka Valley campgrounds is on a big open flat with the Stanislaus flowing around it on three sides. The sites near the water are filled with the sounds of the stream and will lull you to sleep in the quiet of the evening.

Past Eureka Valley and Douglas picnic grounds the Kennedy Meadows turn-off marks the end of the road for camping trailers: The Sonora Pass Road is too high, too narrow, and too steep.

Immediately after you turn on to the Kennedy Meadows road, **Baker** Campground beckons from the right. Widespread, shady campsites and easy access to trails into the back country, make this camp a popular one with backpackers and day hikers alike. Next to it is **Deadman** Campground where Deadman Creek flows into the Stanislaus. Smaller and more secluded than Baker, it sits at the base of granite monoliths towering high on the western side of the river.

The Big Oak Flat Road is an adventure in itself. It parts company with Highway 49 near Moccasin Creek Fish Hatchery and climbs Priest Grade. In about four miles the road twists and turns and switchbacks and doubles back on itself about seventy-seven times, while climbing close to 1,000 feet. Halfway up brave miners have dug into the side of the mountain and the remains of their corrugated iron buildings and tailings from the shafts still mark the slopes.

Take the Lumsden Bridge Road north before you reach the Buck Meadows Ranger Station. At the Bottom you'll come to **Lumsden Bridge** Campground, where white-water rafters gather for the eighteen-mile trip crashing down the Wild and Scenic Tuolumne River.

Halfway from Buck Meadows to the Yosemite Park line Forest Road 1N07 turns north and drops down into the canyons of the Tuolumne. At about mile five the road splits. The right hand fork goes on to Mather and into Yosemite to Hetch Hetchy Reservoir. The left hand road continues on in the National Forest to Cherry Lake, the largest on the forest.

At the lake you'll find **Cherry Lake** Campground, boat launching ramp and a pack station with burros as well as horses and mules.

When you enter the Stanislaus National Forest on Ebbett's Pass Highway, stop at the **Calaveras District Ranger Station** at Hathaway Pines. The rangers have maps and other literature and know the answers to questions about the forest.

The first developed campgrounds you come to on the Ebbett's Pass Road aren't in the forest, but in **Calaveras Big Trees State Park**. Both campgrounds in the State Park can be reserved through Mistix, and during the summer season it's virtually a necessity on week-ends.

Above the community of Ganns, at about 6,000 feet, you come to **Cabbage Patch** and **Big Meadows** campgrounds. Thickets of young lodgepole pines crowd the meadows and road along here and make for gratifying camp sites in the flats adjacent to the highway.

Highway 4 is closed for the winter at the Bear Valley/Mt. Reba turn-off, but during the summer you can go on to Lake Alpine. This old reservoir at 7,400 feet has been the summer home to generations of families who have been coming to the Ebbett's Pass country since before there was a Bear Valley, and their captivating vacation cabins are scattered all along the north shore. You can camp at the eastern end of the lake, sheltered in groves of lodgepoles with sunset views out over the basin in **Pine Martin** and **Silver Valley** campgrounds. At the western end of the lake, **Lake Alpine** Campground has space for twenty-seven families. All three campgrounds have trailer space, but beyond this point trailers had best be left behind as the pass is a steep and narrow one.

Beyond Lake Alpine you'll cross Pacific Summit, and descend sharply through a narrow canyon to **Pacific Valley**, once a resting place for teams of mules or oxen pulling freight along the Emigrant Road. A small unimproved campground welcomes fishermen.

A mile before the top of Ebbett's Pass, Forest Road 8N01 turns south past Tryon Peak and Tryon Meadow to Highland Lakes. These alpine pools perch on the divide between the Mokelumne River and Highland Creek drainages. 10,000-foot peaks surround you on three sides, their glaciated flanks shining with the first light of dawn, and glowing pink and salmon with the last light of dusk. Because of the remoteness, **Highland Lake** Campground at the lower lake is seldom crowded and quality fishing in both of the lakes and the streams below them is usual.

On The Trail

One of the best ways to get acquainted with Stanislaus National Forest is to take advantage of the National Recreation Trails and the portions of the Pacific Crest Trail that pass through the forest.

Just a few steps below the top of Ebbett's Pass, and actually on the Toiyabe National Forest and not the Stanislaus is access to the **Pacific Crest Trail**. The trail follows the crest of the Sierra crossing and recrossing the serrated ridges, all along the eastern edge of the forest until it enters Yosemite National Park at Dorothy Lake Pass. Other access points are at Sonora Pass and Blue Lakes. In addition, many of the trails in the Mokelumne, Carson Iceberg, and Emigrant Wildernesses connect with the PCT on top of the Sierra.

National Recreation Trails

During Gold Rush days, miners from Sonora and Columbia dammed the South Fork of the Stanislaus and several of its feeder creeks with wood cribbing dams to provide water for the mines lower down the mountain. Each of these little dams created ponds behind them, and the remains of some can

STANISLAUS NATIONAL FOREST

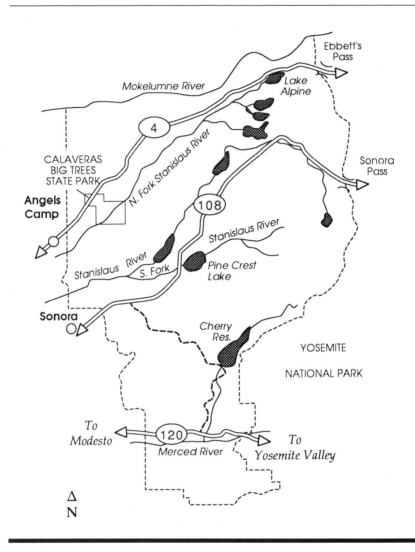

Ebbett's Pass

Mokelumne River

Lake Alpine

4

CALAVERAS BIG TREES STATE PARK

Sonora Pass

N. Fork Stanislaus River

Angels Camp

108

Stanislaus River

Stanislaus River

S. Fork

Pine Crest Lake

Sonora

Cherry Res.

YOSEMITE

NATIONAL PARK

To Modesto

120

Merced River

To Yosemite Valley

Δ
N

still be seen. Then, early in this century, a large concrete dam was built across the South Fork, and Pinecrest Lake was formed in a natural bowl among the peaks. There's a beach for swimming and sunning, and the twenty-mile-an-hour speed limit makes it great for sailboats and small outboards.

One of the best ways to get acquainted is to take the **Pinecrest Lake National Recreation Trail** around the lake. To reach the trailhead from the swimming beach parking area you head southwest along the southern shore. Lots of granite exposures mark this relatively level 3.5 mile loop. A mixed conifer forest—mostly ponderosas and red firs—offers shade on the south side of the lake, but the north is more open with patches of manzanita, whitethorn, and chinquapin. The trail gets heavy use in summer, but late spring or September hikers can have it all to themselves. The shining granite basin that encircles the lake reflects from its surface on calm days, and the thunder from occasional summer storms reverberates in the bowl.

Columns of the Giants National Recreation Trail is about fifteen miles up Highway 108 from Pinecrest at the Pigeon Flat Campground. This short trail, just over a half-mile, take you to some huge basalt columns, a result of volcanic activity. Geologic and glaciation processes are explained by exhibits at the trailhead and at the columns. This is the same kind of phenomenon as that revealed at Devil's Postpile National Monument.

Emigrant Wilderness Trails

Bell Meadow, Crabtree Camp, Aspen Meadow, and Gianelli Cabin behind Dodge Ridge serve hikers, backpackers, and pack trains as major getaway points for trips in the Emigrant Wilderness, far and away the most popular destination for backcountry camping on the forest.

You can make a loop trip from any one of the starting points, traveling east to Huckleberry Lake near the Yosemite border, then north to Emigrant Lake and Emigrant Meadows, before heading back through forest-circled meadows, and along tumbling creeks, and by the side of granite-bound lakes. The contrast between the volcanic flows that make up the ridge to the north and the glacially reexposed granite on the rest of the forest gives you a walking geology lesson.

From Niagara Creek Campground you can drive up FR 5N01 to Eagle Meadow, starting point for trails over the top of Eagle Pass to the south and down to Dardanelle Campground on the north. Corrals and barns made from local pine, bright yellow in the sunshine, mark a summer camp of cattlemen with grazing permits on the forest.

The walk to the top of Eagle Pass is about four miles one way, and after the first half mile is uphill all the way. The lower part of the trip is through Eagle Meadow with the waters of Eagle Creek always near at hand. The trail follows the creek as it starts its climb and finally leaves it less than a mile from the top of the pass. From the top Cooper Meadow is directly below the pass and Cooper Pocket, where fishermen get big trout in a little creek, is just out of sight to the east. Beyond the near meadows, the wilderness stretches out to the horizon of peaks south to Yosemite, beckoning the adventurous.

The second **Eagle Creek** hike is an absorbing downhill ramble from Eagle Meadow about four miles to Dardanelles Campground and Resort. After it leaves the meadow, the trail keeps to the side of the canyon of Eagle Creek. Deep forest cover with ferns and foot-thick accumulation of needles and leaves marks the way. The dappled sunshine filtered through the branches high above you, falls on stellar jays and nuthatches, and chickarees scold loudly as you pass. Someone has to drive up and back, because it's best as a one-way walk—downhill.

At the end of the road along the Clark Fork is Iceberg Meadow. The trail leading into Carson Iceberg Wilderness here is a remnant of the emigrant road leading over **St. Mary's Pass**, a route used before Sonora Pass Road was completed. Early in the season, the Jeffreys at the edge of the meadow shelter hundreds of snow flowers and pine drops whose bright pink stalks and blossoms are among the first sure signs of spring in the Sierra.

Going back down the Clark Fork Road just before it climbs back up to Highway 108, FR 6N06 turns west through Fence Creek Campground and on to Montgomery Meadow. At the upper end of the meadow a trail climbs steeply over the ridge topped by the Dardanelles and drops down to **Lost** and **Sword Lakes** at the edge of Carson-Iceberg Wilderness. These little meadow-bound lakes are a wonderful destination for a day hike, or a lunch stop on the way to Gabbot Meadow and Highland Creek.

From Kennedy Meadows Resort a heavily-traveled trail leads over a slight rise and down into the meadows for which the resort is named. The broad, green, grassy meadow has islands of trees scattered across it, and the wide Stanislaus winding through it. Beechey ground squirrels, or "picket pins," scurry through the grass at your approach, diving into their burrows at the last minute. Above, on all sides, the Sierra peaks—Leavitt, Kennedy, Relief—soar into the atmosphere almost 12,000 feet, their north slopes holding fields of perpetual snow.

Ebbett's Pass Hiking Trails

A mile or so above Big Meadows on the Ebbett's Pass Highway, you come to the Hell's Kitchen overlook. Park here and spend some time taking in the magnificent valley of the North Fork of the Stanislaus River and Highland Creek. The southern horizon is marked by the Dardanelles, looming above the Middle and Clark Fork. Three huge reservoirs are in the valleys below you—Utica, Union, and Spicer Meadow—controlling the flow of the streams below them.

A mile above the Hell's Kitchen overlook, FR 7N01 branches southeast from Highway 4 providing access to the valleys and reservoirs below. You can get to all three lakes by auto, although the Utica road is best suited for four-wheel drive vehicles. Camp a night or two on the North Fork where the road crosses and enjoy the sounds of the river as it flows around the boulders crowded into the bed of the stream.

At the very end of FR 7N01 are two parking places for hikers who want to enter Carson-Iceberg Wilderness. Trails lead to **Rock Lake, Gabbott Meadow**, and all of the **Highland Creek** drainage. A wilderness permit is required, even for day use, and can be obtained from any ranger station on the forest.

Lake Alpine is the terminous for trails that go north into the Mokelumne Wilderness and south into Carson-Iceberg Wilderness. The **Camp Irene Trail**, which leads from the lake down into the canyon of the North Fork of the Mokelumne, starts just behind the resort or, on another branch, from the Chickaree picnic area at the upper end of the lake. At the end of the road to Silver Valley Campground, the trail for **Duck Lake**, and all points south and east in the Carson-Iceberg takes off.

At the top of Pacific Summit, you'll come to Mosquito Lake, a shallow tarn so close to the edge of the road you often have to dodge fishermen. From the parking lot at the west end of the lake a well-marked trail goes south 2.5 miles through open stands of red fir and Jeffrey pines, past tiny **Heiser Lake** to **Bull Run Lake**. About halfway into the trip you cross over into the wilderness. From the ridgetop above Heiser Lake, you'll have a view of Bull Run and Henry's Peak soaring almost to 10,000 feet, with Peep-sight Peak coming into view toward the top of the range.

Halfway between Pacific Valley and Hermit Valley, a trail and four-wheel drive route heads north into a break in the Mokelumne Wilderness. This trail is an actual remnant of the old hand-built Stockton and Big Trees Road. Walking

Long Valley Creek plunges into Middle Fork Stanislaus River.

a few miles on it will cause you to reflect again on the difficulties of making the crossing in 1949.

The way passes through **Deer Valley** and **Clover Valley** on its route to the Blue Lakes, and Faith, Hope, and Charity valleys in neighboring Eldorado National Forest.

From the Highland Lakes, a very scenic and often solitary loop trail through Hiram Meadow, Jenkins Canyon, across the top of the Dardanelles, and back up Arnot Creek between Iceberg Peak and the long ridge of Lightning Mountain, starts at the parking lot near the lower lake.

Touring, Sightseeing, and Special Programs

Just before Highway 108 climbs to the 6,000-foot level, you will arrive at

Pinecrest and the **Summit Ranger Station**. These can really be called the activities center of the forest, because so much revolves around them. Pinecrest Lake and Dodge Ridge Ski Area are the focal points that bring people back year after year, winter and summer.

Vacation homes fill the western section of old "Strawberry Flat" and extend part way around the lake on both the north and south shores, many of them first constructed before 1920. Forest Service campgrounds, the University of California's Camp Blue, and two resorts provide accommodations.

Centered in the Summit Ranger Station is one of the National Forest Service's most interesting and complete recreational programs. "Free Adventures" is the title of the program which features interpretive walks and tours, camp-fire programs, and opportunities to learn about the human as well as natural history of the area.

The largest Jeffrey pine, sugar pine, and western juniper in the world arc growing on the Stanislaus National Forest. The sugar pine and juniper take quite a bit of effort to see, but the Jeffrey is one of the destinations around which an interpretive trip is based. Each week a ranger or docent leads a scenic and fairly gentle hike over open terrain to view the giant. An array of wildflowers graces the route, and the leader points them out along with other wonders of the forest. He'll show you a kind of yellowish mistletoe in the pines, and a mammoth wind row of fallen giants where winter storms raging down from Sonora Pass have blown over full-grown trees like so many sticks.

One of the unqiue features of the "Free Adventures" is the appearance at unexpected moments during the tours of the "ghost" of historically impor-tant people from the forest's past. Dressed in appropriate costume, Ranger Gary Hines impersonates the original Stanislaus Ranger, Charles Taggart, or a 49'er searching for gold, or even Gifford Pinchot, the first chief of the Forest Service.

The portrayals are so authentic that once, as Taggart, he told a group that it wouldn't do any good to take photos of him, because, being a ghost, he wouldn't show up in the picture. And nobody did!

Along Herring Creek Road above Pinecrest, at the six mile mark, a dirt road leads off to the left to the **Trail of the Gargoyles,** one of the many self-guiding interpretive trails on the district. Beginning millions of years ago and ejected from numerous vents along the east side of today's Sierra crest, large quan-tities of volcanic ash mixed with snow or water and formed hot, oozing mud. Small cinders and stones were swallowed up until the steaming liquids finally cooled into the concrete-like *lahar* of today. The lahar has been twisted and eroded into the grotesque shapes you'll see at the "Trail of the Gargoyles."

Park under the junipers in the turn-around at the end of the road and walk out to the edge of the horseshoe shaped canyon. You'll find yourself looking over a 90-degree drop from a platform of eroded lahar, and on both sides of you, stretching to the open end of the canyon, monstrous shapes form the near horizon.

Leaving Herring Creek Road and climbing up Highway 108 toward Sonora Pass, high on your left will appear the spectacular formations called "The Dardanelles," the most prominent deposits of lahar in the area. You will know when you see them that eagles nest there, secure in the crenelated battlements of their stony aerie.

Eureka Valley is the site of one of the earliest stage and freight stops on the Sonora Pass. A marker on the left side of the road just past the campground

The tip-top of Sonora Pass looks out over the White Mountain Range of the Nevada-California border.

shows where Dave Hays built his "road house." It was fifty feet long by eighteen wide, according to one early account, and made of logs, squared and dovetailed at the ends. Hays served as "landlord, cook, chambermaid, and barkeeper." If you look sharp, you can trace the outline of the building with your eyes, spotting the corner posts and a few pieces of the foundation still visible.

Highway 108 rises steeply from the Kennedy Meadows turn-off, following Deadman Creek as it plunges down from the top of the range. In the 1800s the creek got its name when a young man tried to walk across the pass from Leavitt Meadow on the east side to Hays Station at Eureka Valley too late in the season and was trapped in a storm which closed the pass for the winter.

Pull off the road at the two overlooks provided and look down into the canyon. The first overlook, called **Que de Porka**, is directly above Kennedy Meadows, and provides sight-lines deep into Emigrant Wilderness. Relief Peak, named when an emigrant party was rescued below it, stands out against the southern horizon, and the waters of the Stanislaus reflect in the afternoon sun.

At the second overlook, **East Flange**, you can look down the canyon that carried the original emigrant road through Relief Valley, and past Flange Rock and Granite Dome. Far below you, Deadman Creek makes its way down the slopes.

Just past Chipmunk Flat, it's possible to pull off the road again. Here, across Deadman Creek, remnants of the old road can be seen where it wound its way over the pass. This is also a favorite place for rock-climbers to practice their sport. You can watch from the willow-lined creek as they make their way with rope and hardware up the sheer face of the cliffs above.

Over on Highway 4, Ebbett's Pass, you'll come to the fast-growing resort communities of Arnold and White Pines. Above the towns you'll come to **Calaveras Big Trees State Park**. Although strictly speaking it's not a part of the National Forest system, it's certainly worth a stop.

Within the 6,000 acres of the park are two magnificent groves of Big Trees (*Sequoiadendron giganteum*), some wonderful hiking trails, and good State Park campgrounds—which means hot showers. Near the entrance is the museum and educational building where docents from the Calaveras Big Trees Association operate a book store, the exhibits, and a well-made audio-visual program explaining the park to its visitors.

Besides the Sequoias you'll find a variety of Sierra trees, including sugar pine, red and white fir, ponderosa, and incense cedar in the park. Deep in the forest shade, flowering dogwood blooms glow in phosphorescent radiance. If you'll leave a self-addressed post card with the docents of the association, they'll mail it to you in plenty of time for you to make it back at the peak of bloom—usually late May or early June. It's a display of beauty seldom rivaled.

Under the direction of park rangers, the association conducts classes and discovery walks for kids of all ages, as well as the campfire programs in the evening. Among the self-guided hikes, you can do some walking in the footsteps of the pioneers here within the park. A portion of the original Stockton and Big Trees Road passes through the park. Beginning in the 1850s, a hotel sat where the parking lot is now. The tourists from all over the world came to stay, including future President Ulysses S. Grant.

Sports

Dodge Ridge is the closest ski area to most parts of the San Francisco Bay Area; close enough that you can drive up for the day and return in the evening. With beginning, intermediate and advanced runs, and half a dozen lifts, you can get all the exercise you want at any skill level.

On the Ebbett's Pass road, just beyond Onion Valley, you cross into Alpine County, California's smallest in population, and arrive at **Bear Valley**, and the Bear Valley/Mt. Reba Ski Area. With a total of nine lifts this destination resort can handle a good sized crowd of skiers without seeming crowded.

Cross-country skiing, snowmobiling, and snow play are all popular winter sports on the Stanislaus. On Ebbett's Pass just below Bear Valley, you'll find **Tamarack** and **Onion Valley** summer home tracts. Above Dorrington, near Calaveras Big Trees, is **Cottage Springs**, one of the favorite winter sports areas. **Ganns Meadow** and along Highway 108 near Pinecrest are other winter sports areas, with miles of unplowed forest roads.

Boating and Water Skiing

Pinecrest Lake, and **Lake Alpine**, with their colonies of vacation homes, are very popular boating centers. To promote the serenity of the areas, and for safety's sake, both of these relatively small impoundments have speed limits which make them suited for sailing, windsurfing, and canoeing.

From Highway 108, turn down the Beardsley Road for a 2,000-foot drop in six miles to the bottom of the fabulous Stanislaus River Canyon. The lake created by damming the river here is the second largest in the National Forest and home to some whopper rainbows. A boat ramp allows both fishermen and water-skiers to launch their craft, and the lake is big enough that both can enjoy themselves without interfering with the other.

Other launch ramps on the Stanislaus National Forest are at **Cherry Lake** and **Lyons Reservoir**, and car-toppers can be launched at both **Union** and **Spicer Meadow Reservoirs.**

Fishing and Hunting

The Stanislaus is a very popular National Forest, and any fishable water that can be reached by automobile is going to get heavy usage. Consequently, if you can get away from roads, you're going to get better fishing for wild trout. One of the forest roads that will take you into this kind of country is FR 4N01, which leads to Fraser Flat on the South Fork Stanislaus and Sand Bar Diversion Dam on the Middle Fork.

Below Beardsley dam in the afterbay and in the stream below the afterbay dam there's more good fishing. You can't drive all the way to Donnell's Lake, but if you park at the base of the dam you can climb up to the water's edge. Some fishermen carry inflatable rafts and launch them on the surface of the lake. Fishing here is even better than at Beardsley.

Resorts, Lodges, and Hotels

Pinecrest Lake Resort advertises itself as the perfect family resort, and they may be correct. It certainly is the most complete on the Stanislaus. Located on the shore of the lake, it includes the Stream Donkey Restaurant, a snack bar, motel, cabins, townhouses, market, tennis courts, sport shop, service station, lounge, and marina.

Pinecrest Chalet, another resort at the lake, has the closest accommodations to Dodge Ridge, with "European Style" lodging for groups and individuals in the winter. In the summer, the accomodations expand to include cabins, tents, and RV spaces, a swimming pool, huge lawn, and dance floor.

Leaving Pinecrest and starting up Highway 108 again, you come almost at once to the community of **Strawberry** where the road crosses the South Fork of the Stanislaus River.

Two resorts and a grocery store share "downtown" Strawberry with a couple of gas stations. One of **Strawberry Inn's** big attractions is its location high over the south fork of the river. Especially in the restaurant, you get to look out over white water and quiet pools of the stream while you eat. The chalets and cottages at **Sparrow's Resort** are also built out over the south fork, and the swimming pool is heated in the summer.

Stop in the old-fashioned grocery store and purchase supplies for a picnic. Then walk across to the flat below the bridge and spread your feast on a rock at the water's edge. Both the downy woodpecker and Williamson's sapsucker make their summer homes here, and you can watch them busily feeding while you dangle your feet in the snow-chilled stream.

Higher up Sonora Pass, across the street from the Forest Service campground, is **Dardanelle Resort**, complete with grocery store, restaurant, lounge, cabins, and RV campground. This quaint old stopping place has been serving visitors for almost a century. The cabins were built for the Hollywood epic *For Whom the Bells Toll*. Each has a "set and whittle" front porch where you can lean back of an evening and watch the sun's last light creep up the slopes of Bald

Peak across the canyon. In the meadow between the cabins and the resort building, flakes of obsidian work their way to surface each year, making you realize you aren't the first people to visit here.

Still higher on the Pass, **Kennedy Meadows Resort** is at the end of the side road past Baker Campground. The rustic old forest-green buildings are home to a grocery store and restaurant, hotel rooms, cabins, a lounge, and most of all a pack station. There is always some activity around the barns and corrals behind the resort, as packers and "dudes" get ready for extended trips into Emigrant Wilderness.

On Highway 4, **Bear Valley Resort** is located on an enclave of private land in the Forest. Many people have taken advantage of its location at the edge of huge meadows to build comfortable summer homes. In July and August, a major summer music festival is hosted by the resort, "Music from Bear Valley." The surrounding peaks echo with the sounds of operatic arias, chamber quartets, and pop tunes, as the festival draws performers and audiences from around the world.

Among the buildings and businesses at Bear Valley, you can find a grocery store, automobile garage and gas station, souvenir shop, real estate office, and rentals for skis and snowmobiles.

Halfway up the north shore of Lake Alpine sits **Lake Alpine Lodge**. This rustic, family-oriented resort has house-keeping cabins on the slope behind the store and restaurant. Each of them boasts a fire-place for chilly nights and a broad veranda for warm ones. For lunch, sit out on the lodge's wide front porch for a superb view over the lake to the ridges beyond. The Sierra blue butterfly, perfectly matching the sky, flits among the trees and shrubs.

STANISLAUS NATIONAL FOREST CAMPGROUNDS

Ebbett's Pass Area	Piped Water	Camp Sites	Trailer Space	Fishing	Boating	Swimming	Store	RV Dump Station	Reservations	Special Attractions
Big Meadow	•	68	•							
Bloomfield		10		•						
Board's Crossing	•	5		•						
Hermit Valley		6		•						
Highland Lakes		10		•	•					
Lake Alpine	•	27	•	•	•	•	•			Restaurant near
Pacific Valley		6		•						
Pine Marten	•	33	•	•	•	•	•			Restaurant near
Sand Flat		4		•						
Silvertip	•	23	•	•	•	•	•			
Silver Valley	•	25	•	•	•	•	•			Restaurant near
Sour Grass	•	6	•	•						
Stanislaus River		5	•	•						

STANISLAUS NATIONAL FOREST CAMPGROUNDS

	Piped Water	Camp Sites	Trailer Space	Fishing	Boating	Swimming	Store	RV Dump Station	Reservations	Special Attractions
Sonora Pass Area										
Baker	•	44	•	•						
Boulder Flat		23	•	•						
Brightman Flat		30	•	•						
Cascade Creek		7	•							
Chipmunk Flat		2	•							
Clark Fork	•	88	•	•			•			
Dardanelle	•	32	•	•			•			Restaurant
Deadman	•	17	•	•			•			Restaurant near
Eureka Valley	•	26	•	•						
French Creek		8	•	•						
Fraser Flat	•	38	•	•						
Herring Creek Reservoir		6		•						
Hull Creek	•	11	•	•						
Meadowview	•	100	•	•	•	•	•	•	•	Full Resort near
Mill Creek		12	•	•						
Niagara Creek		5	•	•						
Pigeon Flat Walk-in		6		•						
Pinecrest	•	200	•	•	•	•	•	•	•	Full Resort near
Sand Flat	•	48	•	•				•		
Big Oak Flat Road										
Carlon	•	16		•						
Cherry Valley	•	46	•	•	•	•				
Lost Claim	•	10		•						
Lumsden		10		•						
Lunsden Bridge		8		•						
Middlefork		25	•	•						
South Fork		5		•						
Sweetwater	•	13	•							
The Pines	•	5								

TOIYABE
NATIONAL
FOREST

Sacramento

San Francisco

Los Angeles

Toiyabe National Forest

The word "toiyabe" in Paiute means **black mountain** and the forest is more in the Great Basin than in California. It is the largest of our National Forests south of Alaska, and almost all of it is within the state of Nevada. However, two of its ranger districts—Carson and Bridgeport—have large and important sections in California.

Camping

North of Lake Tahoe an isolated section of the Toiyabe enters California along the Truckee River and north in the Dog Valley region. There is only one campground in this historically interesting portion of the forest, **Lookout**.

The Donner Trail came through Dog Valley on its way to California and emigrants in later years followed this part of the trail west from near Verdi, Nevada. The canyon of the Truckee River narrowed to the point where the wagons of the pioneers had to cross and recross the boulder-strewn stream repeatedly, and the Dog Valley route was easier on livestock and wagons alike.

Rockhounds will find a good source of quartz crystals at the Crystal Mine north of the Lookout Campground. Check with the ranger to make sure it's still open for gleaning, as there are plans afoot to reopen the mine.

South of Lake Tahoe and still in the Carson Ranger District are several more campgrounds, mostly along Highway 88, the Carson Pass Highway, which was designated a National Scenic Byway in 1988. About six miles below the crest of the range, the road through Hope Valley turns south to **Hope Valley** Campground. Spread out along the West Fork of the Carson River, This campground is often full. Aspens, willows, and lodgepole pines make appealing campsites near the river, and both sunrise and sunsets are glorious here.

Back on Highway 88 below Hope Valley, a series of campgrounds follow the tumbling waters of the West Carson River. These campgrounds, **Kit Carson, Snowshoe Springs**, and **Crystal Springs**, become more developed as you go down the canyon. Crystal Springs Campground is the most developed of the three with paved parking spurs suitable for trailer camping. In addition, you'll be greeted by a campground host at Crystal Springs. All three campgrounds give access to exciting fishing on the swift, dancing stream flowing by the camps, littered with boulders that have crashed into the canyon bottom from the surrounding cliffs.

Silver Creek Campground is near the site of the old mining town of Silver Mountain on Highway 4, the Ebbett's Pass road. The Silver Creek Campground is just above the end of the road for trailers, as the pass beyond is steep, narrow, and too strenuous for them to go any higher.

There are some tent sites at **Little Antelope** Pack Station west of Highway 395 at the trailhead for Silver King and Corral Valley trails. Located at about 8,500 feet altitude it is surrounded by aspens and pinons and junipers typical of the eastern slope.

Bridgeport Ranger District has more developed campgrounds than does the Carson and also gets a lot more recreation traffic. From Highway 395, several roads lead up into the mountain valleys, and at the end of almost every one of them is one or more developed Forest Service campgrounds. **Leavitt**

Meadows and **Sonora Bridge** campgrounds along Highway 108, the Sonora Pass road, are eight and three miles from Highway 395 respectively, and are popular stopping places. Leavitt Meadows, especially, because of the pack station located there, and its proximity to the West Walker River trailheads. Big granite boulders, rough-barked lodgepoles, and sage thickets mark the camp sites.

Going south from the intersection of Sonora Pass road and Highway 395, you very shortly come to the dirt road leading west to **Obsidian** Campground, and just before the town of Bridgeport, the road to **Buckeye** campground and Buckeye Hot Springs turns off. Buckeye is a large campground at about 7,100 feet. It's close to the green meadows and grey granite of the Sierra crest and is one of the major entrances to the Hoover Wilderness.

The next turn-off right in Bridgeport is the busiest, leading to Twin Lakes with five Forest Service campgrounds along the stream below the two popular lakes. Robinson Creek alternates between crashing noisily over granite boulders and through narrow rock chutes, to rippling quietly through meadows and gravel bars. All of these camp sites are near enough to the stream that you'll be lulled to sleep by its music. **Robinson Creek** and **Paha** campgrounds are the most developed. The Forest Service has an amphitheater at Robinson Creek and an interpretive program operates all summer. At 7,000 feet, these campgrounds serve as entrance points for both the Hoover Wilderness and Yosemite National Park's east side. Also, fishermen gather here for the purpose of trying to catch the world record brown trout that hang out in Twin Lakes.

Two more turn-offs lead to two more important campgrounds and Wilderness trailheads. These are at **Green Creek** and **Trumbull Lake** campgrounds. Both are at the edge of the wilderness, and you can be at the tip-top of the Sierra in a few hours walk or ride from eight of them. Trumbull Lake is above the timberline and your campsite is in the willows. At night you can pick the stars, you're so close.

If you want to stay at a lower altitude near Highway 395, both **Bootleg** and **Chris Flat** campgrounds will suit your needs. Both are in the sagebrush flats along the West Walker River.

On the Trail
Pacific Crest Trail
The Echo Summit-Yosemite segment of the Pacific Crest Trail extends ninety miles along the crest of the Sierra from Echo Summit south to Yosemite National Park. It crosses and re-crosses the spine of the range sometimes in Stanislaus National Forest, sometimes in Eldorado, but mostly on the Toiyabe. scenic peaks and snowfields are common along this alpine ecosystem, much of it above 10,000 feet. Primary access points are Little Norway on Echo Summit, Carson Pass, Blue Lakes, Ebbett's Pass, and Sonora Pass. Almost every road that leads up the side canyons also ends in a trail that connects with the PCT system.

Many of the day hikes possible in this region are along portions of the PCT for at least a part of the time. If you go north on the PCT from Ebbett's Pass about three miles you will come to the slopes of **Reynolds Peak**. A short jaunt takes you to the top from where you can see just about forever. Below you to the east are the Kinney Lakes and the Silver Creek Canyon; to the west Deer and Clover Valleys and the drainage of the Mokelumne River. The color contrast is remarkable, from the gray and tan tones of the arid eastern side to the green of the well-watered west.

Either north or south along the PCT from Carson Pass in July will take you into a wildflower paradise. Paintbrush, lemon-yellow buttercups and bright pink pygmy shooting stars are among the favorites. South from the **Blue Lakes trailhead** you pass the Sunset Lakes and keep going another two miles to the turn-off to **Raymond Lake**. This little charmer tucked into a glacial bowl has been planted with golden trout, and early in the season they will rise nicely to a fly and give you a lot of fishing entertainment.

The PCT does tend to get busy in the peak of the season, so searching out some of the other trails of the Toiyabe is worthwhile. One of the nicest is the **Pleasant Valley Trail** south of Grover Hot Springs State Park. The trail begins at the end of Pleasant Valley Road, which turns south from Hot Springs Road about a mile-and-a-half from Markleeville. This six-mile trail meanders up Pleasant Valley Creek through sagebrush flats, Jeffrey pines and aspen groves to a connection with the PCT a third of the way between the Blue Lakes trailhead and Ebbett's Pass.

The **East Carson River** and **Silver King Trails** will both take you into some interesting and not very well known country. Llewellyn Falls and Carson Falls are big cataracts on Silver King Creek and the East Carson River respectively. Both of these trails lead into Paiute Trout Management Area and no fishing is allowed from the points on the streams where the management area begins. The Paiute trout is a threatened species and survives only in its native habitat in the upper reaches of Silver King Creek.

Both of these two trails can be accessed from Little Antelope Pack Station or from Wolf Creek Meadows off the Ebbett's Pass Road.

Hikers interested in history can walk on several sections of emigrant passes that aren't covered with asphalt. Sonora Pass, especially is available in its original form. One long section of **Sonora Emigrant Trail** starts at Mill Canyon Road which turns off the Little Antelope Road south of Coleville. The pioneer trail leaves the road a mile-and-a-half from the junction with Mill Canyon Road at Little Lost Canyon and goes south up Lost Cannon Creek to Summit Meadow and then down along Silver Creek to the U.S. Marine Mountain Warfare Training Center on Sonora Pass at Pickle Meadow. You can pick up the trail again where it leaves Leavitt Meadow following the West Walker River to the headwaters of the West Fork and over Emigrant Pass into Emigrant Wilderness on the Stanislaus National Forest. Minerals in the rock have turned the granite tannish, and the pass is a green-and-tan meadow on the Sierra crest. Eventually, the trail comes out near Pinecrest, and is the longest unpaved section of emigrant road in the Sierra. Unless you're trying to break some speed records, the trip will take a week.

Mokelumne and Carson Iceberg Wildernesses

About 82,000 acres of the Carson Iceberg Wilderness lie along the spine of the Sierra with Toiyabe National Forest, from the region of Ebbett's Pass on the north down toward Sonora Pass. This is wild country, and truly a wilderness. To give an idea of how lightly these two wildernesses are used, in 1987 Hoover Wilderness received about 60,000 visitor days, while the Mokelumne and Carson Iceberg combined received only 9,000 visitor days.

Hoover Wilderness

The Hoover Wilderness, consisting of 42,800 acres within Toiyabe and 9,000

A pack train loads up at Cinko Lake high on the Sierra crest.

more on the Inyo National Forest, is characterized by rugged mountains, alpine lakes, and rushing streams. The steep canyons lead to glacial meadows and winding streams stocked with rainbow and eastern brook trout. It is the home of deer, bears, bobcats, and coyotes, as well as an occasional mountain lion. The air above the meadows and cliffs is owned by hawks and eagles. In the forested sections, porcupines, squirrels and chipmunks make their homes. Twin Lakes, Green Creek, and Virginia Lakes are the major Tioyabe entrances to the Hoover.

Touring, Sightseeing, and Special Programs

Campfire programs are held regularly at the Robinson Creek amphitheater below Twin Lakes on Saturday evenings. A ranger-naturalist presents a slide-show or film on the natural history of this area, as well as the usual songs and fun. For the kids, there are Junior Ranger Walks. They explore the plants and animals, rocks and streams. On Wednesday evenings there are "star parties" presented by a ranger-naturalist. An evening of star-gazing and folklore is presented.

Along Highway 88 at the top of Carson Pass, history buffs will find the **Odd Fellows Monument**. One of the pioneer wagon trains that crossed here was made up of a party of Odd Fellows. They named the valleys below "Faith, Hope, and Charity" for the tenets of their lodge. In addition, they took white lead that they had carried with them to make paint and scribed their initials on a group of boulders beside the trail. Modern-day Odd Fellows keep up the initials with additional coats of white lead.

At the foot of the pass, you'll come to **Red Lake**. Forty-niners had their "nooning" here after the pull up the slope from Hope Valley and got ready for the last big pull over the top. In 1849 and 1850 the traffic was so thick the emigrants worked all night to cross, setting whole trees on fire to light their way. Along the original trail, south of the lake, you can see trees damaged by the chains used to help haul the heavy wagons up to the top.

The Nevada Emigrant Trail Marking Committee, a section of the Nevada Historical Society, has placed markers all along the two major historical trails through Nevada and up to the top of the Sierra. Marker numbers 27, 28, and 29 can be seen in Hope Valley, at Red Lake, and at the top of the pass.

Touring in the Markleeville region in the fall of the year is a journey of color. The aspens, willows, alders, and other trees put on their annual pre-winter show, especially the aspens, which turn brilliant yellow and shimmer at the slightest breeze, turning the meadow edges and each water course into golden motion.

In Markleeville, stop at the **Alpine County Historical Complex** where there is a museum, the old Webster School, an old log jail, and a library/archives room. Since 1963 when the Alpine County Historical Society was founded, volunteers from the community have put together a fascinating collection of

Grover Hot Springs State Park, which is surrounded by Toiyabe National Forest, is enjoyed by summer and winter visitors alike.

logging, mining, and ranching artifacts housed in old buildings they have moved to this hilltop site on the edge of town.

Hot Springs Road runs past the historical complex and also takes you out to **Grover Hot Springs State Park**. The 519-acre park lies in Hot Springs Valley at an elevation of almost 6,000 feet, with shining basalt and granite mountains rising abruptly on three sides. The area is one of alpine beauty set in the midst of the greenest meadow you can find. But it is the hot springs that are the major attraction.

The hot springs are a phenomenon associated with the faulting that developed when the Sierra began to rise. The springs here leave the ground at 148° Fahrenheit. The hot water is mixed with cold to enter the concrete pool at a temperature between 102° and 105°.

Grover Hot Springs State Park is open all year round, except for Thanksgiving, Christmas and New Year's Day. The two campgrounds have seventy-six sites equipped with stoves, cupboards, and tables. Each site is close to piped water and restrooms with showers. As with all of the State Parks, reservations can be made through Mistex, and are advisable during the summer season. The campgrounds themselves are closed from October to May, but you can camp in the picnic grounds in the winter and have access to the water and restrooms—no showers. It's a favorite winter sports area.

Another drive that historians like is to head east into the desert mountains from Bridgeport. There are ghost towns, real ones, like **Masonic** and **Monte Cristo** in the Sweetwater Mountains, and miles of jeep roads. Four-wheelers, especially, enjoy this section of the Toiyabe.

In the same area, but surrounded by Bureau of Land Management land instead of Forest Service Land is **Bodie State Historic Park**. This fascinating ghost town was actually occupied and the mines and mills working until World War II. Now in a state of "arrested decay" it presents a wonderful opportunity to see how men and women managed to wrest a living from the high desert, which was often buffeted by frigid fifty-mile-an-hour winds called the "Washoe Zephyrs."

Sports

The most popular area for winter sports on the Toiyabe are centered in the Hope Valley and Grover Hot Springs regions. In Hope Valley, **Sorenson's Resort** has more than ten miles of cross-country ski trails through varied terrain, some of which is on private property and some on National Forest land. The cabins at Sorenson's are unique. One of them—Norway House—was build in Norway and shipped directly here. It's a replica of a 13th century Scandanavian home. The smell of wood smoke lingers over the cabins from the stoves that most of them provide.

The ownership of several parcels in the area has just recently come into the forest's possession. Included in the recent acquisitions is **Burnside Lake**, a popular destination for Nordic skiers from both Sorenson's and from Grover Hot Springs. At the end of a long day of cross-country skiing, the hot springs really feel like Heaven.

Snowmobiling is starting to come into its own on the Toiyabe, with the Faith, Hope, and Charity valleys the most popular spots. The forest's Off-Highway Vehicle Recreation Plan is being developed and will no doubt include snowmobile areas as well as roads and trails for four-wheelers and motorcycles.

TOIYABE NATIONAL FOREST

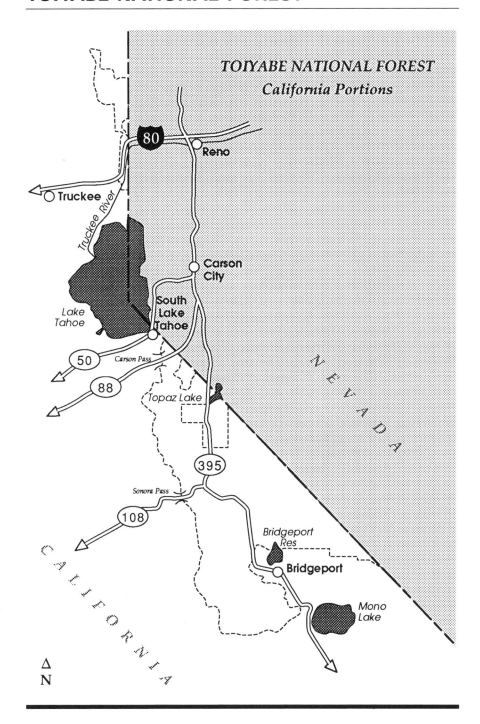

TOIYABE NATIONAL FOREST
California Portions

Reno

Truckee

Truckee River

Lake Tahoe

Carson City

South Lake Tahoe

50

88

Carson Pass

Topaz Lake

NEVADA

395

Sonora Pass

108

Bridgeport Res

Bridgeport

Mono Lake

CALIFORNIA

N

Boating and Waterskiing

The **Twin Lakes** provide a place for boating, especially for fishermen who like to troll the two lakes. A resort on private land at the head of Upper Twin Lake, Mono Village, has rentals and launch ramp. **Bridgeport Reservoir** is another big fishing lake, and touches national forest land at its northern tip. **Topaz Lake**, on the California-Nevada border, provides sport for both water skiers and fishermen. Most people who like speed-boating and waterskiing tend to travel on to Lake Tahoe to practice their sports.

In the spring, there's exciting whitewater rafting and kayaking on the **East Fork** of the **Carson River**. In 1988 there were seventeen commercial outfitters using the East Fork, as well as several hundred private rafters.

Off Highway Motoring

Although not too many people take advantage of it there is excellent off-highway vehicle travel in the mountains east of Highway 395 throughout the forest. The **Bodie Hills**, which are mostly in BLM lands, the **Sweetwater Mountains**, and the area immediately north of **Monitor Pass** on the west side, are especially inviting. Remains of mines and mining towns dot the draws and canyons. The spring wildflower displays are a marvel of color, especially the Douglas iris, Indian pinks, and wild asters.

Hunting and Fishing

Fishing and hunting are the major draw in the forest, with mule deer the most important game being hunted and trout by far the most important fish sought.

Four pack stations, Little Antelope, Leavitt Meadows, Wolf Creek, and **Virgina Lakes** provides trips into the back country for both hunters and fishermen. Besides the packers, there are back-packing opportunities for people of every capability, not to mention day hikes that will get you to where the trout are biting.

Every stream, from the Carson River on the north to the creeks draining into Bridgeport Reservoir on the south have fish in them, and only those in the Paiute and Lahontan cutthroat management streams are closed. Every canyon on the Sierra front, and every hidden spring in the high desert marks a place where that trophy buck is hanging out.

TOIYABE NATIONAL FOREST CAMPGROUNDS

	Piped Water	Camp Sites	Trailer Space	Fishing	Boating	Swimming	Store	RV Dump Station	Reservations	Special Attractions
Bridgeport Ranger District										
Bootleg	•	63	•	•						
Buckeye	•	65	•	•						
Chris Flat	•	15	•	•						
Desert Creek		13								
Green Creek	•	11		•						
Honeymoon Flat	•	47		•						
Leavitt Meadows	•	16		•		•				
Lower Twin Lakes	•	17	•	•	•	•				
Obsidian	•	14		•						
Paha	•	22	•	•						
Robinson Creek	•	54	•	•						
Sawmill	•	8		•						
Sonora Bridge	•	23	•	•						
Trumbull Lake	•	45		•						
Carson Ranger District										
Lookout	•	30								
Shoeshoe Springs		13		•						
Kit Carson	•	12		•						
Hope Valley	•	20	•	•						
Crystal Springs	•	25	•	•						
Markleeville	•	10		•						
Silver Creek	•	26	•	•						

*ELDORADO
NATIONAL
FOREST*

Sacramento

San Francisco

Los Angeles

Eldorado National Forest

A variety of landscapes, activities and experiences as diverse as rock climbing, gold panning, and auto touring are yours to discover on the Eldorado National Forest. Within an hour's driving time you can travel from the oaks of the foothills, through the conifer forest, and into the rocky sub-alpine regions of the "high Sierra." More than 586,000 acres of national forest land, plus more than 200,000 acres of private land lay within the confines of the forest.

Hundreds of miles of tumbling alpine streams and 175 secluded lakes dotting the landscape are evidence that water is a valuable forest resource. And clanging cowbells and gigantic logging trucks remind forest visitors that this, like all of our national forests, is a multi-use area, managed for the greatest good of the public.

Camping

The Eldorado has a wide variety of campgrounds, many of them operated by concessionaires. And, of course, almost all of the forest is open for dispersed camping. The only parts not open to dispersed camping are those in the developed portion of recreation areas such as Crystal Basin and Wrights Lake region.

Georgetown Ranger District

Most of the camping places on the Georgetown Ranger District are dispersed in the forest along the creeks and streams. There are, however, two big reservoirs with developed campgrounds. At low altitude, and easy to reach is the Stumpy Meadows Campground at Stumpy Meadows Lake on the Wentworth Springs Road east of Georgetown. Located close to the water in a yellow pine forest, the camping places are in open country but sheltered from sun and wind.

Hell Hole Reservoir is more difficult to reach, being in the far northeastern tip of the forest. Two campgrounds serve the area. First is Big Meadow Campground, located about 1.5 miles northwest of the lake and about ten miles southeast of French Meadows Reservoir on adjacent Tahoe National Forest. Hell Hole Campground is nearer the lake, but much smaller, with only ten units. At Big Meadows, the camp sites are in the fir and pine forest and look out over the meadows dotted with huge granite boulders and clumps of willows.

A short walk east of your campsite at Hell Hole will take you to a vista point where you'll look out over Hell Hole Reservoir and up the canyons of the Rubicon River and Five Lakes Creek to the shimmering peaks of the Sierra crest beyond.

Pacific Ranger District

The Crystal Basin Recreation Area, on the Pacific District, has several hundred camp sites in developed campgrounds. All but three are operated by a concessionaire under special permit from the forest.

Three of the Crystal Basin campgrounds are on the shores of big Union Valley Reservoir—Sunset, Wench Creek, and Yellowjacket. Sunset is located at the tip of a peninsula that protrudes into the middle of the lake from the east shore. Firs, incense cedars, and Jeffrey pines shelter the camp sites and campers practically surrounded by the blue waters of the lake. There's a picnic area, swimming beach, boat ramp, and trailer dump station nearby.

Yellowjacket is on the north shore of the lake and has its own boat ramp. The forest here comes right to the edge of the lake, and the camping places have the advantage of large boulders and clumps of manzanita and whitethorn separating them.

Each of the other lakes and reservoirs in the basin has its own campground, beginning with Ice House. Dominated by the high granite peaks of the Crystal Range to the east, the pine and fir forest in which the camp sites are makes each site seem unique and special. There's a picnic area and boat ramp here, too.

Loon Lake Campground is close to Desolation Wilderness and at 6,500 feet escapes the summer heat of lower areas. Right at the edge of lovely Loon Lake, the sites are on the northwestern slopes of Brown Mountain above the South Fork of the Rubicon River. Across the Lake is Pleasant Campground, accessible only by boat or trail. This camp is a popular entry point for the Rockbound Valley region of Desolation Wilderness two miles to the southeast.

The only family campground in the Basin where you'll need reservations at this time is at Wrights Lake. Write Mistix, P.O. Box 85705, San Diego, CA, 92138-5705, (800) 444-PARK, at least ten days in advance and no sooner than eight weeks in advance. Cliffs of the Crystal Range rise from the meadows at the edge of this small lake just under 7000 feet. It's a nugget for fishing and swimming, and motorboats are prohibited. Red firs and both Jeffrey and lodgepole pines are scattered through each of the two campground sections. Chokecherries and willows grow near the lake, and the white bark of aspens shines through the crevices in the granite.

Placerville Ranger District

Sand Flat is the only campground along Highway 50. It sits on the banks of the South Fork American River a mile west of The Sugarloaf and is a favorite site of rock climbers. The Sugarloaf, an immense upthrust granitic dome, along with Lover's Leap a few miles to the east, are climbers' meccas.

China Flat and Silver Fork campgrounds are both located along the Silver Fork of the American River south of Kyburz. Hiking, fishing, and OHV trail access are the big attractions. The road south from Kyburz is paved, and trailers can easily be pulled to both campgrounds.

Both campgrounds are within sight and sound of the Silver Fork as it splashes down through the valley around massive boulders and through thickets of alders, chokecherries, and willows. Back from the stream, ceanothus, manzanita, whitethorn, and mountain misery blanket the forest floor under the canopy of sugar pines and white firs.

Amador Ranger District

Fishermen and hunters heading for the Salt Springs Reservoir country have three adjacent campgrounds to choose from along the banks of the north fork of the Mokelumne below the dam. They are Mokelumne, Moore Creek, and White Azalea. At about 3,200 to 3,500 feet, these camping spots are in the transition zone with oaks and ponderosas above and many of the chaparral plants in the understory.

Up along Highway 88 there are fully developed campgrounds at Silver Lake

Boats of all sizes and description can be found on Silver Lake. Bob Henley photo.

and Caples Lake. These are high altitude camps, way up in the granite, lodgepole, and aspen country. Especially at Caples Lake, campers will be enraptured with the views out over the lake to the serrated crest beyond, from one part of the campground, and into the dark and light of the ridges and canyons from other parts.

A little further away from the highway, campgrounds at Lower Bear River Reservoir, called South Shore, and at Woods Lake just below the top of the pass, attract their share of campers. At Woods Lake, tent campers will find themselves near the shores of a tiny lake. Small granite domes, their sides exfoliating from repeated frost and thaw, dominate the campground and separate the sites into private nooks and crannies sheltered under red firs and lodgepoles.

At the very crest of the Sierra, and only accessible by crossing Carson Pass into Toiyabe National Forest and turning south through Hope and Faith valleys, are the Blue Lakes. Three Pacific Gas and Electric Company campgrounds serve this alpine eden. Emerald meadows, gray granite peaks laced with veins of pink and white quartz, sparse clumps of whitebark pines, and both red and white heathers tell you you're at the top of the range.

On The Trail

The Pacific Crest Trail on the Eldorado National Forest extends south approximately fifty-three miles from the southern boundary of the Tahoe National Forest to Border Ruffian Flat on the Toiyabe National Forest. It includes segments that pass through the Eldorado and Toiyabe and the Lake Tahoe Basin Management Unit. Elevations range from about 7,000 feet to over 9,500. Because of the heavy snow pack it is normally not feasible to hike this area before mid-June, and the higher passes may not be completely free of snow until mid-July or later.

National Recreation Trails

Both of the National Recreation Trails on the Eldorado are historically connected. First is the Emigrant Summit Trail. This trail is thirty-two miles south of Lake Tahoe along Highway 88. Access is at Tragedy Springs and the Caples Lake Spillway. The trail averages 8,600 feet in altitude and is about eighteen miles long. It was used by emigrants from 1849 until the Carson Spur Road was blasted out of the cliffs in 1863. It was the highest of all the passes across the Sierra, and wagon ruts and rust marks from the iron-bound wheels are still visible in some locations. One such location where the rust marks can be seen is just south of tiny Mud Lake near the western terminous of the trail.

Ten miles of the Pony Express Trail parallel Highway 50. This designated section is only a portion of the existing route, but it is the longest publicly owned segment. Along the trail you'll be able to see examples of old trail construction and communities dating back to the 1800s. The trail was part of both the Pony Express route and the Johnson's Cut-Off Wagon Road. One good place to get on the trail is at White Hall, about two miles east of the turn-off to Crystal Basin.

Hiking the Georgetown Ranger District is basically low-altitude walking. The country is steep and cut with creeks and canyons. The Rubicon Trail is a beautiful ten-mile walk along the Rubicon River Gorge with many swimming and fishing holes along the way. The stream banks are lined with ferns and mosses in the shady spots, and wild currant and azalea shrubs cover parts of the canyon walls. To get to the trailhead, take the Wentworth Springs Road to the 11 Pines Road and continue up the route five miles to the trailhead at the Ellicott's Bridge.

Close to the top of the range along Highway 50, the Bryan Meadow and Sayles Canyon Trails open up an especially scenic loop. From the parking lot just off the Sierra Ski Ranch Road, you can walk up Sayles Creek to the Bryan Meadows Trail, which continues easterly for about three miles to a junction with the PCT, traveling through stands of lodgepole pines and mountain hemlock. From the duff under foot and the bark and needles of the conifers comes the smells only associated with the Sierra. A mile south on the PCT you'll come to the Sayles Canyon Trail intersection. This trail will take you back through exquisite Round Meadow, filled with penstemons, monkey flowers, and columbines, and back and forth across Sayles Creek to your starting point. It's about an eight-mile walk. Take a picnic lunch to enjoy along the creek among the wild roses and snow flowers blooming in the early summer.

At Kyburz, the Silver Fork Road turns south along the Silver Fork American River into some of the best hiking, fishing, and exploring country along Highway 50. The Caples Creek Trail is just one of the trails you can get to from this road. After travelling about ten miles south of Kyburz you'll come to the Fitch Rantz Bridge. A four-wheel drive road turns left just before the bridge about a quarter-mile to the trailhead. The trail follows along the north side of Caples Creek through virgin forest, intersecting the Silver Fork Trail and continues through Jake Schneider's Meadow to the Old Silver Lake Trail.

Over on Highway 88, both Silver Lake and Caples Lake are near trailheads that will take you into the backcountry on either little "strolls" or though alpine hikes. The Emigrant Lake Trail starts at the west end of the spillway of Caples Lake and proceeds on the south side of the lake for about 2.5 miles. The trail then joins the old Emigrant route and climbs steeply up the ridge south of the lake to a junction. Go left at the junction, cross the stream and continue to the lake. It's 4.5 miles to the lake from the dam. There are campsites along the shores and plenty of fishing—but not much catching.

A really pleasant loop hike starts at the outlet of Woods Lake and goes south up the ridge to Winnemucca Lake about two miles. This trail makes its way out of the aspens and lodgpoles at about the half-mile mark and for the rest of the trip you'll be walking through meadows ablaze with wildflowers. In July it's like walking through a wildflower nursery. Sierra Indian paintbrush, shooting stars, asters, and blue-eyed Marys glow under the summer sun. At Winnemucca Lake, the trail turns west for a mile to Round Top Lake—more meadows shining with the yellows and golds of marsh marigold, monkey flowers, and dwarf daisies. Whitebark pines, marvelously twisted by winter's snows and winds clump in sheltered spots and make wonderful campsites. One branch of the trail goes up a slight incline and then drops sharply into 4th of July Lake in the Mokelumne Wilderness. The other branch returns to Woods Lake near abandoned mining buildings leaning precipitously and thick forests. It's about a six-mile trip.

Mokelumne Wilderness

Recently enlarged to more than 105,000 acres, the Mokelumne Wilderness is located between highways 88 and 4 in the Eldorado, Toiyabe, and Stanislaus national forests. It is characterized by massive granite formations and deep canyons. In contrast with the Desolation Wilderness to the north and the Emigrant Wilderness to the south, the Mokelumne does not have as many high alpine lakes. Until recently, the Mokelumne was one of our little-used wilderness regions. However, it is receiving increasing use and wear by more and more backcountry travelers each year, especially in those parts of the wilderness that are accessed by the PCT.

Desolation Wilderness

Desolation Wilderness was originally established as a "Primitive Area" in 1931, and included the portion of the current wilderness that lies between the crest of the range and Mt. Tallac in the Eldorado National Forest and the Lake Tahoe Basin Management Unit. The current wilderness became part of the national Wilderness Preservation System in 1969, and is the single most-visited wilderness in the country.

Because Desolation is extremely attractive and easily accessible from the Bay Area and the Sacramento Valley, as well as the Reno-Carson City area, over-use was endangering the wilderness experience. Consequently, a quota system was established, and beginning in 1978, a quota of 700 overnight users per day was put into effect. Permits for 50 percent of the quota can be reserved up to ninety days in advance, and the other 50 percent are issued on the day of entry.

Hiking in Desolation Wilderness is a wonderous experience. This is glaciated,

ELDORADO NATIONAL FOREST

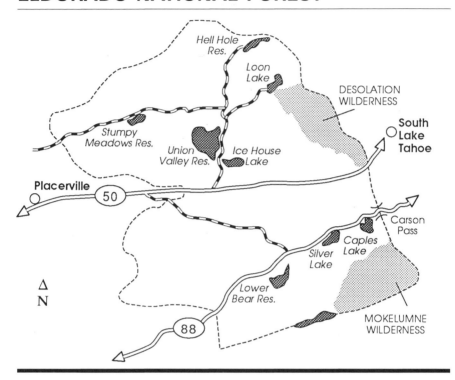

high Sierra country, with vast open meadows filled with granite and wild flowers surrounding more than a hundred sparkling lakes. Tiny creeks drain the snow fields and thread their way through the boulders tinkling over hidden falls and cataracts.

There are entry points on the Eldorado all along the western side of the wilderness. The favorite is at Wrights Lake where the trails to Twin Lakes and Rockbound Pass start. The Horsetail Falls and Ralston Trails go into the wilderness from Highway 50.

Touring, Sightseeing and Special Programs

In the fall the Sierra passes and the high meadows associated with them turn to gold as the aspens feel approaching winter. An ''aspencade'' is a wonderful way to spend an October weekend. Drive to Silver Lake on Friday evening and spend the night at one of the resorts there. Then on Saturday, drive the highways and byways at the top of the range, crossing into Toiyabe National Forest at Carson Pass and around into the Lake Tahoe Basin over Luther Pass. Spend Saturday night at the lake, and then Sunday come back into the Eldorado via Echo Summit, stopping to admire Echo Lake and the Twin Bridges aspens on your way. Go into the Crystal Basin all the way to Loon Lake. The first frosts of the season will have turned the forests to gold and green. There are few visitors, and a sense of peace pervades the atmosphere.

In the summer, the picnic grounds along highway 50 are frequently jammed, especially Bridal Veil on the South Fork American River just below the turn-off for Crystal Basin. Hikers can enjoy a short section of the original Pony Express Trail and everyone can enjoy the quiet pools in the river. Anglers should have good to excellent success downstream from the crossing.

Robbs Peak, in Crystal Basin, at 6,686 feet, has been used as an observation point for detecting forest fires since 1915. The present facility on the peak was constructed in 1934 and was manned every summer until 1978.

Recently with the help of Recreation Equipment Incorporated (REI), and over seventy volunteers, the bunkhouse was converted into a mountain hut, Robbs Hut. The Forest Service is currently offering the mountain hut for personal recreation on a permit basis. Reservations for a small fee are made through the Eldorado Information Center in Camino. The bunkhouse is equipped with a wood stove, firewood, a small propane stove and lantern, three double bunks, six wool blankets, among other things, and can house six persons comfortably. During winter and early spring access is over the snow, via skis, snowshoes, or snowmobiles. The rest of the year the hut is used by hikers or bicyclists.

Sports

There are a number of winter recreation areas on the Eldorado. These "designated" areas are in Crystal Basin and along both Highways 50 and 88.

Loon Lake winter recreation area is forty-five miles northeast of Placerville in the Pacific Ranger District. It offers a variety of winter recreational opportunities, including cross-country skiing, snow play, and winter camping. The greatest asset lies in its potential for providing many miles of marked and unmarked ski touring routes. The trails are signed with trail name, mileage, kilometers, and difficulty. Route markers are blue diamonds with intermittant pink flagging. A warming room is available on weekends.

Snowmobilers will enjoy the Silver Bear Snow trails on the Amador District along Highway 88. There are three staging areas: Bear River Reseroir, Iron Mountain Sno-Park, and Kay's Silver Lake Resort. There is a groomed trail leading from Silver Lake to Bear River Reservoir and Bear River to Iron Mountain Sno-Park.

The Strawberry Canyon Nordic Trail System is located about a quarter-mile west of Strawberry Lodge along Highway 50 at Forty-Two-Mile Recreation site. The system encompasses eleven miles of cross-country trail from beginner to intermediate skiers. Three marked trails from 1.5 to five miles long provide enough variety that everyone in your party will find the correct terrain for himself.

Alpine skiers will find three major ski resorts, Kirkwood and Iron Mountain, on Highway 88 and Sierra Ski Ranch on Highway 50. A proposed enlargement of Sierra Ski Ranch will enable it to accommodate many more skiers than its current maximum.

Boating and Water Skiing

Nine major reservoirs on the Eldorado have boat launching ramps, and boating and water skiing are major summertime recreation activities on the Forest. In addition, car-toppers and inflatable rafts can be launched on many of the smaller bodies of water, making the Eldorado one of the most water-oriented of all our forests.

Plans are in the making for the Lower Bear River Reservoir to be raised by thirty-four feet. This will open up more back country to boat-in camping.

At the time of completion, it would rank with Loon Lake as best on the Forest for boat-in camping.

Resorts at Bear River, Silver Lake, and Caples Lake have boats for rent for fishermen, either with or without outboard motors. For the others you'll have to bring your own. Late in the season, some of the reservoirs are drawn down to the point where launch ramps are no longer in the water. The Eldorado has a weekly "Recreation Report" that gives all sorts of information about the forest, and especially for boaters, lists the lakes where boating is best.

Off Road Motoring

The Eldorado National Forest is one of the state's most popular for off-highway vehicle enthusiasts. Four-wheelers, all-terrain vehicles, and motorcycles all have their backers, and the Eldorado provides room for all.

Wentworth and Rubicon Springs in the far northeastern part of the forest are the centers of a very active four-wheel drive community. As many as 200 jeeps at one time may be on the Georgetown-Rubicon Springs Road. Special jamborees for clubs take place very frequently on the Georgetown and Pacific ranger districts, such as the Toyota 4WD jamboree and others like it.

Motorcyclists, too, have their special trails and special meeting places on the forest. South Fork Campground in Crystal Basin is one of the cyclists' favorites. Open from Memorial Day through Labor Day it provides access to hundreds of miles of road and trail suitable for the two-wheelers.

Newest sport on Eldorado National Forest is mountain bicycling. The opportunities abound for cyclists wishing to test their skills off the paved roads on the Eldorado. There are skid trails and abandoned road beds scattered throughout the forest and offer the all-terrain bike rider a challenge. Most roads and trails outside of congressionally designated wilderness areas and developed recreation sites are open to bike riding unless posted as closed. The Pacific Crest Trail is closed to mountain bikes from Oregon to Mexico.

Fishing and Hunting

Most of the lakes and rivers of the Eldorado are stocked with catchable trout on a regular basis, and just as regularly, there are fishermen to catch them. This is a popular forest, and the California State Fish and Game Department does its best to see that the fishable waters contain fish. And they do a remarkably good job.

Your problem is to find fishable water that isn't too crowded. The biggest reservoirs, such as Union Valley, Hell Hole, and Lower Bear River, are almost always a good place to try, especially in the early and late seasons, and for those who are willing to go on foot, the Rubicon River offers great fishing.

Hunting

Like the Tahoe National Forest to the north, the Eldorado is very popular, and the large numbers of people that are in the forest make hunting difficult. Deer hunters do come into the Eldorado in season, and the good ones—and sometimes the lucky ones—will get their buck. But it's really not the place for the casual buck hunter to try his luck.

Resorts, Lodges, and Hotels

Two of the resorts on the Eldorado are on Forest Service land and operate under special permit from the Forest Service. Both are along Highway 88 at the big lakes. Caples Lake Resort is open in summer only sixty miles east of Jackson. They have guest cabins as well as rooms in the lodge itself. They also operate a store and marina where you can launch your own boat, or rent one from the resort. If you sit out on the deck, or in the restaurant, you look out over the waters of Caples Lake with sunlight glinting off the waves. Beyond the lake, you can trace the route of the Emigrant Trail up the monolithic wall below Thimble peak.

Largest and most "upscale" of the resorts along Highway 88 is Kit Carson Lodge at Silver Lake. Two types of accommodations are offered. The hotel rooms have a bedroom and bath and private sundeck overlooking the lake, the trees, and the mountains beyond. The housekeeping cottages with both fireplaces and barbecues are completely furnished except for bath towels and linens. The cottages too, have big sundecks overlooking the lake. The restaurant has an antique clock collection which establishes a warm and quaint atmosphere for dining. They also have a general store, post office, and laundromat. Sailboats and fishing boats with or without motors can be rented.

Plasse's Resort, on private land at the lower end of Silver Lake, has been operated by the Plasse family since 1853, and is open from June through September. They have an RV and tent campground with forty-five sites. Water hook-ups, hot showers and a laundromat are available. They also have a fully stocked store, plus gasoline, propane, and a dump station. The bar and restaurant are open every day of the season.

Kay's Silver Lake Resort, on P.G. & E. land, has studio and one or two-bedroom cabins, and they're open all year, although you may have to hike through the snow to get to the cabins, which are on top of a hill overlooking Silver Lake. The grocery store has a complete stock of groceries, over-the-counter drugs, hardware, and fishing tackle. The coffee shop and the marina, perched on the granite adjacent to the dam that holds back the water of the South Fork American River, are only kept open in the summertime.

ELDORADO NATIONAL FOREST CAMPGROUNDS

	Piped Water	Camp Sites	Trailer Space	Fishing	Boating	Swimming	Store	RV Dump Station	Reservations	Special Attractions
Amador Ranger District										
Caples Lake	•	35	•	•	•	•	•			Resort near
Kirkwood	•	13		•	•	•	•			No motors
Lower Blue Lake	•	16		•	•	•				PG&E
Lumberyard	•	8		•	•					
Middle Creek	•	5		•	•	•				PG&E
Mokelumne		8		•		•				
Moore Creek		8		•		•				
Pipi	•	51		•	•		•			Handicapped
Silver Lake	•	97		•	•	•	•	•		Resorts near
South Shore	•	22		•	•	•	•	•		
Upper Blue Lake	•	25		•	•	•				PG&E; PCT Trailhead
White Azalea		6		•		•				
Woods Lake	•	25		•	•	•				No motors
Georgetown Ranger District										
Big Meadows	•	55		•	•				•	
Hell Hole	•	10			•	•				
Stumpy Meadows	•	40		•	•	•	•	•		
Pacific Ranger District										
Gerle Creek	•	50		•	•	•				No motors
Ice House	•	83		•	•	•	•	•	•	Handicapped
Loon Lake	•	34		•	•	•				
Pleasant		10		•	•	•				Walk or boat in
Silver Creek		11		•		•	•	•		
South Fork		17		•		•				
Sunset	•	131		•	•	•		•		
Upper Hell Hole		15		•	•	•				
Wench Creek	•	100		•	•	•		•		
Wentworth Springs		8		•		•				
Wrights Lake	•	71		•	•	•			•	No motors
Yellowjacket	•	40		•	•	•				
Placerville Ranger District										
Capps Crossing		10		•		•				
China Flat	•	23		•		•				
Sand Flat	•	29		•		•				
Silver Fork	•	35		•		•				Handicapped

TAHOE
NATIONAL
FOREST

Sacramento

San Francisco

Los Angeles

Tahoe National Forest

The Tahoe is an immense forest with highly developed recreational facilities. At the same time, it is so large that it's possible to get completely away from the crowds that follow the main highways by simply turning down one of the hundreds of side roads and "getting lost."

Gold mining—basically river dredging and panning—are important recreational activities on the forest, along with OHV travel. The other typical forest activities—fishing, camping, sightseeing, boating, winter sports, hunting—are all well represented, too.

You are never very far from some of the most important sites in the history of California when on the Tahoe: Included on the forest are the scene of the Donner Party disaster, the Gold Rush towns of Camptonville, Goodyear's Bar, Downieville, and Alleghany, and the first transcontinental railroad.

Camping

There are eighty-two campgrounds within the boundaries of the forest, including several that are owned and operated by the Pacific Gas and Electric Company, and some by public irrigation and power districts. A few, too, are in the two state parks—Malakoff Diggins and Donner Memorial. The forest itself operates sixty-eight family and nine group campgrounds.

About four miles above Oregon Creek where you first enter the forest on Highway 49, a good paved road turns left for Bullard's Bar Reservoir, one of the Mother Lode's least used recreational lakes. The sixteen-mile-long lake has oaks, pines, and madrones right to the water's edge and is one of the prettiest reservoirs in the foothills. You can camp in a national forest campground at **Schoolhouse** Campground. Schoolhouse has plenty of room for boats and trailers, and the camp sites are on a bluff that overlooks the lake. Spring and fall are the best times to visit here.

Back on Highway 49, you will reach the North Fork of the Yuba at Indian Valley. From this point to the top of Yuba Pass some forty miles to the east, the road follows the course of this historic, gold-spotted river. Camping along the river is restricted to established campgrounds, and there are lots of them—twelve along the highway itself, and a half dozen more just off the road.

Depending upon what you like to do and the time of the year, you can choose to camp at relatively low altitude along the lower river or climb into the higher regions of pines and cooler weather. Campgrounds like **Upper** and **Lower Carlton** are frequently filled with recreational miners and their families. The North Yuba from Indian Valley to Downieville is chock-a-block with dredges from June to October. Between Downieville and Sierra City, there is far less mining action in the rougher water of the more rapidly falling river, and **Union Flat** and **Loganville** campgrounds are usually not as busy as those below.

At Sierra City, a short road leads up Haypress Creek to **Wild Plum** Campground. Here forty-seven sites along the banks of the creek wait for family campers. Alders, willows, and some other water-loving plants line the creek, and ponderosas, incense cedars, black oaks, and big-leaf maples shade the camp sites. You'll be able to fish the creek, and hike the well-maintained trails, including a portion of the Pacific Crest Trail.

At Bassett's Station about five miles east of Sierra City, the road from Gold Lake and the Lakes Basin Recreation Area intersects Highway 49 from the north. There are six campgrounds in the region on Tahoe National Forest and another one or two in neighboring Plumas National Forest. All six are easy to get to and almost always very busy on summer weekends. **Snag Lake, Berger, Packsaddle**, and **Diablo** are undeveloped as far as water is concerned, and campers either have to bring their own, or use lake or creek water, which should be boiled for three minutes before being used in order to protect the users from giardiasis infections.

Also in the Lakes Basin are **Salmon Creek** and **Sardine** campgrounds. The serenity of the imposing Sierra Buttes, overlooking the lakes and campsites, is a marked contrast to the hubbub of civilization only an hour away. The Salmon Creek Campground is along the creek of that name while the Sardine Campground is just below Sand Pond, one of the most attractive swimming holes in the Sierra. The sand bottom of the pond and the extreme clarity of the water reflect the granite peaks and the pine forest almost photographically.

Beyond Bassett's Highway 49 climbs more rapidly toward Yuba Pass. Some three or four campgrounds mark the route. **Chapman Creek** and **Yuba Pass** campgrounds are both above 6,000 feet in altitude in the red fir forest. Both have widely spaced sites so that there's lots of privacy because of the architectural design of the campground which has taken advantage of trees and rock outcroppings. Yuba Pass Campground is at the top of Yuba Pass amidst behemoth red firs and lodgepole pines.

From the top of Yuba Pass, Highway 49 descends to the flat floor of Sierra Valley, where it joins Highway 89 coming down from Plumas National Forest. Highway 89 goes on south, reentering the Tahoe through a mixed forest of lodgepole pines and an occasional juniper.

Climb along Cold Stream to the top of a small pass separating the Feather River drainage from the Little Truckee. On the way are two campgrounds, **Cold Creek** and **Cottonwood**. From Cottonwood, larger of the two, you can walk an interpretive nature trail that loops around the south end of the camp. Both camps are heavily used during the deer season, much less during other times of the year.

Just below the top of the pass, a road turns west for Webber Lake and Jackson Meadow Reservoir. This is the original Henness Pass Road. Follow carefully, and it will take you across the crest of the Sierra and down to Marysville in the Sacramento Valley. It's a good paved road as far as Jackson Meadow, but very tough and suitable for four-wheelers beyond that point.

Camping at Jackson Meadow is excellent, because the camping places were designed and laid out to take advantage of the site. Trees, meadows, and forested mountainsides can be seen from each of the campsites. A concessionaire manages them, which means that there is always someone around to help enforce the national forest regulations. **Pass Creek** and **East Meadow** are the easiest to get to; both have paved interior roads and spurs, and there is an RV disposal station, too.

Webber Lake, along the way to Jackson Meadow from Highway 89, is all on private property and the camping there is also private. Just before the road returns to the highway, a branch leads southwest to Independence Lake. This large lake is in the hands of a power company, and the campground is open to the public. There is a boat ramp, and fishermen can almost always be seen here in the summer.

Gold dredges are a common sight along the branches of the Yuba River.

Along Highway 89 before it reaches Truckee you'll come to **Upper** and **Lower Little Truckee** campgrounds right along the river in a very pleasant white-and-green meadow-and-aspen location. Easy to get to, they are frequently filled with campers in the summer, because the location is relatively close to Lake Tahoe, yet without the crowds.

Downstream from the Little Truckee campgrounds the turn-offs for Stampede and Prosser Reservoirs lead to camps near these popular fishing lakes. The best of these are **Prosser** at Prosser Lake and **Logger** Campground at Stampede. Logger is the biggest campground on the Tahoe Forest, with 252 sites. They are so well laid out that you'll seldom be aware that so many campers are there all at once. The three lakes in the region, Prosser, Stampede, and Boca, are all located in what used to be meadows, and are not very deep. Consequently in years of little rainfall, they lose a lot of water and the shorelines shrink and become less attractive. As the lakes shrink, so do the numbers in the campgrounds, and late in the year you may find yourself one of the very few people to be using them.

Exploring above Stampede Reservoir is fun for history buffs. It's here that the ill-fated Donner Party first entered California.

Across Interstate 80, Highway 89 follows up the Truckee River to Lake Tahoe and the Lake Tahoe Basin Management Unit. The corridor of the Truckee is busy: Rafters and tire tubers splash down the stream in the daytime, anglers try their luck in the evening, and cyclists speed along the cycle path at all

TAHOE NATIONAL FOREST

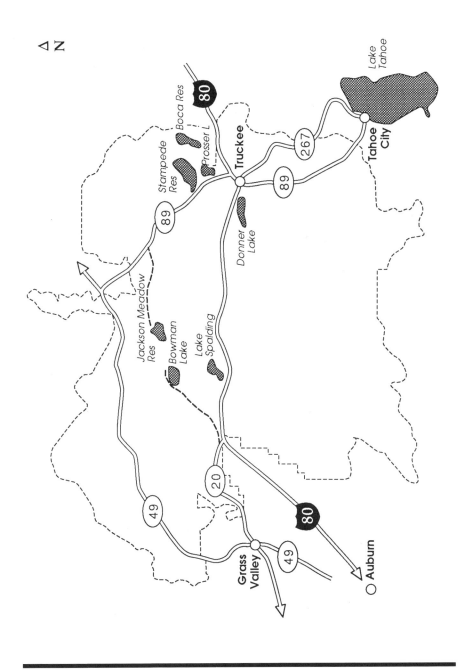

hours. All three of the campgrounds along the Truckee, **Granite Flat, Goose Meadow**, and **Silver Creek**, are almost constantly filled during the summer season. Some are in bad shape from overuse. Granite Flat has been reconstructed and is wheelchair accessible.

Coming into the forest from the west is more quickly accomplished if you come in on Highway 20 from Nevada City. Highway 20 parallels Interstate 80, finally joining it at Yuba Gap. On the way are two special campgrounds, **White Cloud**, and **Skillman**. White Cloud, at about 4,800 feet, is in a forest of black oak, white fir, Douglas fir, sugar pine, ponderosa pine, and incense cedar. All interior roads are paved, as are the parking spurs at the camp sites. Immediately adjacent to White Cloud is a logged-over area that is home to at least four varieties of woodpeckers—downy, acorn, Williamson's sapsucker, and northern flicker. This is a very quiet camping place, and it's easy to get some time to meditate and reflect.

Four miles before the intersection with Interstate 80, the Bowman Lake Road heads north into one of the most interesting parts of the Tahoe. The Grouse Lakes area is a mecca for fishing, camping, and hiking. There are literally dozens of little lakes and ponds scattered about among the granite and pines. Some of the bigger lakes—Bowman, Sawmill, Faucherie, and Meadow—can be reached by backcountry roads. Your sedan will take you to Bowman and Sawmill lakes, but it might be a little tired before arriving at Faucherie or Meadow lakes which are more suited for pick-ups or four-wheelers.

Camping in the region is excellent. There are plenty of developed sites and plenty of room for dispersed camping along the multitude of streams, ponds and lakes. Trailer camping is limited in the entire area. **Jackson Creek** Campground is marked for trailer spaces on the Forest Service map, but the road is so uncertain, that probably only small folding trailers should attempt the trip.

Grouse Ridge Campground, at the end of Forest Service Route 14 off the Bowman Lake Road, is an enchanting campground almost at the top of the ridge. Just a short walk will take you to a fire lookout station that has incomparable views west to the Sacramento Valley and east to the crest of the Sierra. It's great to take a thermos of coffee to the top in the evening to watch the sunset turn the forest into a magic shadow land.

Another mile up Highway 20 past the Bowman Lake turn-off, the road for Lake Spaulding heads north. This big impoundment is large enough to launch fishing boats, and some whopping big trout are landed here every year. The Pacific Gas and Electric Company operates the campground near the lake, and boaters and fishermen use it all summer long.

Once you reach Interstate 80 there are several choices for camping near the highway. **Indian Springs**, the first one you'll come to after Yuba Gap, is also one of the best. It's on a branch of the Yuba River and far enough from the highway that its noise isn't too much of a bother. From this camp, you can fish down toward Lake Spaulding through a canyon where almost no one bothers to go. It ain't easy, as the saying goes, but it surely does get fish.

To get to **Woodchuck** and **Sterling** campgrounds, take the Cisco Grove exit off I-80, turn north, and proceed to Rattlesnake Road. Woodchuck is three miles up this improved light duty dirt road beside Rattlesnake Creek. Sterling is another three miles up a steep and rocky road by the shores of Sterling Lake. Both of these more remote sites allow plenty of room amidst the granite, whitethorn, and manzanita; neighbors will be few.

Across the highway, just east of Cisco Grove, is **Big Bend** Campground. It's located right on the Yuba adjacent to the ranger station, and along with neighboring **Hampshire Rocks** Campground, is very frequently full in the summer months. Trying to get in on a weekend can be a lesson in frustration. But if you do get a site, you'll find good camping in private locations among the riverside trees and shrubbery.

Two PG&E Co., campgrounds, **Lodgepole** and **Silvertip**, can be accessed at the Yuba Gap turn-off on the south side of I-80. They have comparable amenities and about the same fees as National Forest campgrounds in this area, and both provide entrance to Lake Valley Reservoir and Kelly Lake for fishing, hiking, and exploring.

These are the last easily reached campgrounds along the interstate, although side roads do lead to areas of dispersed camping, especially on the north side of the highway.

Be prepared for some wild and remote country when you venture into the Foresthill Ranger District. Even though there are some good paved roads, in some places they are not for the faint-hearted. Clinging to the edge of thousand-foot cliffs, and twisting to the tops of remote ridges and deep into bottomless canyons, some of them are enough to give heart attacks to the most jaded backcountry traveler.

Developed campgrounds in the district are centered around French Meadows and Sugar Pine reservoirs. Sugar Pine and Big reservoirs near the western edge of the forest at the 3,500-foot level, attract campers and fishermen from spring through fall. They can be pretty hot in the summer, but there's always a place to swim and cool off.

Shirttail Creek and **Giant Gap** campgrounds at Sugar Pine are frequently crowded on summer weekends, but they're worth it. Oaks, madrones, and ponderosa pine trees shelter most of the sites, and the boat ramp across the lake allows lots of water activity. Giant Gap Campground, especially, has perfect lake views from many of its sites.

French Meadows Reservoir is at the end of one of those long, winding roads over ridges and down canyons described earlier. The reservoir is very large, and four good-sized campgrounds serve to take care of all the campers and fishermen who make the drive. **French Meadow** Campground is the first one you'll come to, and for attractive camping, you don't have to go any farther. It's located on the south shore of the lake up on bluffs where you can camp and look out over the water in the evening. The concessionnaire is there all summer long to help you enjoy camping, fishing, and the hiking and off-highway vehicle trails in the region. **Poppy** Campground, on the northwest shore of the lake is only accessible by boat or trail. Because of its relative remoteness, you'll have to purify your water and pack out your garbage.

Ahart and **Talbot** campgrounds are located along the Middle Fork of the American River above the reservoir and make good jumping-off places for entry into Granite Chief Wilderness.

On The Trail

From the heights of the Sierra Buttes to the solitude of the American River Canyon, hikers on the Tahoe National Forest will be rewarded with beautiful scenery, glimpses of wildlife, and trails suited to every taste and experience. Some of the trails have been used for thousands of years by Indians and more recent times by miners traveling to and from their claims. The trails have been built and maintained to help travelers explore and enjoy the Tahoe.

Pacific Crest Trail

The Pacific Crest Trail extends through the Tahoe for ninety-seven miles, entering the forest from the north at The A-Tree northwest of Gold Lake at the Tahoe-Plumas National Forest boundary. It leaves the forest on the south about a mile northwest of Sourdough Hill on the Eldorado National Forest boundary. The trail can be accessed at numerous points on the Forest, and crosses major roads near Sierra City, Jackson Meadows Reservoir, and Donner Pass. Several trails in the Lakes Basin Recreation Area intersect with the PCT, as do the trails in the Granite Chief Wilderness.

National Recreation Trails

The two National Recreation Trails on the Tahoe are both very short, and relatively easy walking. The first **Donner Camp** National Recreation Trail is only .4 mile. You can follow it through a meadow about three miles north of Truckee on Highway 89 to visit some of the places where parts of the party camped in the dreadful winter of 1846-47.

Big Trees Trail, the other National Recreational Trail on the forest is in the Placer County Grove of *Sequoiadendron giganteum*, the northernmost such grove. The interpretive trail is in two loops and will carry you through the small grove of six of the native trees. As impressive as the sequoias are, the forest in which they stand would be worth spending some time in even without the giants. Touch the bark, feel the leaves and needles, listen to the wind in the branches. To get to the trail, drive the Mosquito Ridge Road east from Foresthill about twenty-five miles. Interpretive brochures are available at the trailhead.

Hiking on the Forest

There are seven hiking areas with maintained trails, one of the most of any of the forests in the state. Hiking areas are the North Fork of the American River in the Wild and Scenic sections, Grouse Lakes, Big Bend, Donner Summit, Highway 49—Nevada City to Sierra Buttes—Highway 89 north of Truckee, and Granite Chief.

Because the American River Wild and Scenic River is in such a relatively low altitude, the heat really builds up in the summer, and hiking is better in the fall and spring. The Wild River offers a variety of scenic camping and fishing opportunities. The diversity of this unique canyon is seen in its deep, vertical-walled gorges and high bluffs, in its placid pools and cascading rapids, and through its mixture of conifer and hardwood forests.

Sections of the river contain an abundance of historical features that are remnants of the Gold Rush era. Some of the early townsite locations, cabins, and mining equipment can still be found at various sites along the stream and its trails. Of course, all of the sites and equipment are protected under federal antiquities laws.

Most trails into the canyon are extremely steep, with 2,000- to 3,000-feet elevation losses, and quite rocky in places. While traveling down to the river is a relatively easy task, coming back out can be very strenuous.

The **Euchre Bar** Trail is one of the few that cross the river and offer access from both sides. From I-80 you can get at it from the Alta turn-off, and from Foresthill Road on the south via Elliott Ranch Road.

The Donner Party faced this view of the infamous Donner Pass.

Probably the most popular trip down to the river goes down the **Sailor Flat Trail** to the bottom, then along the river on the **American River Trail** and back up on the **Mumford Bar Trail**. It's a good two-day trip, and affords a look at some mining remains, and leaves time for exciting evening fishing in this wild trout stream.

The Grouse Lakes area is located west of the Sierra crest, with elevations ranging from 5,200 feet along Fordyce Creek to over 8,000 feet at the Black Buttes. The southernmost trailhead at **Eagle Lake** is only four miles from I-80, but over a rough, four-wheel drive road. Five other trailheads provide access points into this 19,000-acre scenic area, which is closed to motor vehicles.

Trailheads at **Carr Lake, Lindsey Lakes**, and the **Grouse Ridge Lookout** can be reached by driving north on the Bowman Lake Road, four miles west of I-80 on Highway 20. The **Sawmill Lake** trailhead is reached by taking

Bowman Lake Road to the Faucherie Lake Road, and on to Sawmill Lake. The road is not recommended for low-clearance vehicles. **Beyers Lake** trailhead can be reached by driving south from Jackson Meadow Reservoir.

The **Loch Leven Lakes Trail** starts across the road from the Forest Service information center at Big Bend. Stop in for all kinds of books, maps, and pamphlets that help to interpret the National Forest. The trail leads south up the walls of Devils Peak to five alpine lakes at about 7,000 feet elevation. The trail is moderately steep, and during weekends gets high use, but it's nevertheless worth the effort to get into the high country. Vistas of ridges and valleys, high alpine meadows, and glaciated mountain terrain can be seen in all directions. For a really tough hike, the **Cherry Point** and **Big Granite trails** lead down into the North Fork of the American River Wild and Scenic section. They drop 2,600 feet in less than five miles, which isn't so bad until you realize you have to climb back out.

In 1987, the Forest Service constructed a new trailhead with restrooms and water to provide access to the trails in the **Donner Summit** area. To reach the trailhead, take the Castle Peak/Boreal Ridge Road exit immediately west of the highway's Donner Summit Roadside Rest Area. On the south side of the highway there is a sign pointing the way to the trailhead and access to the PCT.

One of the trails reachable at Donner Summit is the **Glacier Meadow Loop Trail** which offers a relaxing and informative half-hour stroll. Interpretive signs along the route explain how glacial action carved and polished the surface landscape.

The **Warren Lake Trail** leads to an out-of-the-way destination. The trail traverses a unique glaciated basin which offers a sense of back country remoteness rarely found in the Tahoe Sierra. There are creeks to cross with spectacular displays of subalpine wildflowers, rock climbing, and some fishing. Seven miles one way, it is ideal for the weekend backpacker.

Some of the wildest country on the Tahoe National Forest lies along its northern edge, and can be reached by trails in the Downieville area. To reach the **Empire Creek Trail**, the **Second** and **Third Divide trails**, and the **Butcher Ranch** and **Pauley Creek Trails**, follow Upper Main Street through the historic Gold Rush town of Downieville. About a half-mile east of the town post office you will cross the Downie River bridge. Continue up this road to the Empire Creek, and the Second and Third Divide Trails. The Pauley Creek and Butcher Ranch trails are accessed by the Divide Trail.

Another way to reach the **Butcher Ranch Trail** is from the Lakes Basin Recreation Area above Packer Lake.

Granite Chief Wilderness

The Granite Chief Wilderness is among the newest in the country and was formerly the "Granite Chief Vehicle Closure Area" on top of the Sierra crest to the west of Lake Tahoe. Due to its proximity to the lake, it is a popular area for hikers and equestrians but as yet not so popular that quotas have been set as they have in the adjoining Desolation Wilderness.

You can reach the trail system from three points. Two of these are on roads which lead off Highway 89 between Truckee and Tahoe City. The **Tinker Knob Trail** begins near the fire station in Squaw Valley. The **Five Lakes** trailhead will be found on the Alpine Meadows road, approximately a half-mile before the ski resort.

148

At the south end of the wilderness, the **Powderhorn Trail** can be reached by driving south from Tahoe City about four miles to the Kaspian Picnic Area, and turning west on Forest Road 15N03 for about eight miles.

An excellent shuttle trip can be made in the wilderness by going in on the Tinker Knob Trail to its intersection with the PCT, then south on the PCT to its intersection with FR 15N03 near Powderhorn trailhead. This 16-mile jaunt is fairly easy, and good campsites with water are frequently available.

Touring, Sightseeing, and Special Programs

What will strike most summer travelers immediately about the North Fork of the Yuba along Highway 49 is the number of gold mining dredges floating in the stream. From Shennanigan Flats far upstream, virtually every place that will float a suction pump has been claimed by miners. According to Forest Service sources, the Tahoe is the most active in this kind of mining activity of the California National Forests. Although the miners have filed legal claims to their portion of the stream, and technically are commercial miners, basically they are weekenders or hobby miners.

If you'd like to try your hand at panning or working a rocker or long tom, make sure you're not on a portion of the stream that's been claimed. Although "claim-jumpers" aren't hanged from the nearest oak any more, as was once the case, they still aren't treated very well. At the North Yuba Ranger Station at Camptonville, you can get a series of maps showing the places along the river where no claims are allowed, and recreational mining is wide open for you.

Downieville is a charming old Mother Lode town situated on the banks of the Yuba. Less visited now than it once was just a few years ago, it's worth spending some time in. Some of the buildings along Main Street date 'way back into argonaut times. Northeast of Downieville, you'll come to Sierra City, last stop before Yuba Pass takes you out of the Northern Mines. Just past Sierra City, Sierra County operates the **Kentucky Mine Museum**. An operating stamp mill is the center of the attractions. Listening to the noise of the mill, you begin to understand what it must have been like living in hard-rock mining towns like these. The mills ran twenty-four hours a day, crushing quartz and granite to powder so the gold could be extracted. People became so accustomed to the constant pounding, that they would awake from a sound sleep if the mill should suddenly shut down in the night.

The **Lakes Basin Recreation Area** north of Highway 49 contains about three dozen lakes, of which twelve or more are on Tahoe National Forest and the rest in neighboring Plumas. They form a recreation area for all seasons and all ages. Rising from the Mohawk Valley in Plumas National Forest, most of the more than thirty lakes lie between 5,000 and 6,000 feet, with Eureka Peak at 7,447 feet and the Sierra Buttes at 8,587 feet silent north-south sentinels overlooking the basin.

The lakes are regularly planted with trout, and in a few of them self-sustaining fisheries have been established. Swimming and boating are summer-long activities in all the lakes, but swimming is really best in Sand Pond just below Sardine Lake. The pond is a result of gold mining operations at Young America mine just upstream. Long since abandoned, the mine tailings were dumped here and then reworked in later years for any remaining gold. There are benches in the picnic area where you can sit to enjoy your meal while looking out across the pond to the peaks of the Sierra Buttes. The loop interpretive trail around the pond is an enjoyable addition to the area.

Highway 20, east of Nevada City, takes you to several interesting stops. First, just as you enter the forest, is the **Rock Creek Nature Study Trail**. It's in the yellow pine belt forest, a transitional zone through which Rock Creek flows. Rock Creek is the home of many animals and plants and even man has lived and worked here in the past. The trail is cool and shady on the hottest days and there aren't any hills to climb.

The length of the trail is about .75 mile and the journey should only take forty-five minnutes to an hour depending upon how much you stop to look and listen. To help you enjoy the trail, the Forest Service has placed wooden posts with numbers on them that correspond to numbers in an explanatory pamphlet. The trail makes a complete loop, crossing Rock Creek twice along the way.

About ten miles east of Rock Creek, a county road branches left down to the town of **Washington** on the banks of the South Fork of the Yuba River. There are two picnic areas maintained by the Forest Service—Keleher and Golden Quartz—where you can enjoy a swim in the river or try your luck with a gold pan. The Alpha and Omega mines were located near here and remains of Gold Rush days are everywhere. There are also privately operated campgrounds in Washington.

The two State parks, **Donner Memorial** and **Malakoff Diggings**, both offer complete interpretive programs as well as camping. Donner, especially, is the center of a vacation region. Winter and summer, the state park rangers have programs going here, ranging from snowshoe hikes to history walks in the footprints of the pioneers.

Sports

Winter Recreation

Winter is a beautiful time to explore the Tahoe National Forest. Miles of roads and trails on the forest offer excellent cross-country skiing and snowmobiling routes. Several commercial downhill ski resorts are operated with special-use permits on National Forest land. Snow play, sledding, and winter camping can be enjoyed near any of the major highways.

Squaw Valley, site of the 1960 Winter Olympic Games, is the largest and most popular of the commercial alpine skiing resorts, with more than 8,300 acres of skiable terrain, and a total of twenty-seven lifts. Other downhill areas are **Alpine Meadow** , **Boreal Ridge**, **Sugar Bowl** , and **Donner Ski Ranch** Two more downhill resorts, **Soda Springs** and **Tahoe Donner**, are located on private land surrounded by the National Forest.

Cross-country and snowmobile enthusiasts have an embarrassment of riches on the Tahoe, from unmarked logging roads and trails to groomed and graded routes.

Starting in the north along Highway 49, the **Lunch Creek-Yuba Pass Ski Trail** is a nine-mile marked ski trail. It leads north and west from Yuba Pass through Beartrap Meadows and out along Lunch Creek Road. Hills along the way lend themselves to telemark practice. The route is marked "more difficult," but many sections are all right for beginners.

In the same general area, the **Gold Lake Road** provides seventeen miles of snowmobiling for all degrees of experience. Since it goes along a county road, the slopes are moderate enough that even raw beginners can enjoy themselves.

Lakes in the Grouse Lakes Recreation Area carry trout up to a foot long.

Cross-country skiers also use the first part of the route to get to trails heading for **Sardine Lakes** and **Packer Lake**

Over on Highway 89, the **Little Truckee Summit-Yuba Pass** snowmobile trailhead opens out on to three marked routes totaling 110 miles.

Boating and Water Skiing

Donner Lake, although technically not on the National Forest, is the most popular boating lake in the area. There are marinas and launch areas all along the northern and western shores, and both sailers and motorcraft are represented. **New Bullard's Bar Reservoir** in the far western part of the forest is also very popular. There is a marina near the dam called Emerald Cove where you can rent a houseboat or small boat such as a fishing craft or patio boat for fun on the lake.

The Forest Service has provided launch ramps for boats on several other lakes on the Tahoe, including **Jackson Meadow, French Meadows**, and **Sugar Pine** reservoirs. In the eastern part of the forest north of I-80, the three big reservoirs of **Stampede, Prosser**, and **Boca** also have launch ramps maintained by the Forest Service. Pacific Gas and Electric Company has also provided launch ramps on some of their reservoirs, such as **Lake Valley Reservoir** and **Lake Spaulding.**

Smaller bodies of water in the area lend themselves very well to launching cartop boats and canoes for fishermen and other water sportsmen. On some of the lakes, it takes a boat to get out "to where the big ones are." Bowman

Lake, Sawmill, and Faucherie in the Grouse Ridge area are frequently the scene of cartoppers and inflatables, as are the Sardine and Salmon Lakes in the Lakes Basin Area.

Off-Road Motoring

Historic gold mining areas, tall trees, mountain creeks, and easy-to-challenging experiences await you on off-highway trails on the Tahoe. Many new miles of trail have recently been completed and older portions closed. The results are new challenges for riders of all skill levels.

Most of the trail development, construction, and maintenance is funded with State of California OHV funds, in cooperation with the national forests. A really good example of this inter-agency cooperation is the **Parker Flat Staging Area** on the Foresthill Divide. There are four loops starting from the staging area averaging about six miles each, and ranging in difficulty from easiest to more difficult. All are for motorcycles, and two of them also accept all-terrain vehicles. Ramps are provided at the staging area for loading of vehicles, and camping is permitted, although the area has been developed primarily for on-and-off loading of vehicles.

Another special unit on the forest is **Old Gravel Pit**, near Prosser Reservoir, which has been set aside for concentrated OHV use.

Information on these trails is available at Tahoe National Forest offices.

Fishing and Hunting

Hunting, especially deer hunting, is a very popular activity on the Tahoe, although perhaps because of the large numbers of people who visit the forest each year, hunters are not as successful here as they are in the forest farther north. Those hunters who are most successful shoot on the east side of the forest in the region north of the big reservoirs.

Fishermen have much better success on the Tahoe than hunters, generally speaking. there are many lakes, reservoirs, and streams planted with catchable-sized trout on a regular basis. Indeed, the "put-and-take" plantings along popular streams and lakes bring many people into the forest.

Many of the lakes are open for ice fishing in the winter and sportsmen hike or ride snowmobiles to get to them.

Resorts, Lodges, and Hotels

Most of the recreation lodges and resorts that are on Forest Service land are in the northern portion of the forest in the Lakes Basin region. **Sardine Lakes Resort** has modern conveniences in a rustic setting. The dining room is locally famous, and people drive up from Reno just for the dinners. This is the kind of lodge where families continue to come year after year, and reservation are made as much as a year ahead. From the Fourth of July until Labor Day, reservations are an absolute must, and you'll be turned away if you show up without them.

The same is true at **Packer Lake Lodge** on Packer Lake. Rates at the Packer Lake Lodge not only include accommodations in cabins overlooking the lake, but a rowboat per cabin to get out on the lake for the brown, rainbow, and brook trout.

Salmon Lake Lodge has been in operation for nearly a century on the opposite shore of Upper Salmon Lake. You have to park and call for the lodge's barge to come get you on arrival. You may stay in a duplex tent cabin with stove and heat, or in one of the more deluxe cabins. Upper Salmon Lake is located in the glaciated high country. First occupied by hard-rock miners, the area is now exclusively recreational.

Sierra Shangri-La is a small resort on the North Fork of the Yuba River at 3,100 feet elevation carved out of the mountainside at the exact spot where Crow City once was a rip-roaring mining camp. Just outside the quaint mining town of Downieville, the cabins cluster at the edge of the river and you can almost cast from the front porch.

TAHOE NATIONAL FOREST CAMPGROUNDS

	Piped Water	Camp Sites	Trailer Space	Fishing	Boating	Swimming	Store	RV Dump Station	Reservations	Special Attractions
Downieville Ranger District										
Berger		10	(*)							
Carlton Flat-Lower		30	(*)	•						
Carlton Flat-Upper		12	•	•						
Chapman Creek	•	29	•	•						
Diablo		8	•							
Fiddle Creek		13		•						
Garden Point		7	•	•						
Frenchy Point		8	•	•						
Indian Valley	•	17	•	•						
Loganville		20	•	•						
Packsaddle		8	•							
Ramshorn	•	16	•	•						
Rocky Rest		7	•	•						
Salmon Creek	•	31	•	•	•	•				
Sardine	•	29	•	•	•	•				
Schoolhouse	•	67	•	•	•					
Sierra		18	•	•						
Snag Lake		16	(*)	•	•	•				
Union Flat	•	14	•	•						
Wild Plum	•	47	•	•						PCT Trailhead
Yuba Pass	•	20	(*)							
Foresthill Ranger District										
Ahart		12	(*)	•						
Big Reservoir		19	(*)	•						
French Meadows	•	75	•	•	•					
Lewis	•	40	•	•	•					
Poppy		12		•	•					
Robinson Flat		6								
Secret House		2								

TAHOE NATIONAL FOREST CAMPGROUNDS

	Piped Water	Camp Sites	Trailer Space	Fishing	Boating	Swimming	Store	RV Dump Station	Reservations	Special Attractions
Talbot		5		•						Granite Chief Trialh.
Giant Gap	•	30	•	•	•	•				Sugar Pine Res.
Shirttail Creek	•	30	•	•	•	•				Sugar Pine Res.
Nevada City Ranger District										
Big Bend	•	15	(*)	•						Visitor Center
Bowman Lake		7	(*)	•	•	•				
Canyon Creek		20		•						
Fuller Lake		9	(*)	•		•				
Grouse Ridge	•	9		•						
Hampshire Rocks	•	31	•	•						
Indian Springs	•	35	•	•						
Jackson Creek		14	(*)							
North Fork	•	17	(*)	•						
Skillman	•	16	•							
Sterling Lake		6		•		•				
White Cloud	•	46	•							
Woodchuck		8		•						
Sierraville Ranger District										
Cottonwood	•	25	•	•					•	Reservations for group site only
Cold Creek	•	13	•							
Bear Valley	•	10	•							
Upper Little Truckee	•	26	•							
Lower Little Truckee	•	15	•							
Annie McCloud		10	•	•						
Lakeside		30	•	•	•					
Prosser	•	29	•	•	•					
Prosser Group	•	50	•	•	•					
Pass Creek	•	30	•	•	•	•				
East Meadow	•	46	•	•						
Wood Camp	•	20	•	•	•	•				
Findley	•	14	•	•						
Fir Top	•	12								
Silvertip Group	•	50		•		•				
Aspen Group	•	100				•				
Truckee Ranger District										
Boca		20	•	•	•	•				
Boca Rest		25	•	•	•	•				
Boyington Mill		10								
Emigrant Group		10				•		•	•	
Logger	•	25				•				

LAKE TAHOE BASIN MANAGEMENT UNIT

Sacramento

San Francisco

Los Angeles

Lake Tahoe Basin Management Unit

The Lake Tahoe Basin Management Unit was established in 1973 by the Forest Service to manage all the National Forest lands in the Lake Tahoe Basin.

Lake Tahoe is about twenty-two miles long and twelve miles wide with seventy-two miles of shoreline. It is the third deepest lake in North America and the tenth deepest in the world, 1,645 feet at its greatest depth.

The lake's average surface elevation is 6,225 feet above sea level making it the highest lake of its size in the United States. The water in the lake is enough to cover a flat area the size of the state of California to a depth of fourteen inches and enough to supply every one in the U.S. with fifty gallons a day for five years.

The Lake Tahoe Basin offers an ideal alpine climate with warm dry summers, a mild spring and fall, and snowy winters. Despite its approximate 213 inches of snowfall a year at the level of the lake—much more at high elevations—the basin still manages 307 days of sunshine a year.

Camping

There are more than eighteen campgrounds, public and private, within the California portion of the Lake Tahoe Basin, with room for more than 1800 camp units. A concessionaire operates all the campgrounds by special permit on Forest Service land. The State of California operates five of the campgrounds in state parks and state recreation areas. Two more are municipal campgrounds run by local governments.

Because of the intense level of use in the basin, it's almost mandatory to get reservations if you want to be assured a place to camp. Fallen Leaf, Bay View, Kaspian, Meeks Bay, and William Kent campgrounds are on the Mistix system. Camp Richardson, one of the old-time resorts that has been acquired by the Forest Service, and is now operated by a concessionnaire, has 230 camp sites on a non-reservation basis. Hook-ups are available at Camp Richardson.

There are 205 widely separated camp sites in the Fallen Leaf Campground, and its location near the Forest Service visitor center and public beaches makes it an ideal family campground. Tall, mature sugar and Jeffrey pines grow in the flat where the camps are located, with cottonwoods, aspens, and alders along Taylor Creek.

General Creek Campground in Sugar Pine Point State Park, is on a gently sloping forested promontory, and extends 3.5 miles up the General Creek watershed. Principal trees are the sugar and Jeffrey pines, red and white firs, and incense cedar. Lupines, Indian paintbrush, penstemon, and red columbine bloom in spring and early summer. Chickarees, chipmunks, and golden-mantled ground squirrels zip through the camp sites, gleaning seeds and leftovers.

One of the municipal campgrounds, South Lake Tahoe-Eldorado, operated by the City of South Lake Tahoe, is located right on the lake shore within the city limits. Your view is of the southern and eastern parts of the lake. The lights of the Nevada casinos sparkle in the night.

The historic Valhalla Estate at the Pope-Baldwin Recreation Area.

Almost all of the private campgrounds are located at the southern end of the lake, and as might be expected, range from the vary simplest parking places to deluxe RV parks.

On The Trail

Most famous of the hiking trails in the Lake Tahoe Basin is the Tahoe Rim Trail, which will eventually encircle the basin completely. As you hike along portions of this trail you meander through areas rich in history, wade through waist-high grasses, stands of red fir and Jeffrey pine, and alongside gurgling mountain streams. These are old Washoe hunting grounds and long vanished game trails, as well as trails made by early settlers. You'll wander high above mysterious places with names like Marlette Lake and Franktown. You'll skirt the largest bog in the Sierra at Grass Lake, and most of the time you'll be able to view the Lake itself. You can't imagine how many shades of blue there are until you've seen Tahoe from this aspect on a bright, sunny day.

Some of the sections of this trail are yet incomplete, but there are enough finished sections that it will take several days to hike them all. The visitor information centers have maps that show where the completed sections are and how to get to them.

There are two national recreation trails in the basin—Hawley Grade Trail and Lake Tahoe Bike-Pedestrian Trail. Hawley Grade is in Christmas Valley, just south of Lake Tahoe. It was the first easy-grade trail in the central Sierra to connect the east side with the west side. Constructed in the 1850s, it also became a part of the Pony Express route. The trail begins at Upper Truckee Road and climbs through chaparral and conifer stands to a point just below Echo Summit.

The Lake Tahoe Bike-Pedestrian Trail is a 3.3-mile jaunt along Highway 89 west of the lake. Scenic views include a marsh, coniferous stands, the lake itself, and the surrounding peaks. At the half-way point, the Forest Service Tahoe Visitors Center attracts thousands of visitors each year.

The Lake Tahoe Basin management Unit maintains 115 miles of trail in the south shore region of the lake. These range from trails of three-quarters of a mile through Tallac Historic Site, to strenuous six-mile climbs to the top of Mt. Tallac, with a gain of over 3,000 feet altitude.

One of the more popular trails, and one that will get you into the high country south of Desolation Wilderness, is the Meiss Meadow Trail. This hike is a gentle to moderate six-mile climb through creekside meadows to reach "Meiss Country," which although not designated as "wilderness," is nevertheless wild. There are some six lakes that can be reached with short side trips from the main trail, including Round, Dardanelles, Meiss, Showers, Elberts, and the Four lakes.

On the west shore of the lake, the Rubicon Trail is a 4.5-mile walk between D. L. Bliss State Park and Emerald Bay. It follows the lake's shoreline from Rubicon Point to Emerald Point and into sparkling Emerald Bay. Vikingsholm, considered the finest example of Scandinavian architecture in the western hemisphere marks the end of the trail.

Many of the trails available along the western shore go into the Desolation Wilderness and consequently require a permit, even though you may not plan to stay overnight. Day use permits can be obtained right at the trailheads, or from ranger stations. Among the best of these is the Lake Genevieve Trail. Take the Meeks Bay trail five miles up to pine and granite circled Lake Genevieve and then continue on this trail to a chain of lakes which include Crag, Stony Ridge, Hidden, and Rubicon Lakes. This ten-mile round trip will take at least a half-day each way, and longer is better. You'll be in a part of the northernmost glaciated High Sierra-type landscapes with shining granite peaks, wildflower-filled meadows, and scattered groves of mountain hemlock and whitebark pines.

For a hike similar to the Lake Genevieve Trail but with a lot fewer people, consider the Duck Lake Trail, also known as the Lost Lake Trail. This walk starts from General Creek campground in Sugar Pine Point State Park. Rangers at the entrance station will tell you where to park for this six-miler. Plan on at least a half day. Better yet, take a picnic and spend the entire day at the lakes.

For directions to several more maintained trails in the Tahoe Basin, drop in at the William Kent Information Center just south of Granlibakken and Tahoe Tavern on the west shore. Ask about the Twin Peaks Trail and others of the Crystal Range.

Desolation Wilderness

Administration of the Desolation Wilderness is shared between Eldorado National Forest and the Lake Tahoe Basin Management Unit, but by far the most use of this wilderness occurs within the Basin Unit. There is a quota for overnight use in effect, which means you should apply for your entry permit ahead of time at any National Forest office, even though half of the permits

LAKE TAHOE BASIN MANAGEMENT UNIT

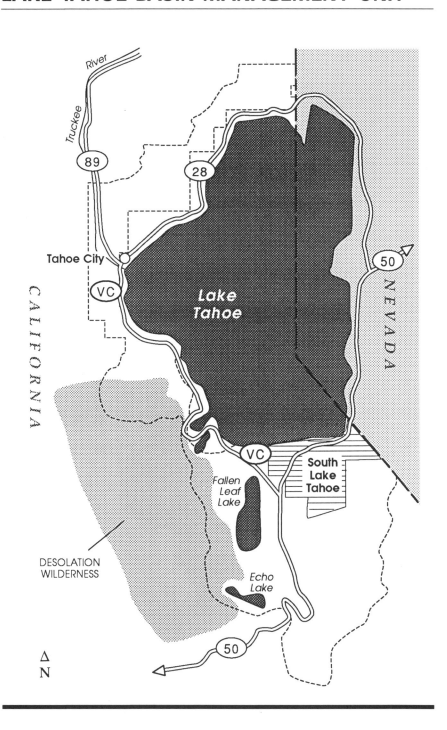

for any one day aren't issued until that day. (For more information on the Desolation Wilderness, see Chapter 10, El Dorado National Forest.)

Touring, Sightseeing, and Special Programs

Four of the old Lake Tahoe resorts have been purchased by the Forest Service in order to keep the shoreline open to the public. Otherwise the land would have gone to commercial or residential development. All were purchased in run-down condition and permittees continue to have to economic difficulty because of very high maintenance costs. The four resorts, Meeks Bay, Camp Richardson, Glen Alpine Springs, and Zephyr Cove, on the Nevada side, can all be visited.

Pope-Baldwin Recreation Area

The Lake Tahoe Basin Management Unit has one of the Forest Service's finest interpretive programs. In the Sierra and northern California, only Inyo and Stanislaus national forests offer as much. First, there is the visitor center where virtually any question you can think of concerning the Lake Tahoe area can be answered.

Associated with the visitor center are six interpretive trails, the stream profile chamber where you can watch trout and kokanee salmon from under water, and an amphitheater.

Each of the six interpretive trails has a different theme. On the Rainbow Trail, you travel from Jeffrey pine forest to a cool mountain meadow. You'll discover wildflowers along the way and learn the importance of marshes and meadows to the clarity of Lake Tahoe. Halfway down the Rainbow Trail, it passes through the stream profile chamber. As you go underground, plate glass windows along one side of the chamber give you a glimpse into the underwater world of the trout. Other displays in the chamber tell about the life cycle of the fish, and more of the history of the stream and associated marshes. Just outside the chamber, you will be walking along Taylor Creek where twice-a-week walks are led by a forest ranger-naturalist.

To discover the ways of Tahoe's first inhabitants, take the Trail of the Washoe. Learn how these Native Americans lived off the land for thousands of years with little impact on the environment.

On the Forest Tree Trail you'll discover the Jeffrey pine, the dominant tree in the basin. The life cycle of this pine, from germination to decomposition is explained along this enjoyable trail. Stick your nose into one of the cracks in the Jeffery's bark and inhale. What do you smell? Pineapple? Vanilla? Whatever it is, you'll not soon forget the Jeffrey's aroma!

Smokey's Trail is for the kids. Safe campfire construction is the theme on this trail that begins just outside the visitor center. Children who walk the trail and can remember the procedures for a safe campfire will receive a reward from the visitor center staff.

Historically rewarding is the Tallac Historic Site Trail. From the Kiva Beach Picnic Area, you stroll along the historic promenade by remains of the Lucky Baldwin Tallac House, gambling casino, and Tallac Hotel. Then you enter the grounds of the Baldwin, Pope, and Valhalla estates. Here, too, ranger-led walks will help you discover the romance of the lake. The Pope House tour takes you through the grand estate of an affluent family who lived on the southern shore of Lake Tahoe during the summers at the turn of the century. In the same area, the Lucky Baldwin Historic tour takes you back in time to experience some of the lake's past. You'll learn something about early mining efforts, the logging era, and the influence of Lucky Baldwin and his daughter in California, as well as the efforts of his daughter to save some of the beauty of the lake.

As you might expect, the evening campfire programs are both informative and exceptionally entertaining. Friday and Saturday evenings in the amphitheater, rangers and their seasonal helpers entertain campers and visitors with well-designed programs that include the familiar sing-along of campfires everywhere, as well as interpretive programs on such things as the history of transportation around the lake, mammals you might run into in the surrounding forests, and the human history of the Sierra.

Altogether, there are about sixteen different ranger-led programs each week as well as the six self-guiding trails. In the visitor center, you can learn where to hike, where the fish are biting, the best places to take your mountain bike. You can even ask what's the best number to play when they spin the big wheel at the casinos. You won't get an answer, but you can ask.

Auto Tours

Want to discover more about Tahoe while driving at your own pace? The visitor center has two taped tours, one for around the Lake and the other to

Children view salmon spawning along the nature trail near the Lake Tahoe Basin Management Unit visitor center. Jean Hawthorne photo.

Angora Fire Lookout. Tapes and players can be rented for $1 each. The drive around the lake takes about three hours, and between the National Forest, State Parks and a wide variety of tourist attractions, there will be something for everyone. If you have a little more time, you can travel outside the basin to such attractions as Squaw Valley, site of the 1960 Winter Olympics, or historic downtown Truckee. Visit the site of the tragic Donner Party at Donner State Park, or cross over into Nevada. Nearby Virginia City relives the "boom-town era" of the Comstock silver strike. Or try for a strike of your own in the casinos of Reno or Carson City.

Special Programs

The paddlewheeler M. S. Dixie and the catamaran Woodwind out of Zephyr Cove on the Nevada side, provide a variety of lake tours and are National Forest permitee operations. Up on Echo Lakes, the Forest Service operates a tour each week during July and August. The two glaciated lakes serve as the backdrop for this hour-and-a-half tour. A naturalist recounts the natural and human history of the scenic region. Seated in the boat, you're right at water level looking up at peaks above 9,000 feet. Halfway up you can see the line of demarcation between glaciated and unglaciated rock. Avalanche chutes scar the sides of the mountains, and the guide points out where one vacation cabin was wiped out by masses of sliding ice and rock.

Two stables, Camp Richardson Corral, and Zephyr Cove, operate with Forest Service permits, providing guided horseback rides across the Basin lands.

The Tahoe-Tallac Association (a non-profit organization) in partnership with the Forest Service offers a variety of cultural events at the Tallac Historic Site. The rustic mountain homes of the historic site create unique environments that showcase concerts, chamber music, jazz, and bluegrass as well as fine art and historic exhibits. There is an "Artist in Action" program where artists of varying disciplines display their work, create and respond to public questions. Fiber arts and folk arts are the headliners at the "Honeymoon Cabin" at Pope House, and there are art workshops for children each morning through the summer.

Sports

The Lake Tahoe Basin is a mecca for winter sports; thousands of visitors crowd the slopes of the alpine ski resorts, and just as many huff and puff their way around the miles of cross-country ski tracks and slip through the powder in out-of-the-way places around the lake.

Heavenly Valley Ski Area will accommodate some 18,000 skiers on a busy day, with the record being over 15,00 skiers at one time. Ski Incline, on the Nevada side, has recently doubled in size and capacity and has expanded into National Forest land. Granlibakken and Homewood ski areas along the west shore, and Echo Summit at the top of the pass on Highway 50 are additional alpine ski areas that operate within the Basin.

Within the Basin, Nordic skiers will enjoy the trails at Sugar Pine Point. The roads in the state park are especially good for exploring the back country along General Creek. The park trails are marked but not machine groomed. Two commercial operations in the Basin are Tahoe Nordic Ski Center and Echo Summit Nordic. Echo Lakes, near Tahoe's south shore, offers moderate terrain, perfect for family excursions.

Boating and Water-skiing

The Lake Tahoe Basin offers a variety of boating environments to suit almost everyone; from the deep turquoise waters of the Lake itself to the rugged alpine heights of the Echo Lakes. Also quite popular is the serene, wooded Fallen Leaf Lake near the south shore. Each of these lakes offers a variety of boating opportunities.

There are twenty-three launching ramps around the lake where you can put your craft into the water. Some are free, the majority have a small charge for use. Most of these marinas associated with the ramps also offer berths, some for the season, some for as short as a week.

Two very popular areas for canoeing, kayaking and rafting in the Basin are the Upper Truckee River flowing into Lake Tahoe on the south shore, and the Lower Truckee River flowing out of the Lake on the north shore. Indeed, the Truckee River corridor on the north shore sometimes looks as if a traffic cop would come in handy on sunny summer weekends.

The elements which make up the attractive Lake Tahoe Basin environment create significant hazards for boaters, especially on the big lake. Sudden, high gusty winds of sufficient intensity to capsize a small craft occur at times. There are many underwater and waterline obstructions, such as rocks and old pilings. Also the water in the Lake Tahoe Basin is very cold. Surface temperature is about forty degrees during December through April, although during the summer, the temperature may reach close to the 60s near shallow shorelines.

Bicycle Touring

Mountain bikes are a relatively new development in forest recreation. Consequently, new regulations are constantly popping up. Basically, however, if you're a mountain bike enthusiast, you can count on certain kinds of places being closed to you. Wilderness and the Pacific Crest Trail—except on roads—and self-guided nature trails are closed to bike riding; and persons riding in these areas can be cited.

Areas that provide good riding include: abandoned logging roads, areas designated for off-highway vehicles, non-wilderness trails, and paved backcountry roads. Some suggested rides include Meiss/Big Meadow, Angora Ridge Road, McKiney-Rubicon OHV Roadway, and the Broadway Summit to Martis Peak Trail.

For those wanting to go for a casual bicycle ride or an extensive touring trip, there is a variety of bike paths and bike lanes around Lake Tahoe, as well as numerous shops and stands where bikes can be rented. The Forest Service maintains a nearly flat 3.3-mile path located on the south end of the Lake called the Pope-Baldwin Bike Trail. Parallel to Highway 89, the path starts where the four-lane highway narrows into two lanes. This trail offers several scenic side trips including Pope and Baldwin Beaches, the Tallac Historic Site, the Lake Tahoe Visitors Center and Fallen Leaf Lake.

Another bike trail goes along the west shore from General Creek to Kale Forest, passing through Tahoe City. A branch of this trail leads down the Truckee River from Tahoe City, and a bike lane along one shoulder of the highway goes all the way into the city of Truckee from the Squaw Valley turn-off.

Off-Road Motoring

Because there is so much development, and because the undeveloped land

The Forest Service tour boat loads up at the Echo Lake Chalet.

in the Lake Tahoe Basin is so fragile, off-highway vehicle travel is limited. What little opportunity there is, is restricted to designated areas only and no vehicular cross-country travel is permitted. A complete brochure is available that lists OHV rules and available routes from the Forest Service.

Fishing and Hunting

The many streams and lakes of the basin provide an abundance of fishable waters. In addition to native populations, some waters are stocked with rainbow trout periodically by the California Department of Fish and Game. Most of the streams that flow into the basin are closed to fishing each year until the middle of July to protect delicate spawning areas.

Lake Tahoe is open to fishing year around with either a California or Nevada fishing license. Surrounding lakes and streams require a license from the state in which they're located.

The Truckee and Upper Truckee rivers provide fishing for those willing to try it, but the best fishing in the region is probably in the remotest lakes of the Desolation Wilderness such as Fontanillis and Dick's Lakes.

Hunting

There is little opportunity for hunting in the basin. There are too many people, too much private property, and many closures. Hunters have far better luck in the National Forests outside the Basin.

Resorts, Lodges, and Hotels

The Forest Service has purchased several of the old resorts that have served travelers for many years, such as Camp Richardson, Meeks Bay, and Zephyr Cove on the Nevada side. These are operating under special use permits issued by the Forest Service. They were all bought to protect the Basin from further commercial development or turning the land over to further private home building.

The lodges at these resorts, as well as at Angora Lakes, still cater to the public, and a stay in one of them is akin to stepping back in time to what was perhaps an easier era, albeit a short-sighted era in terms of conservation of natural resources.

All the rest of the multitudinous hotels, lodges, resorts, campgrounds, bed-and-breakfast hostelries, and whatever else qualifies, are on private property and beyond the purview of the National Forest, and better described in a chamber of commerce publication.

LAKE TAHOE BASIN
MANAGEMENT UNIT CAMPGROUNDS

	Piped Water	Camp Sites	Trailer Space	Fishing	Boating	Swimming	Store	RV Dump Station	Reservations	Special Attractions
U.S. Forest Service Campgrounds										
Bayview		13	•	•						Two nights only
Fallen Leaf	•	205	•	•	•	•			•	
Kaspian Recreation	•	10	•	•	•					
Meeks Bay	•	40	•	•	•	•	•		•	
William Kent	•	95	•	•	•	•	•	•	•	
Nevada Beach	•	54	•	•	•	•			•	in Nevada
State Parks; Other Public										
D.L. Bliss	•	168	•	•	•	•		•	•	
Eagle Point	•	100	•	•	•	•			•	
General Creek	•	175	•	•	•	•		•	•	
Lake Forest	•	21	•	•	•					
So. Tahoe-Eldorado	•	170	•	•	•	•		•	•	
Tahoe State Rec. Area	•	39	•	•	•	•	•		•	
Camp Richardson	•	230	•	•	•	•	•	•	•	Privately operated
Zephyr Cove	•	170	•	•	•	•	•		•	in Nevada

MENDOCINO NATIONAL FOREST

Sacramento

San Francisco

Los Angeles

Mendocino National Forest

Mendocino National Forest is the southernmost of the series of forests that cover the northwestern coastal ranges of California from the Oregon border southward. It is more than a million acres in size, and altitudes range from 1,100 feet to a little over 8,000 feet at the top of Mt. Linn in the South Yolla Bolly Mountains. Two-thirds of the forest is heavily timbered, and the Mendocino produces enough timber each year to build about 9,000 average three-bedroom homes.

Two wilderness areas, the Yolla Bolly-Middle Eel and Snow Mountain shelter parts of the forest for the hikers, equestrians, hunters, and fishermen, and especially those who seek solitude. Although close to centers of population, neither of the wildernesses is highly used, consequently wilderness permits are not currently required for either place.

Off-highway vehicle recreation forms a large part of the visitor-day count; there is even a National Recreation Trail for motorcycles. There are six major organized OHV events each year centered around Middle Creek and Davis Flat.

Camping

There are twenty-five developed campgrounds in the forest containing in all about 400 units. Most of the camping places are relatively small, but only during hunting season are you likely to find them all full. There are areas where campgrounds are clustered: Letts Lakes, Plaskett Recreation Area, and Lake Pillsbury. Over most of the forest, however, camping places are few and far between, leaving lots of room to roam.

Corning Ranger District Camping

The Corning Ranger District is the northeastern quadrant of the forest. The major point of entry is from Paskenta about twenty miles west of Corning on County Highway 56. Most of the camping places on the Corning District have piped water, and many are "OK" for trailers. If you pull a trailer, however, be advised these are dirt roads, and some of them quite rough. Be aware too, that there are no hook-ups.

The largest campground on the Corning District is Wells Cabin; it's also one of the easiest to access. It's surrounded by a red fir forest at an altitude of 6,300 feet. A mile away is Anthony Peak Fire Lookout from where you can see the Pacific Ocean on clear days. The misty outlines of darkly forested mountain ridges, each silhouetted against the next, fill the miles in between.

Three Prong Campground is situated among tall fir and pine trees at the edge of a wide meadow twenty-five miles west of Paskenta on Forest Road 24N13 in Three Prong Valley below Ball Mountain. Whitlock Campground is only sixteen miles northwest of Paskenta, and like Three Prong, is set at the edge of a large green meadow. The units are sheltered under spreading oaks and ponderosa pines. Hunters like both Whitlock and Three Prong sites and both deer and bear seasons find them fully utilized.

Covelo District Camping

The three developed campgrounds on the Covelo Ranger District can all be reached relatively easily, especially Eel River, which is located adjacent to the USFS Work Center on State Highway 162. This campground is in an oak woodland on a flat-iron shaped bluff at the junction of the Middle Fork of the Eel River and Black Butte River and is a favorite place for steelhead and salmon fishermen. One of three National Recreation Trails on the forest, Traveler's Home Trail, begins just up a side road from this site.

Another fisherman's camp is Hammerhorn Lake Campground. Situated at the edge of a five-acre lake at 3,500 feet elevation, this campground is especially attractive in early summer. Douglas firs, ponderosa pines, and incense cedars grow around the lake, sheltering small green meadows which are filled with early wildflowers. You'll see fairy lanterns, blue brodiaeas, and several lilies, among others. Hikers can get to the Smokehouse Trail entrance to Yolla Bolly-Middle Eel Wilderness quite easily.

Titanic sugar pines tower over Little Doe Campground, which shares the road to Hammerhorn. Howard Lake, regularly stocked with trout, sits nearby in a small tree-lined bowl.

Stonyford District Camping

Both the Plaskett and Letts recreation areas are on the Stonyford Ranger District. Families return to these delightful camp spots year after year to enjoy the boating and fishing on the lakes.

Plaskett Lake Campground is 6,000 feet above sea level, which makes for cool camping even on the hottest days of summer in the valleys. Both red and white firs and Jeffrey pines grow around the shores of the two small Plaskett Lakes. The lakes, about three and four acres in size, are for fishing and non-motorized boating only; swimming is not permitted. Trout are planted regularly through the season. There are a number of summer homes nearby, and one of the finest views on the forest can be had by driving or hiking up to the shoulder of Black Butte. You look out over Snow Basin, Plaskett Lakes and Meadow, and Upper Cold Creek Canyon. Chimney Rock stands out on the far side of Cold Creek, an imposing sentinel over the Plaskett complex.

Because the Letts Lake campgrounds are about 1,500 feet lower than Plaskett Lakes, they open about two months earlier each year. There are actually four small camps around the lake: Main Letts, Saddle, Stirrup, and Spillway. Tall, stately ponderosa pines, mixed with digger pines shade the campsites, and from every site there's a view out over the blue-green waters of thirty-five-acre Letts Lake. Like Plaskett Lakes, motors aren't permitted on the lake, but rowboats, canoes and small sailboats are frequently seen.

About a mile before you reach the Letts Lake area, you'll come to Mill Valley Campground. This is the closest campground to the Deafy Glade entrance to Snow Mountain Wilderness. It has access to both Summit Springs and Bathhouse trails. The ponderosas and digger pines grow tall here and the red-and-green bark and bright green leaves of manzanita make up much of the understory, along with the ever-present chamise and whitethorn.

Birders camp in this area for the chance to see both hawks and eagles. Swainson's hawks live here, along with the more frequently seen Cooper's, sharp-shinned, and red-tailed hawks and the kestrals. Both golden and bald eagles can be seen occasionally.

Between the Letts Lake complex and Stoneyford Ranger Station and Work Center, you'll come to three of the most popular camping places for motor-cycle enthusiasts. Dirt bikers congregate at Fouts, Mill Creek, and North Fork campgrounds in order to use the myriad trails set aside for them in this portion of the forest. Stony Creek flows through all three camps and can be counted on early in the season to have some catchable trout. Fouts and Mill Creek are located in chaparral with some digger pine cover, and North Fork is in a grove of oaks alongside the stream.

Another camping place on the edge of concentrated OHV use is Digger Pine Flat. It's popular in winter because being 1,500 feet above sea level it is not subject to closure by the snows as some other campsites are.

Upper Lake District Camping

Lake Pillsbury is a major attraction on the Upper Lake Ranger District, attracting forest users of every stripe. There is a large concentration of vacation homes on both sides of the lake, some on private property, some on Forest Service permit land. Three big campgrounds, Pogie Point, Fuller Grove, and Sunset provide more than 130 units for family camping. There's also an overflow campground at Oak Flat for heavy weekends. The surface of Lake Pillsbury is at about 1,850 feet elevation, and summer temperatures soar over 100 degrees on occasion. However, the campsites are all shaded by oaks, Douglas firs, madrones, bay laurels, and a few ponderosas. Pogie Point Campground is on a flat that extends along the northwest shore of the reservoir, and individual units are widely spaced, so that even on crowded weekends you're still a long way from neighbors.

At Sunset, the camp units have a thick growth of both trees and underbrush, making your visit cooler and shadier. Fuller Grove is much like Pogie Point in location and layout.

Bear Creek Campground along one of the major tributaries to the Eel River is another favorite OHV camp. From here, both motorcyclists and four-wheelers can reach many miles of OHV trails in the Elk Mountain area.

At the edge of the forest eight miles north of the city of Upper Lake, Middle Creek Campground anchors one end of Sled Ridge National Motorcycle Recreation Trail. Located in an oak grove, this camping place is one of the few on the forest that can be reached via paved road. Dirt bikers and jeepers use this campground as headquarters to roam the challenging trails of Elk Mountain ORV Area.

On The Trail

Both hikers and horseback riders make use of the trails of Mendocino National forest and its two wilderness areas. Except for the Snow Mountain Wilderness, most of the hiking and horseback riding is confined to the northern half of the forest on the Covelo and Corning Ranger Districts.

National Recreation Trails

From Toomes Campground, you can reach the Brown's Camp or Ide's Cove parking areas for Ide's Cove National Recreation Loop Trail by taking Forest Road 25-1 (M22) six or seven miles northwest. Quickest access is from Corning. This trail is part of the Yolla Bolly-Middle Eel Wilderness system and dates back to Indian times. The Pomo Indians used portions of the trail as part of the communication link between the valleys of the Sacramento and Eel rivers. Except for a half-mile stretch near one end, gradients are gentle. The loop is just short of eight miles and you'll spend your time alternating between green meadows filled with corn lilies and buttercups, and stands of mixed firs. You'll

The nature trail along Comanche Creek. Activities include wildlife and bird watching, photo opportunities, and painting the fall colors. Gary Norcross photo.

see a stand of foxtail pines near Long Lake. In the near distance, the North Yolla Bolly Mountains stand out on the horizon, and in the far northeast clear days reveal Mt. Shasta's glimmering peak.

On the western edge of the forest near Eel River Work Center, Travelers' Home Trail attracts horsemen much of the year. Averaging 3,000 feet, it's the remnant of a pioneer route built around the turn of the century. The 9.5-mile trail follows the Middle Fork of the Eel, winding through stands of Douglas firs, their drooping limbs weighed down with pendulous cones. Ancient, twisted oaks, and smooth-limbed madrones fill the spaces between. Underfoot are countless bushes of lupine sprouting wherever they find sun and space. Make a loop trip out of this by crossing the Eel at the end of the trail and returning by way of Hell Hole Canyon.

Wilderness Areas

On the Mendocino Forest, there are basically three entry points for the Yolla Bolly-Middle Eel Wilderness; Indian Dick, Green Springs, and Ide's Cove. Both Indian Dick and Green Springs can be most easily reached via the town of Covelo on the west side of the forest. From Eel River Station, Indian Dick Road (FR 1N02) proceeds about twenty-eight miles to Indian Dick Station. Along the way, the turn-off for Hammerhorn Lake and Green Springs is on your right at the twenty-mile mark. From any of the entrances, you'll be able to get deep into one of the least used of California's Wildernesses. The words "Yolla Bolly" come from Wintun Indian Languages and mean *high, snow-covered peaks*, which is exactly what they are in the winter.

Unlike the granite and basalt crags of the Sierra and the lava domes of the Cascades, the Yolla Bolly Mountains are metamorphic schist, composed of sediments deposited eons ago on ocean bottoms that have been pushed high onto the continental mass by tectonic pressure. Glaciers, rain and landslides act to erode them into the shapes visible today. Jeffrey, sugar, and foxtail pines grow in the wilderness, along with Dougles firs, and true firs—both red and white. You'll see wild onions, lupines, shooting stars, and mules' ears growing in the numerous meadows. The wild onions are edible, incidentally, and a handful of sauteed onions will spice up your backpacker's stew.

Mountain quail and chicadees will be your companions along the wilderness trails. Up among the peaks, the grey and white Clark's nutcracker will call back and forth from the highest branches of the trees.

Far in the southern half of the forest, the Snow Mountain Wilderness, established in 1984, already gets as much use as the Yolla Bolly. It's less than a four-hour drive from San Francisco, Santa Rosa, or Sacramento, and the hiking trails are free of snow a month or more before its Sierra counterparts.

A large and prosperous population of mountain lions makes its home on the wilderness. They are very secretive, you might spend years here without spotting one. Pacific blacktail deer are very numerous, as is the black bear. Hunters come after both deer and bear in their season.

Many hikers use Snow Mountain as a day hike area, but there are a number of places where you can camp within the wilderness.

One of the best viewing spots in California is the top of Snow Mountain East. It's a complete 360-degree panorama. You can see the Yolla Bolly Mountains at the far northern end of the forest. To the north-northeast is Shasta's perpetual snow cap, and to its right the massive bulk of the sawtooth Sierra Nevada looms up on the eastern horizon beyond the flat Sacramento Valley, Its flatness is broken only by the jagged Sutter Buttes. The view in the other half of the circle from southeast all the way around to northwest is of mountains—one range after another—as you take in with your eye much of the north coastal ranges.

Touring, Sightseeing, and Special Programs

Most sightseeing is done on foot after a short drive on this forest. The tops of forest fire lookouts are favorite spots, and visitors are encouraged to visit during daylight hours from mid-June to October. Goat Mountain, behind Cedar Camp on the Stonyford District and Anthony Peak, on the Covelo District, are among the most popular. The Goat Mountain lookout is temporarily closed, but hikers can still walk up to it.

One interesting drive you can make is the cross-forest drive from Covelo

MENDOCINO NATIONAL FOREST

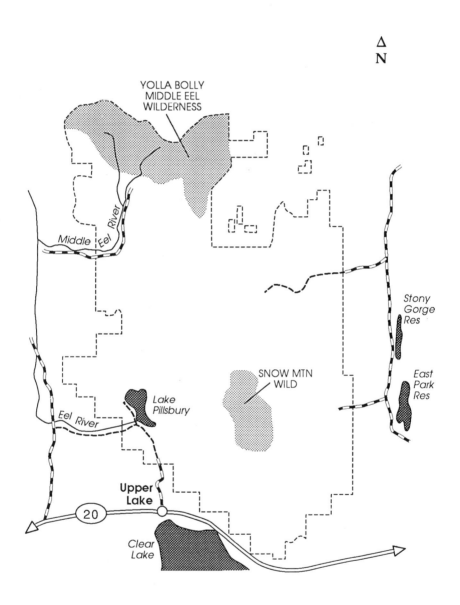

Δ
N

YOLLA BOLLY
MIDDLE EEL
WILDERNESS

Middle Eel River

Stony
Gorge
Res

East
Park
Res

SNOW MTN
WILD

Lake
Pillsbury

Eel River

Upper
Lake

20

Clear
Lake

to Stonyford. This drive crosses the top of the ridge at Mendocino Pass and then drops down to the Plaskett Recreation Area with its two tiny lakes and on out of the forest past Alder Springs.

An alternate route from Upper Lake to Lake Pillsbury follows designated Forest Route M-1 by way of Middle Creek. You'll travel through low altitude forests of firs, madrones, oaks, and bay laurels, dipping down to cross summer-dry streams and climbing slightly to meadow-topped ridges.

A summer interpretive campfire program is offered at the Letts Lake Recreation Area. Forest Service personnel conduct the programs Saturday evenings during the camping season. Films, slides, and lectures about the forest and its history, both human and natural, are the principal features.

Sports

Of all the opportunities for sports on the Mendocino National Forest, those that are most taken advantage of are hunting and off-highway vehicle travel, especially dirt bikes. During the long, split deer season, many of the camping places will be full, and dispersed camping will handle many more hunters. And some motorcycle events will be limited to 750 participants, they are so popular.

Opportunities for winter sports are limited because of the shortage of paved roads within the forest boundaries. There is room for both cross-country skiing and snowmobiling from the snow line by way of Forest Highway 7 east of Corning, and on the west side, there is some snowmobiling activity in the Mendocino Pass and Anthony Peak areas.

Boating and Water Skiing

Lake Pillsbury on the Upper Lake Ranger District is the only spot on the forest where motorboats are permitted. The lake was constructed in the 1920s for the primary purpose of producing electricity, with boating, fishing, swimming, and water skiing secondary. Now operated for power use by the Pacific Gas and Electric Company under a Forest Service permit, there is a private resort on the western shore which has launching facilities. Fuller Boat Launch is adjacent to Fuller Grove campground.

Kayakers gather at Mill Creek campground below Letts Lake in the spring for a brief opportunity when run-off is highest to try the run down to Mine Camp. There's also some innertubing on Stony Creek.

The small lakes of the forest, especially Plaskett and Letts, are fun for small boat owners and their kids. Rafts, rowboats, canoes and kayaks all appear at one time or another at these family recreation areas. So long as there's no motors, they're all welcome.

Off Road Motoring

The Mendocino offers off-highway vehicle enthusiasts beautiful scenery, challenging terrain, and a memorable camping experience. In addition, there are about six organized OHV events sponsored by various organizations each year, and "green sticker" funds continue to be used to build motorcycle trails and to reclaim land damaged by abuse.

There are three major OHV areas on the forest, **Lake Pillsbury, Elk Mountain**, and **Davis Flat**. The designated trails on each of the special ORV Areas, as well as those for the forest as a whole, are diagrammed completely on the "Mendocino National Forest Off Road Highway Vehicle Map." Any ranger station on the forest can see to it that you get a copy of the map, as well as answer any questions you have and fill you in on changes or closures.

As in all of the forests, wilderness areas are off-limits to all motorized vehicles and bicycles. However, practically all other roads on the Forest are open to OHV's. You might want to be aware, too, that the Mendocino is a *working* forest, and that logging trucks or cattle on the roads are a fact of life, and drive accordingly. Detours can be expected when timber sales are active.

Fishing and Hunting

Essentially, this is a "dry" forest, especially at low altitudes. Many of the streams are seasonal, fading away to occasional pools or nothing when summer's heat appears. Still, there are some places where water stays through the year and trout can be caught. Furthermore, the Eel River below Lakes Pillsbury and the Middle Fork have an annual salmon and steelhead run.

Letts Lake and Plaskett Lakes in the recreation areas are planted regularly, as are a couple of other small lakes—Hammerhorn and Howards. There's also trout fishing in both wildernesses. Lake Pillsbury has a good population of trout, as well as green sunfish, and trollers working early and late bring home some nice catches.

It is hunting, however, that brings sportsmen into the forest in the largest numbers. Deer hunters especially like the Mendocino. The forest lies in two hunting time zones, and consequently when you add archery seasons and open seasons you get almost three months of deer hunting somewhere on the forest each year. Both Wildernesses are open for hunters with the Yolla Bolly being the favorite. Blacktail deer, a large bear population, feral pigs, and upland birds bring many hunters into the Mendocino every year.

MENDOCINO NATIONAL FOREST CAMPGROUNDS

Corning Ranger District	Piped Water	Camp Sites	Trailer Space	Fishing	Boating	Swimming	Store	RV Dump Station	Reservations	Special Attractions
Dead Mule	2	•								
Del Harleson	2									
Kingsley Glade	5	•								
Rocky Cabin	4	•								
Sugar Springs	2	•								
Three Prong	5	•								
Toomes	2	•								
Wells Cabin	25	•								
Whitlock	5	•								
Covelo Ranger District										
Eel River	16	•	•							
Hammerhorn Lake	8	•	•							
Little Doe	22		•							

MENDOCINO NATIONAL FOREST CAMPGROUNDS

	Camp Sites	Piped Water	Trailer Space	Fishing	Boating	Swimming	Store	RV Dump Station	Reservations	Special Attractions
Stoneyford Ranger District										
Board Tree	16	•								
Cedar Camp	6									
Digger Pine	7	•								
Fouts	9	•								
Letts Lake	40	•	•							
Mill Creek	5		•							
Mill Valley	15	•	•							
North Fork	6		•							
Old Mill	10	•								
Plaskett Lake	32	•	•							
Upper Lake Ranger District										
Bear Creek	16	•								
Deer Valley	13	•								
Lakeview	9	•								
Lower Nye	6									
Middle Creek	15	•	•							
Oak Flat	17	•	•							Lake Pillsbury
Pogie Point	49	•	•							Lake Pillsbury
Sunset	54	•	•							Lake Pillsbury
Fuller Grove	28	•								

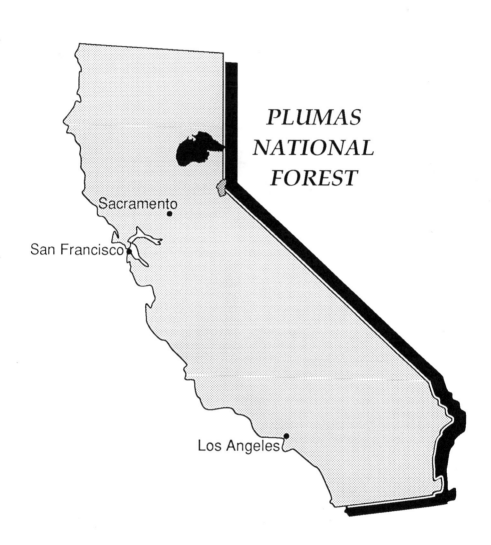

*PLUMAS
NATIONAL
FOREST*

Sacramento

San Francisco

Los Angeles

Plumas National Forest

The Plumas National Forest, a mountain playground, is oriented toward recreation. More than 1,000 miles of rivers and streams, and 100 lakes, all with excellent fishing, beckon vacationers.

Five large reservoirs offer camping, fishing, boating, swimming, and water skiing. You can also enjoy hunting, rock-hounding, gold panning, hiking, and winter sports, including both downhill and cross-country skiing.

Areas of interest include the Middle Fork of the Feather River, designated a part of the National Wild and Scenic River system; Feather Falls, the sixth highest waterfall in the continental U.S.; Lakes Basin, containing many glaciated areas, strikingly scenic lakes and unusual terrain; and historical mining towns and regions of historical interest.

Camping

The Plumas is divided into six ranger districts, and each of them has a "center of interest" in the form of lake or river.

Quincy Ranger District

The Quincy District campgrounds are along the north fork of the Feather River and off the road from Quincy to Bucks Lake. All but two, Silver Lake and Brady's Camp, are low altitude sites that open early in the season around the first of April and stay open until late October.

About two miles east of Belden along Highway 70, Caribou Road turns north, following the north fork of the Feather. Proceed up this paved road to three campgrounds: Gansner Bar, North Fork, and Queen Lily. Ponderosa and sugar pines dominate the tree canopy in these camps, along with incense cedars and black oaks. The stream has alders and willows alternating along boulder-strewn flats. Quiet pools with miniature sand beaches share the stream bed with rapids and cataracts.

One of the most appealing camping places on the Quincy District is Silver Lake Campground off the Quincy-Bucks Lake Road. At 5,800 feet, the camp is located in a white fir forest on the shores of Silver Lake. Clumps of Manzanita and whitethorn separate the campsites. It's very small—only seven units—but perfectly located for hiking, sightseeing, fishing, and relaxing. Its location on the edge of the 21,000-acre Bucks Lake Wilderness makes it an ideal camp for exploring that wild part of the forest, as well as accessing the Pacific Crest Trail which passes within two miles of the lake.

A little more remote, and used more by deer hunters than other recreationists' is Deane's Valley Campground, on the banks of Rock Creek southwest of Quincy. Big pines and firs are scattered across the flats adjacent to the meadows of the valley.

Oroville Ranger District

The center of the Oroville District, as far as recreation is concerned, is the Bucks Lake Recreation Area. This popular destination in the western high country has two campgrounds right on the lake, Sundew and Mill Creek. Whitehorse Campground is east of the lake on the banks of Bucks Creek. All

Group camping at the Lakes Basin Campground. F. A. Sanchez photo.

three are near the edge of one of the large reservoirs for which the forest is famous. They're all up over the 5,000-foot mark and have access to boat launch facilities. Bucks Lake is far to the west of the Sierra crest, but its granite basin could be mistaken for any of the big reservoirs of the high country. Jeffrey pines march up the slopes from the shores, and eagles and hawks own the sky overhead.

Lower Bucks Campground is on Lower Bucks Lake adjacent to the main lake. It is for self-contained recreation vehicles only. Grizzly Creek Campground is a couple miles west of the lake on the Oroville Road. It's meadow country, and beef cattle share the green with the blacktailed deer.

There are three more campgrounds on the Oroville District, at Little North Fork, Milsap Bar, and Rogers Cow Camp. Little North Fork and Rogers Cow Camp are open year-round and are in the far western part of the forest at 4,000 feet. They offer fishing and hunting for those who are willing to drive a little further into the forest on secondary roads. Milsap Bar, at 1,600 feet down in a canyon of the Feather River is really an early eason camp. It is a part of the Feather Falls Scenic Area. It has fishing to offer as well as the striking tableau presented by the canyon of the middle fork of the Feather. While you're there, go look at South Branch Falls, a series of nine waterfalls varying in height from 30 to 150 feet. Rock domes and boulders, interspersed in a wide variety of vegetation, lend contrast and natural charm to the many different falls with their deep green pools.

Beckwourth Ranger District

The Beckwourth District contains both the Lake Davis Recreation Area and the Lakes Basin Recreation Area, two of the most visited sections of the forest. There are three campgrounds at Lake Davis, all three on the shores of the lake. All three of these sites, Grizzly, Grasshopper Flat, and Lightning Tree, are big, new campgrounds with plenty of room to roam. The big pines are far enough apart that they give a particularly open feeling to the camps. The lake itself is a big impoundment almost 6,000 feet up at the edge of the high desert. Jeffrey pines and junipers make up the sparse forest cover, while aspens and cottonwoods grow along the banks of the streams feeding into the lake.

The Lakes Basin Campground on the Plumas portion of the Lakes Basin Recreation Area is in a different setting on a flat adjacent to a creek and Grassy Lake. The area is interspersed with handsome stands of quaking aspens whose golden glow lights up the fall season. It is well located for hikers and fishermen who want to use it as a home base for exploring the Lakes Basin region.

Milford Ranger District

Frenchman Reservoir Recreation Area highlights the Milford District with three campgrounds around the lake and another just below the lake on Little Last Chance Creek. This last, called Chilcoot Campground, is spread along the banks of the creek under cottonwood and juniper trees in the high desert environment. Its forty sites are well-spaced and give a feeling of being in a protected place.

Three campgrounds at Frenchman, Spring Creek, Frenchman, and Big Cove, are on the south shore of this high desert reservoir at an elevation of 5,700 feet. Jeffrey pines and junipers are scattered across the campground areas, along with black cottonwoods. Cottonwood Springs Campground is also a part of the recreation area and is located just to the west of the lake.

This is mule deer country, and the canyons, creeks, and springs of the Diamond Mountains, which rise sharply from the reservoir's eastern shore, shelter parts of a big herd. To the northwest, Dixie Mountain State Game Refuge provides a haven for our largest deer.

La Porte Ranger District

Little Grass Valley Reservoir, on the La Porte Ranger District, in the southwestern part of the forest, has four campgrounds which supply more than 300 camping units on the forested edge of this large lake. The 5,000-foot altitude brings cool nights and warm days.

Little Beaver Campground, just three miles north of La Porte, is a family kind of place, with access to boat ramps, hiking trails, and a ranger interpretive program in the summer. Campers at Running Deer, Wyandotte, and Peninsula walk-in tent camp also have access to the interpretive programs provided by the Forest Service. Both the natural and human history of La Porte District are features of the evening campfire programs.

Across the lake, Black Rock Campground gives access to one of the boat launch ramps and is a favorite with fishermen. White firs dominate the lake's thick forest cover along with ponderosa and sugar pines. At 5,100 feet, it makes a marvelous spot to escape the summer heat of the Central Valley below, as well as offering a good chance to hook into a trophy trout.

Tiny Cleghorn Bar Campground is deep in the Middle Fork Canyon at the end of a four-wheel-drive road. The campground is at one of only three access points to the Middle Fork between Lake Oroville and the Quincy-La Porte Road.

Greenville Ranger District

The Antelope Valley Reservoir Recreation Area in the northeast portion of the Plumas is worth the extra driving time it takes to get there. Boulder Creek, Lone Creek, and Long Point campgrounds provide sites for more than 200 campers. The Forest Service provides ranger interpretive programs including nature hikes and evening campfires during the summer. The camping places share the natural bowl setting with the lake. Pines and firs grow to the water's edge, creating exquisite shadows in the long summer evenings.

On The Trail

Plumas National Forest contains many miles of maintained trails and hikers and horseback riders are an important part of the forest's recreation plans.

The Pacific Crest Trail extends across the Plumas from northwest to southeast for about seventy-five miles, crossing two major canyons, the middle and north forks of the Feather River. The most important access points for the PCT are at Belden on Highway 70, the Bucks Lake-Quincy Road, Quincy-La Porte Road, and the trails in the Lakes Basin Recreation Area.

Mid-June is the earliest that is is feasible to hike the PCT in this area as snow is still prevalent into mid-June and streams are usually high. Mid-October marks the end of the walking season on this length of the PCT, as storms start across the range to blanket the mountains with snow again.

Several parts of the PCT through the Plumas are without sources for water, so hikers should be prepared. This is especially true in the section from Nelson Creek to the middle fork, and from Belden to Three Lakes. This is also rattlesnake country, and because the trail passes through primitive regions, they are more common than in most other parts of the Sierra.

The Lakes Basin Recreation Area, which the Plumas shares with adjacent Tahoe National Forest to the south has many of the rest of the hiking trails favored by back-packers and day-hikers alike. The basin is filled with glacial cirques, volcanic peaks, high meadows, and copses of aspens, red firs, and several different pines. Sharing the region with the national forests is Plumas-Eureka State Park, and the trail systems cross park and forest boundaries in several places. The Little Jamison Creek Trail starts at the Jamison Mine near Upper Jamison Campground in the park and climbs steadily about four miles to the Pacific Crest Trail past the Smith Lake, Grass Lake, Jamison Lake, and Rock Lake trail junctions. It's very well maintained, although it has some steep, rocky stretches that will test you.

Early in the season, the Frazier Falls Trail will take you on a gentle hike from the old Gold Lake Road to a fenced overlook of 100-foot Frazier Falls. As Frazier Creek sometimes dries up later in the year, it's best to go early to see the falls at their most satisfying time. Almost all of the Lakes Basin trails cross other trails, and an almost limitless choice of circular routes can be made through this region of granite and lava grandeur.

While all of the trails in the Lakes Basin, the wild portion of the Middle Fork Feather River, the Feather Falls Trail, and all of the sections of the PCT are closed to all motor vehicles, the trails on the rest of the forest are open to dirt bikes, all-terrain and four-wheel vehicles. Mountain bikes can be ridden everywhere except the PCT and Bucks Lake Wilderness.

Occasionally, closures of specific trails or sections of trails will be made,

PLUMAS NATIONAL FOREST

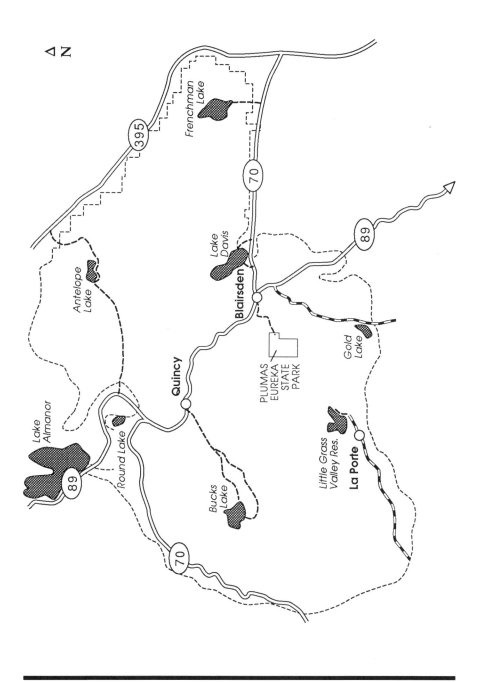

so it's necessary to check with rangers before starting out. Sometimes, too, while a trail is legally open to motor vehicles, it will be in such rough or dangerous condition that the Forest Service will recommend against using it.

A paved road from the community of Feather Falls leads to the **Feather Falls National Recreation Trail**. A well-maintained route extends 3.5 miles to the unique and breathtaking overlook of Feather Falls. The overlook is a real eagle's nest, built high atop a 600-foot pinnacle of rock. Tons of concrete, timbers, cables, anchor bolts, and guard rails were helicoptered in to the site and then assembled into a heart-stopping platform overlooking the falls.

The **Hartman Bar National Recreational Trail** is a four-mile wonder that descends 2,000 feet from Hartman Bar Ridge to the Middle Fork of the Feather River. An extension of this trail also drops into the Feather from the north side of the canyon south of Bucks Lake. Like the Feather Falls Trail, it is best negotiated early in the year, as the heat at the low altitudes can be very intense. An unimproved campground, Dan Beebe, awaits hikers in the canyon, not to mention large numbers of hungry trout in the crystal waters of the Feather. The trailhead can be reached from either Feather Falls or Little Grass Valley Reservoir near La Porte.

The only wilderness in Plumas National Forest is **Bucks Lake Wilderness.** Located in the northwestern portion of the forest, the 21,000-acre wilderness was established in 1984. It has a broad diversity of vegetation and topography. A few small lakes and ponds dot the area at the base of the escarpment that

A blacktail doe wanders through the remains of an abandoned mine at Plumas Eureka State Park.

includes Spanish Peak and Mt. Pleasant. "Difficult access" describes the entire region. Ground cover varies with some bare rock slopes and cliffs or a mix of brush, conifers, and oaks, to pure stands of red firs, and some small mountain meadows. The PCT traverses the wilderness following along the escarpment. From the top you command a spectacular view of the forest to the east and north as far as Mt. Lassen. Canyon and ridge succeed each other under the big, open sky as far as you can see.

Touring, Sightseeing, and Special Programs

Auto touring on the Plumas will take you through some glorious country, and to some wondrous sights. Entering the forest from the west on Highway 70 is a sight-seeing drive in itself. The road snakes along the bottom of the canyon of the North Fork of the Feather River, sharing the space with a railroad. Both cross and recross the river on bridges that seem suspended from skyhooks. The sides of the canyon seem to rise directly from the riverbed. The PCT crosses the canyon at Belden, and hikers have a long, switchback-filled climb to get out. The Pacific Gas and Electric Company operates one of its powerhouses here, and associated with it is the historical site of the Ebbe Stamp Mill—a reminder of gold rush times.

Along the route, sheer granite cliffs provide climbers with room to practice their fun. Both Arch Rock and Elephant Butte know the chocks, ropes, and slings of the climbers.

In the far northern section of the forest a short, steep—but wide and well-paved—road leads to an azure blue gem called **Round Valley Lake**. The road is a fall color kaleidoscope, with big leaf maples, dogwood, black oaks, willows, and aspens all coloring the view with reds and yellows against the green of the conifers. At the lake, besides a resort and marina, there's an excellent nature trail built and maintained by high school students from Indian Valley, and a Chinese cemetery with one marked grave remaining, that of Wong Hank.

The road to **Frenchman Lake** from Chilcoot passes through a spectacular canyon of volcanic mud formations called **Lahar**, which makes it look like a kingdom of gargoyles and eagles' nests. On the Oroville Ranger District, the Oro-Quincy Highway from Meadow Valley to Bucks Lake and the road along the lake itself offer views of the high country on the western half of the forest and the lake.

The **Quincy-La Porte Road**, open only in the summer, will give you a good feeling for this wild and remote part of the Sierra. It's about thirty miles from Quincy over mountains, along knife-edge ridgetops and down into bottomless canyons to the unique 135-year-old mining town of La Porte.

La Porte is an inviting community at 5,000 feet, a wonderful retreat in winter for cross-country skiing, snowmobiling, snowcamping, snow shoeing, and toboganing. **E Clampus Vitus** members in La Porte are remodeling one of the town's oldest buildings into a museum that will house relics from the "lost Sierras" in the southwestern section of the Plumas.

La Porte can be the center for tours on the forest's backcountry road to some other early mining camps such as Howland Flat, Gibsonville, Queen City, and Port Wine. Relics of the days of '49, there's little left but the magic names, the romance, and foundations of buildings long ago reclaimed by the forest.

Plumas-Eureka State Park adjacent to the Lakes Basin Recreation Area, not technically a part of Plumas National Forest, is nevertheless an attraction that you won't want to miss. The mines were over the 6,000-foot mark, and

Rock climbers test their skills next to Highway 70 along the Feather River.

typically buried in snow through the long winter. The remains of the Mohawk Mine buildings have been made the feature attraction in the park. Rangers give talks and guided walks as well as nighttime interpretive programs throughout the summer.

As you travel along the rivers of the national forests, and especially in the Plumas and adjacent Tahoe National Forest, you will see rafts anchored in the stream with gasoline-powered dredges on board. People seeking gold have filed claims on practically every likely looking piece of water in the state. Gold mining methods vary from using a gold pan with a minimum impact on the land, to utilizing heavy equipment which creates major land disturbances. Mostly, however, what you'll see are the dredges.

If you just want to get your feet wet, gold panning by an individual or family is considered a recreational activity and is allowed where other methods would be banned. However, most places where gold mining is permitted have already been "staked out," and you must make arrangements with the claimant if you want to try your luck on his claim.

Sports

Winter sports on the Plumas are the same as in the other forests. Greenville, Quincy, and Blairsden-Graeagle are centers where winter sports enthusiasts can find places to stay as well as trails and roads to explore, whether on skis, snowshoes, or snowmobiles. Bucks Lake has also become a winter playground with two resorts open year round. Access is from Bucks Summit via over-the-snow travel on a groomed track.

There is one downhill center, the Eureka Ski Bowl, located at Plumas-Eureka State Park, which is open Wednesdays, holidays, and weekends.

Boating and Water Skiing

From the southern tip of **Lake Almanor** in the north to **Frenchman** and **Davis** reservoirs in the southeast, the Plumas is loaded with opportunities for boating enthusiasts. Water skiers will find some big water to zip over at the three already mentioned, as well as **Antelope, Bucks Lake**, and **Little Grass Valley**. All of the lakes have launch ramps, and Almanor and Bucks have marinas.

Many of the small lakes are excellent for the kinds of boating that go along with fishing, and the fishing in many cases is well worth it. There is some canoeing and kayaking on both forks of the Feather River, particularly in the Middle Fork Recreation Zone near Portola in the Mohawk Valley.

Off Road Motoring

On the western half of the forest between Johnsville and La Porte is an old freight road straight out of the pioneer west. This route covers what used to be one of the only ways to travel this country, when supplies for the miners of Johnsville and Howland flat were drawn in horse or mule pulled wagons.

This is only one of the roads in this part of the forest that the dedicated off-highway vehicle enthusiast can explore. Others go to Poker Flat, American House, and Race Track Point, not to mention Lumpkin and Mooreville Ridge. And these are only on the La Porte Ranger District.

All five of the remaining ranger districts also have exciting possibilities away from the beaten track. For example, from Milford on Highway 395, Forest Road 26N84 connects with FR 26N16 and a whole network of back roads in the neighborhood of Last Chance Creek, Willow Creek, and Squaw Queen Creek, where you can roam for days without much in the way of company except your own party.

At publishing time, the forest plans to have off-highway vehicle maps available at every ranger station on the Districts.

Fishing and Hunting

Plumas National Forest, like Lassen National Forest to the north, is one of the best in the state for lake fishing for big trout. All of the major reservoirs on the forest contain large numbers of bigger-than-average trout. Lake Davis, Frenchman Lake, Little Grass Valley Reservoir, and Antelope Lake are among the very best places in the state for an angler to hook into a fish to talk about.

Hunting on Plumas National Forest is excellent, especially for deer. Plumas County, which is located in both the Plumas and Lassen National Forests, regularly leads all California counties in the archery deer kill. More and more sportsmen are coming into the forest armed with bow-and-arrow. Both Pacific blacktail and mule deer are taken, with a high degree of success in both the archery and regular deer season.

Resorts, Lodges, and Hotels

The Plumas National Forest has been a recreation center for many years, from the time the railroad first snaked its way up the canyons of the Feather River and the Feather River Inn was established. The Inn no longer caters to the general public, but several comfortable hostelries have jumped in to fill the breach.

Four lodges on national forest property grace the Lakes Basin Recreation Area. **Gray Eagle Lodge** has been in existence for more than sixty years and provides its patrons a modified American plan vacation spot with fifteen cabins with all modern conveniences. The restaurant at Gray Eagle is locally famous for its cuisine.

Elwell Lakes Lodge, and **Gold Lake Lodge** have also been in the area for many years, with some of their patrons being families who come back year after year for vacation time. Newest of the Lakes Basin accommodations is **Mountain Base Camps** on the west shore of Gold Lake. It's a family resort with a riding stable and pack station as well as a dinner house.

Over on the western half of the forest, Bucks Lake is also a resort center. **Bucks Lake Lodge** has been in existence almost as long as the lake has, and provides family vacation fun in an informal atmosphere. The cabins sleep from two to ten people, and are completely furnished. The lodge also has a restaurant and bar, as well as a snack bar and sporting goods department. The marina has boats and motors for rent, and provides launching and gasoline for those who bring their own.

The other resort at Bucks Lake is **Bucks Lakeshore Resort** on Pacific Gas and Electric Company land at the southwest shore. It's lakeshore cabins sleep two to eight people, and are fully furnished. the restaurant overlooks the lake and serves fine dinners and a unique champagne brunch Sundays. It too, has a complete marina with rentals, launching, and gasoline. Both lodges are open for the winter season, and cross-country skiers, snowmobilers, and ice fishermen make use of them on a regular basis. Also, both lodges have spaces for trailers and motorhomes with hookups.

Down in the old mining community of La Porte, the **Union Hotel** accommodates guests in rooms that date well back into the last century. its restaurant and bar are gathering points for locals and tourists alike.

PLUMAS NATIONAL FOREST CAMPGROUNDS

	Piped Water	Camp Sites	Trailer Space	Fishing	Boating	Swimming	Store	RV Dump Station	Reservations	Special Attractions
Beckwourth Ranger District										
Crocker	•	15	•							
Grasshopper Flat	•	70	•	•	•	•	•			Lake Davis
Grizzly	•	55	•	•	•	•	•			Lake Davis
Jackson Creek	•	15	•	•						
Lakes Basin	•	24	•	•						
Lightning Tree		17	•	•	•	•	•			Lake Davis
Greenville Ranger District										
Boulder Creek	•	70	•	•	•	•				Antelope Valley Res.
Greenville	•	23	•				•			Plumas County Park
Lone Rock	•	86	•	•	•	•				Antelope Valley Res.
Long Point	•	38	•	•	•	•				Antelope Valley Res.
La Porte Ranger District										
Black Rock	•	14	•	•	•	•				Little Grass Valley Res.
Burnt Bridge	•	30	•	•	•					
Cleghorn Bar		4	•	•						
Little Grass Valley Tent Campground	•	40		•	•	•				Little Grass Valley Res.
Little Beaver	•	121	•	•	•	•				Little Grass Valley Res.
Running Deer	•	40	•	•	•	•				Little Grass Valley Res.
Wyandotte	•	32	•	•	•	•				Little Grass Valley Res.
Milford Ranger District										
Big Cove	•	28	•	•	•					Frenchman Res.
Chilcoot	•	40	•	•						
Conklin Park		9	•	•						
Cottonwood Springs	•	28	•	•	•					Frenchman Res.
Frenchman	•	62	•	•	•					Frenchman Res.
Laufman	•	8	•							
Meadow View		6	•							
Spring Creek	•	39	•	•	•					Frenchman Res.
Oroville Ranger District										
Grizzly Creek		8	•							
Little North Fork		8		•						
Lower Bucks		5	•	•	•	•				Self-contained RV only
Mill Creek	•	10	•	•	•	•	•			Bucks Lake
Milsap Bar	•	20	•	•						
Rogers Cow Camp		5	•	•						
Sundew	•	19	•	•	•	•	•			Bucks Lake
Whitehorse	•	20	•	•	•	•	•			Bucks Lake

PLUMAS NATIONAL FOREST CAMPGROUNDS

Quincy Ranger District	Piped Water	Camp Sites	Trailer Space	Fishing	Boating	Swimming	Store	RV Dump Station	Reservations	Special Attractions
Brady's Camp		4	•	•						
Dean's Valley		7	•	•						
Gansner Bar	•	14	•	•						
Hallstead	•	20	•	•						
North Fork	•	20	•	•						
Queen Lily	•	12	•	•						16-ft max trailer
Silver Lake		7		•	•					Canoes
Snake Lake		4	•	•	•					

LASSEN
NATIONAL
FOREST

Sacramento

San Francisco

Los Angeles

Lassen National Forest

Located in northeastern California, Lassen National Forest covers 1.2 million acres. It ranges from the oak-covered foothills that form the eastern boundary of the Sacramento Valley to the pine and fir ridges and high peaks of the southern Cascades and the northern part of the Sierra Nevada, and levels off in the Great Basin area of the Modoc Plateau. The diverse topography features sage brush flats and broad, grassy meadows and volcanic lava flows; high sub-alpine peaks and rugged river canyons.

The forest, which was established in 1908 and named for Peter Lassen, a pioneer of Gold Rush times, abounds with wildlife—particularly spectacular are the raptors: eagles, osprey, red-tail and rough legged hawks. But it is the fish that bring sportsmen. Eagle Lake and Lake Alamanor are both home to Leviathan trout, and Hat Creek is one of the famous stream fisheries in the state.

Camping

The Hat Creek District is probably best approached from the west via Highway 44 or Highway 299 from Redding and south on 89, which runs on through the national park and down the center of the forest to Plumas National Forest on the southern boundary. The camping chart lists seven campgrounds on the district, but just as it is in most of the national forests, there's also room for dispersed camping.

An immense lava flow, up to five miles wide and more than twenty miles north to south, underlays this part of the forest. The camping places are sheltered under scattered pines and cedars protruding from brownish-black rocks and boulders that make up the volcanic ground. Alders and willows line portions of Hat Creek, and ceanothus and manzanita grow on the drier soil. Rising abruptly on the east, the creased and doubled battlements of the Hat Creek Rim dominate the skyline.

Cave, Bridge, and **Hat Creek** campgrounds are great for families, and have plenty of room for trailers and other RVs. **Big Pine, Dusty, Rocky**, and **Honn** are more primitive and trailers are definitely not recommended

At the south end of Eagle Lake are four of the most attractive campgrounds in the state—**Christie, Merrill, Eagle**, and **Aspen Grove**. Broad flats covered with widely-spaced Jeffrey pines, white firs and incense cedars stretch back from the edge of the lake. Scattered through the camp units, occasional clumps of manzanita, whitethorn, and aspens provide natural privacy screens and hiding places for white-crowned and fox sparrows. Chipmunks scamper across the flats and gray squirrels scold from the trunks above your head.

There is an amphitheater at Merrill where weekly information programs are scheduled. The host at the campground will know what's going on and when. The programs are presented by Forest Service personnel and students from Chico State University through the University Foundation.

At the north end of the lake among the junipers, sagebrush, and a few widely-spaced pines, the Bureau of Land Management has a campground with seventeen units and a disposal station.

Summer weekends will find most of the sites around Eagle Lake full early, so if you don't have a reservation at Eagle campground, it really is best to arrive a day ahead of time.

Away from Eagle Lake, but still in the Eagle Lake Ranger District, are a number of camping units with only a fire ring and a table. But these can make for great tent camping most of the time, and some of them are accessible to trailer and motorhome campers. Summit Camp, just north of Antelope Mountain, sits on the ridgetop overlooking the Eagle Lake Basin.

West of Eagle Lake and accessible from Highway 44 three campgrounds, **Bogard, Butte Creek**, and **Crater Lake**, hide along side roads. The Crater Lake site sits on the shores of a silvery lake at the center of an old volcano. In the fall, aspen leaves turn a brilliant yellow, framing the basin in gold.

Moving into the Lake Almanor area means more beautiful campgrounds, especially the one called **Almanor** on the west shore of the lake. Built on a series of small hills and gullies extending back from the sandy swimming beach on the lake, the camping places have been situated to take advantage of the terrain. Enormous pines provide shade, and the understory consists of red and green manzanita and silvery whitethorn growing amongst granite boulders. Along one of the interior roads of the campground is a sign saying "Iron Springs—100 Yards," and sure enough, if you follow the trail there is a set of iron springs from an old farm truck.

All of the other campgrounds around the lake itself are either private, or "semi-private" Pacific Gas and Electric Company sites. But away from the lake, and especially up in the area toward the National Park, are additional Forest Service sites. At Silver Lake, at the edge of Caribou Wilderness just east of the Park, campers will find **Silver Bowl** and **Rocky Knoll** campgrounds. White firs dominate the forest cover at both sites, and access to good fishing on both Silver and Caribou lakes attracts campers all season long. In addition, both make good headquarters for day hikes into the wilderness. The Highway 36 entrance to the forest from Red Bluff, takes travelers to several campgrounds, including **Battle, Mill**, and **Gurnsey creeks**. All three campgrounds have access to fishing and hunting, and are handy to the national park entrance.

Along Highway 32 from Chico, which one ranger calls the "prettiest drive on the Forest," are two very good family campgrounds at **Potato Patch** and **Elam Creek**. Both are nestled close to the water and you'll hear the stream gurgling around the boulders and logs in the creek bed. Ponderosa and sugar pines pierce the sky; alders and willows huddle along the canyon floor near the stream. Potato Patch has the added attraction of a well-made and well-maintained nature trail, and both give access to Deer Creek fishing.

Philbrook PG&E Company campground on the shores of Philbrook Reservoir has room for some trailers and is a great place for OHV drivers to make their headquarters for tours of the High Lakes country to the east.

Out in Ishi Country, the campsites are few and far between. **Black Rock**, on Mill Creek, is a magic place with four campsites. Readers of the children's book, *Ishi, Last of His Tribe*, will recognize Black Rock itself and immediately be taken into the mystical world of the Yahi. It's at the edge of the Ishi Wilderness now, and you will know when you're there that the shadows among the trees along the stream are those of the ancestors who haven't gone to the Western Ocean yet.

Silver Lake is perfect for small boat trolling.

On the Trail

The Lassen is one of the best "roaded" forests in the state, yet there are more than 365 miles of hiking trails for you to enjoy in the roadless areas of the forest, and hiking and backpacking can be added to the forests' very real attraction.

Pacific Crest Trail

Two national recreation trails and a 130-mile-long section of the Pacific Crest Trail grace the forest. The Pacific Crest Trail enters the forest through McArthur-Burney Falls Memorial State Park in the north, courses along the Hat Creek Rim, and down into the Feather River Canyon. A fifteen-mile section of the trail over Hat Creek Rim may soon be relocated to provide better access to water.

The five-mile section of the PCT along Hat Creek Rim goes through spectacular territory. To get to it, park at the lot provided where the trail crosses Highway 44 near Mud Lake. Travel south to the Forest Service road east of Big Pine campground and Potato Butte. Along the way you'll see the glittering snows of Mt Shasta, Mt. Lassen's huge bulk, the peaks of the Thousand Lakes Wilderness, and the whole of Hat Creek Valley. Be sure you take water with you, as there is virtually none along the trail.

LASSEN NATIONAL FOREST

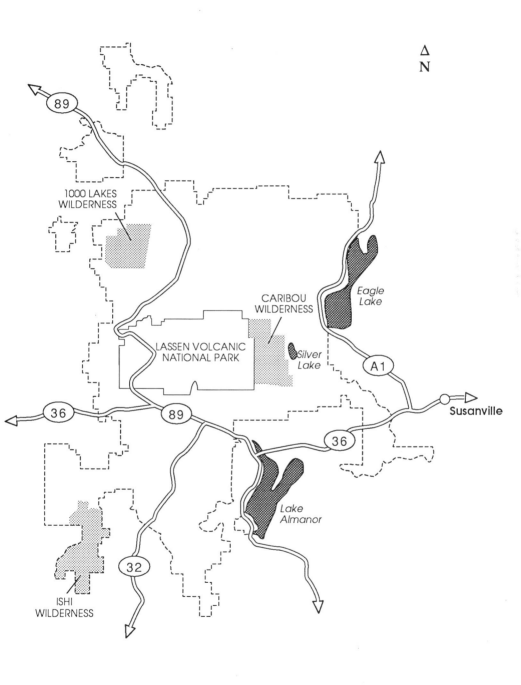

△
N

89

1000 LAKES
WILDERNESS

CARIBOU
WILDERNESS

Eagle
Lake

LASSEN VOLCANIC
NATIONAL PARK

Silver
Lake

A1

36

89

Susanville

36

Lake
Almanor

32

ISHI
WILDERNESS

National Recreation Trails

The **Heart Lake National Recreation Trail** starting point is six miles north of Mineral and Highway 36. The trail passes through mixed conifer stands of virgin red fir and Jeffrey pines. Grades are mostly gentle and include stream and meadow crossings. With two autos, you can make a shuttle trip of about seven miles.

The **Spencer Meadow National Recreation Trail** begins at Highway 36/89 just east of the Mill Creek crossing. It rises gently along a ridge top to connecting trails in Lassen Volcanic National Park, and top elevation is only 6,000 feet. Some seldom-used side trails branch off to good fishing along the upper reaches of Mill Creek. A newly-constructed loop off the Spencer Meadow Trail offers some striking vistas of Mill Creek as it flows through the valley below.

A hidden trail known mostly to "locals" is a three-lake hike, which includes **Homer, Dearheart,** and **Hidden Lakes** on the east side of Keddie Ridge east of Greenville. The trailhead can be reached via Forest Road 28N38 north of Setzer Camp, or by a rough jeep road climbing the eastern side of the ridge from Mountain Meadows Reservoir. Volcanic eruptions left these tiny, cold water lakes trapped in rugged rock formations, which can only be appreciated by viewing them. You'll need 1.5 hours each way for this unique, high altitude walk.

Many of the good hiking trails on the forest are those in the three wilderness areas—Caribou, Ishi, and Thousand Lakes.

Thousand Lakes Wilderness is a land of contrasting topography, many vegetation types, and clear lakes. There are lava and granite formations, as well as dense stands of lodgepole pines, open meadows, and in some areas, brush.

From a gently rolling plateau on the Lassen Forest, the Caribou Wilderness beckons to those who search for solitude. The wilderness is small and can easily be explored by hiking from a camping spot inside or outside the boundary. Silver Lake and Caribou Lake are located at the east trailhead entrance and a good place to start. From here any portion of the area may be reached over a well-maintained trail system. Most of the trails are located on gentle slopes with very few steep pitches.

The Caribou is not an area of lofty mountains and majestic views. It is instead, a primitive wilderness where one may find the earth and its community of life relatively untouched by man. Although it's called a gentle wilderness, the surface of the land is really rough and broken, a reminder of its mostly volcanic origin.

Birders will be rewarded with repeated sightings of at least three different woodpeckers: the downy and white-headed woodpeckers and Williamson's sapsuckers.

Along with the usual golden-mantled ground squirrels and chipmunks, the lucky visitor may catch a glimpse of a pine marten, once a prime target of trappers but now protected.

The Ishi Wilderness was established in 1984 in rugged country on the far western portion of the forest. It's an area of deep canyons where in winter the sun never reaches the bottom. Basically, the wilderness consists of the canyons of Mill and Deer creeks and the ranges that define them. Hiking in the area can be tough, especially in summer when temperatures in open areas regularly break the 100-degree mark, and shade is sparse. The best time to hike the Ishi is the spring when the wild flowers are in bloom, and in fall when the first nips of frost greet approaching winter.

Public access to the wilderness is from Ponderosa Way to trailheads at Mill Creek, Lassen Trail, Moak Trail, and Deer Creek. Four-wheel drive vehicles can reach trail heads at the Rancheria and Table Mountain-Kingsley Cove trails on the north. There is no public access from south or west.

The Ishi Wilderness supports abundant fish and wild life, and a walk down Mill Creek from Black Rock campground will reward the hiker with glimpses of Peregrine falcons, golden eagles, red-tailed hawks, kestrels, and owls, along with sparrows, towhees, and kinglets in the streamside vegetation. The Tehama deer herd, largest migratory deer herd in California, winters in the area. And the only wild horse herd on the west side of the Sierra occurs adjacent to the wilderness.

Touring, Sightseeing, and Special Programs

Travelers in the Hat Creek area won't want to miss **Subway Cave**. Located just off Highway 89 about a quarter-mile north of the junction of Highway 44, the trail is an easy .33-mile walk through a 2,000-year-old lava tube, which begins and ends in the parking lot.

You can visit volcanic spattercones and other interesting lava features along the **Spattercone Nature Trail** across from Hat Creek campground. This trail is a little longer, taking about 1.5 miles to complete the round trip, and you should allow two hours and bring water for this dry trip.

Another nature trail awaits you at **Vista Point** about a .25-mile south of Big Pine campground. You'll learn about different types of volcanoes at the **Deer Hollow** trailhead, and then take a short stroll through a tree plantation to learn a little about forest tree management. If you follow the paved photo trail (300 feet), you'll get an excellent shot of Lassen Peak.

Three other trips a little further afield are really worth the small effort it takes to see them. First is the **Radio Astronomy Observatory** located about four miles up Doty Road off Highway 89 in Hat Creek. Visitors are welcome Monday thru Friday.

Try to arrive at the **Crystal Lake Fish Hatchery** near Cassel at feeding time. The little fish go crazy in a feeding frenzy as the State Fish and Game Department's feeding truck sprays food over the water in the hatchery tanks.

The **West Prospect Fire Lookout** is open to the public and you can get to it by turning off Highway 89 a mile south of Big Pine campground on FR 32N12 for the twelve-mile drive to the top. Here you can learn how forest fires are detected while enjoying a panoramic view of northern Lassen Volcanic National Park and the adjacent Lassen National Forest.

In the Eagle Lake area, the lake itself is a wonder, as are the trout that live in it and the ospreys and eagles that nest near it.

The lake is a mysterious pool that lives in a world of its own, its origins a geological puzzle. Sixteen miles long, it is divided into three distinct sections by peninsulas. In the north, the high desert dominates, while the south shore is edged in towering pines and firs. Wildlife abounds in unexpected diversity because the lake straddles the demarcation zone between forest and desert.

Away from the lake, two important tourist attractions draw visitors. One is the **Antelope Lookout**, the world's first solar-powered fire lookout. It's an easy fifteen-mile drive from the campgrounds at the south end of the lake. The striking view from the top includes Mt. Shasta gleaming on the northern horizon, the bulk of Mt. Lassen, shining Eagle Lake, and east out into the Nevada desert.

Cattle graze along the shores of Eagle Lake. Jean Hawthorne photo.

Brockman Flat lava beds can be reached to the west of the lake along County Road A-1. This is a fairly recent flow, believed to be only about 20,000 years old. You can park your car and wander across the flow, but go carefully. Footing on the lava can be treacherous. Be especially careful when driving off the paved road, as roads in the flow are not marked.

Sports

Boating on Eagle Lake is a favorite recreational pastime. The Gallatin Marina, for more than thirty years a well-used accommodation, is currently undergoing reconstruction and is not scheduled to start regular operations until the summer of 1991, although the new boat ramp will be in use a year earlier. Visitors will be able to use the nearby Aspen boat ramp while construction is under way.

The Almanor area is another center of boating activity. The lake is large, covering more than 28,000 acres, and deep. It has a population of fish—trout, kokanee salmon, and bass. Almanor is a much more "civilized" area than either Hat Creek or Eagle Lake, with commercial activity in the towns of Chester and Westwood north of the lake. There are several vacation home tracts, with Peninsula Village being the largest. Another large resort area is at Big Springs. Launching and marinas can be found at both places as well as Almanor Campground.

You can satisfy your inquisitive nature just by taking a drive around Lake

Almanor; it makes a perfect place for auto touring. The trip around the lake can be made on paved roads the entire distance. You'll see the 130-foot dam at Canyondam, built in 1926-27 that holds back 1,308,000 acre-feet of water, as well as the areas around the Highway 36 causeway, the lava beds, and the Stover Mountain Ski area.

The Forest Service ranger station in Chester will give you a packet of directions for other trips in the area, some of which require experience in driving *real* mountain roads. You'll follow Forest Service roads to places like Humbug Valley, Soda Springs Historical Site, Johnsville, and the ancient mining town of Seneca perched on the banks of the Feather River below the lake.

Snowmobiling is very popular on the forest and three areas with groomed trails and trailheads have been set aside for their use: **Ashpan Snowmobile Area** , north of Lassen National Park, **Morgan Summit**, just to the south of the national park near the town of Mineral, and **Bogard Rest Area** off Highway 44 west of Susanville. There are groomed trails at all three areas with warming huts and parking areas at the first two.

Cross-country skiing gains in popularity with each passing winter, and many of the unplowed roads through the forest are used by the nordic fan. **Eskimo Hill** is near the Ashpan snowmobile area. Eight miles of groomed cross-country trails are available at **McGowan Lake National Recreation Cross Country Ski Trail Area**. Within the national park cross-country skiing can be done in Manzanita Park and Sulphur Works.

Downhill skiers have their choice of three areas on the Lassen: Sulphur Works and Stover Mountain. Coppervale is located outside the park, west of Susanville. All three are small with short lines, even on weekends.

Boating and Water Skiing

Only the two largest lakes, Almanor and Eagle, are large enough for water-skiing. Both have good launching facilities. Some of the smaller lakes are great for the kind of boating you usually associate with fishing. Silver Lake, especially, is a beautiful spot to troll, lying as it does under the rocky eights of the cliffs at the edge of the Caribou Wilderness. Electric motors are recommended by the Forest Service to preserve the quality of solitude of the Wilderness next door. Motor boats are not allowed at Crater Lake, and row boats, small sailboats, and canoes have the place to themselves.

Off Highway Motoring

Because the Lassen is one of the best "roaded" forests in the state, drivers of off-highway vehicles can have a ball. You can take your four-wheel drive car or truck practically anywhere on the forest where there's a road. Many of the trails, including Spencer Meadow National Recreation Trail are open to motorcycles. Because closings change on the forest from year to year, it is always best to check with the forest supervisor's office in Susanville, or with one of the district ranger stations before venturing into the forest.

One especially good four-wheel tour is the High Lakes trip. The region can be reached from Highway 32. Turn east to Butte Meadows, and then take FR 26N10 and 25N02 to Philbrook Lake and follow road signs into the High Lakes country. Forest Service campgrounds are in the area at Cherry Hill and West Branch, and PG&E Company has one at Philbrook Reservoir. It's a challenging area for off-highway vehicle riders, with rough and rocky roads leading to high mountain scenic areas and small high altitude lakes.

On the Hat Creek District, Forest Road 18 follows the Butte Creek Rim from north to south, and gives access to a number of minor forest roads that lead to lakes, creeks and reservoirs. If you're there in deer season, you might expect some company, but the rest of the year you're very apt to have only yourself to talk to.

Fishing and Hunting

Eagle and Almanor provide some of the best trout fishing in the state. In early or late season, the two provide real big game fishing on light tackle. Only in Plumas National Forest immediately to the south, and in the coastal salmon and steelhead streams, are there trout to rival those that come from Almanor and Eagle.

In other parts of the forest, there is first-class stream fishing. Hat Creek is practically always good for fish, even though it is road accessible almost its entire length. It features a four mile "fisherman's access trail" between Cave and Bridge campgrounds. The trail shows off Hat Creek at its best and you'll also find some of the best fishing holes around.

Good fishing can also be found at North Battle Creek Reservoir. Managed by PG&E Company, the reservoir offers boating, camping, and fishing. It's only accessible during the summer.

Hamilton Branch and the North Fork of the Feather River above Lake Almanor are top streams for fishermen, too. Best check with local authorities for seasons and special closings, as both these streams are sometimes shut down to protect spawners from the lake.

Deer hunters have a higher success rate on the Lassen National forest than on the more crowded forests to the south. Typically deer hunters in the more remote areas of the forest are apt to see more bucks and get in more shots. Black-tails on the west and mule deer to the east is the general rule.

Archery deer hunting is an extremely popular activity in the Chester area near Lake Almanor. Plumas County always ranks first in the state in archery deer harvest and most of that harvest is taken from the east Tehama herd in the Chester region.

LASSEN NATIONAL FOREST CAMPGROUNDS

Hat Creek Area	Piped Water	Camp Sites	Trailer Space	Fishing	Boating	Swimming	Store	RV Dump Station	Reservations	Special Attractions
Big Pine		19	•						•	
Bridge	•	25	•	•					•	
Cave	•	46	•	•					•	Subway Cave
Dusty		5		•	•	•				Lake Britton
Hat Creek	•	73	•	•					•	Nature Trail
Honn		6		•						
North Battle Creek Res.	•	15	•	•	•	•				5 walk-in sites
Rocky		8		•					•	

LASSEN NATIONAL FOREST CAMPGROUNDS

	Piped Water	Camp Sites	Trailer Space	Fishing	Boating	Swimming	Store	RV Dump Station	Reservations	Special Attractions
Eagle Lake Area										
Aspen Grove	•	25		•	•	•	•	•		tents only
Bogard	•	22	•	•						
Christie	•	69	•	•	•	•	•	•		Eagle Lake
Crater Lake	•	17	•	•	•	•				
Eagle	•	50	•	•	•	•	•	•	•	Eagle Lake
Eagle Lake (BLM-North)	•	22	•	•	•	•	•	•		boat launch
Merrill	•	181	•	•	•	•	•	•		Interp. program
West Eagle Group	•	150	•	•	•	•	•	•	•	
Lake Almanor Area										
Almanor	•	101	•	•	•	•	•			Interp. program
Battle Creek	•	50	•	•		•				
Benner Creek		8	•							
Domingo Springs	•	18	•	•						
Elam Creek	•	15	•	•						Info. Station
Fox Farm	•	44	•	•	•	•	•	•		Lake Almanor
Gurnsey Creek	•	31	•	•						
High Bridge		12	•							
Hole in the Ground	•	13	•							
Last Chance	•	25	•	•	•	•	•			Lake Almanor
Little Grizzly		5								
Mill Creek		12	•	•						
Mountain View	•	20	•	•	•	•	•			Lake Almanor
Rocky Knoll	•	18	•	•	•	•				Silver Lake
Rocky Point	•	20	•	•	•	•	•			Lake Almanor
Silver Bowl	•	18	•	•	•	•				Silver Lake
Warner		15	•	•						
West Branch	•	15	•	•						
Ishi Country										
Alder Creek		5	•							
Black Rock		4	•							
Butte Meadows	•	12	•	•		•				
Cherry Hill	•	25	•	•						13 walk-in sites
Philbrook	•	18	•	•	•	•				
Potato Patch	•	32	•	•						Nature trail
Soda Springs		10	•							
South Antelope		4	•							

SHASTA-TRINITY
NATIONAL
FOREST

Sacramento

San Francisco

Los Angeles

Shasta-Trinity National Forest

This forest is really two forests in one, the Shasta formed in 1905, and the Trinity formed in 1907, both by President Theodore Roosevelt. Recreation opportunities on the forest are unmatched in their variety. Mt. Shasta, at 14,162 feet, dominates the horizons of northern California, and the Whiskeytown-Shasta-Trinity National Recreation Area affords recreation opportunities for present and future generations around the four huge reservoirs created by the Bureau of Reclamation's Central Valley Project. A hundred miles of Wild and Scenic Rivers, and five National Wilderness Preservation Areas protect our interest in the nationally significant natural resources of the forest.

Camping

Camping on the forest can be divided into two big types: around the big lakes for one, and along the rivers and streams for another. Lake campers tend to be boaters, towing their ski or fishing boats with them, while stream campers follow other outdoor interests.

Lake Shasta Ranger District Camping

Fifteen improved campgrounds and several boat-in sites, complemented by a number of unimproved units and the possibility of dispersed camping almost anywhere around the lake and in the backcountry, means that this ranger district can and does handle a lot of campers each year.

Hirz Bay Campground, on the McCloud arm of the lake, is typical of the lakeside developed camping places. Open all year, it's large, the campsites are spread out away from each other, and you walk out to the edge of your site and get a view out over Shasta Lake. The tree canopy above is basically ponderosa pines with some Douglas firs. Manzanita, contorted, shiny-smooth, red and green, and festooned with long brown needles dropped from the pines, separates the campsites.

There are several more campgrounds along the McCloud Arm, including Ellery Creek, Moore Creek, Pine Point, and McCloud Bridge. Ellery Creek and Pine Point, recently reconstructed, are two of the most attractive. Ellery Creek sits close to the water, with campsites right on the beach front.

McCloud Bridge Campground has been built in an old farmstead. You'll camp at the edge of a broad meadow leading down to the water under a tree cover of walnuts—both English and black—figs, apples, and plums. Across from the camping places, a vast field of blackberries ripens in the early summer sun.

Farther to the north on the lake, along the Sacramento Arm, Antlers Campground attracts lots of visitors. It's close to I-5, open all year, and has plenty of space for trailers. Here, too, boaters like to stay. There's a resort and launch ramp adjacent to the campground, and people who enjoy being out on the water find the convenience enticing. Pines and firs are spread throughout the campground, and both scrub jays and stellar jays will come around for a handout, along with ground squirrels.

Two more camping places are nearby, Lakeshore East and Gregory Creek. Like Antlers, these units are close to the lake. They received less traffic than Antlers, and tent campers will find them particularly attractive. Immense black

Mt. Shasta dominates views from all of northern Callifornia.

oaks, mixed in with the pines and firs, shelter the individual units, and the impression is one of being isolated a little more from other people.

A little harder to get to, but worth the trip is the Lower Jones Valley Campground on the Pit River Arm. A boat ramp and marina are nearby, along with a resort, and boaters have access to both the Pit River and Squaw Creek arms of the lake.

The boat-in campgrounds, situated on all four arms of the lake, offer an opportunity to camp in secluded cover away from crowds and noise.

Away from Lake Shasta, Deadlun Campground is on the north shore of Iron Canyon Reservoir. To get to it, travel east on Highway 299 to the Big Bend turn-off, then north to Big Bend and seven miles beyond to Iron Canyon. Your campsite will be in a grove of ponderosa pines next to Deadlun Creek. Both anglers and hunters like to travel out here away from the numbers of people around Shasta Lake. You're very apt to see an osprey dive into the waters of Iron Canyon and fly off with a trout clutched in his talons, or even a golden eagle soaring over in search of small mammals.

Mt. Shasta Ranger District Camping

Two of the Mt. Shasta District campgrounds are on the flanks of the mighty mountain itself: McBride Springs and Panther Meadows. Both campgrounds are small, and because of high altitude are usually not open until about the 1st of July. Panther Meadows is almost at the treeline, and the camps are scattered through clumps of weather-dwarfed lodgepole pines. In the open grasslands on Mt. Shasta, more than 400 kinds of alpine wildflowers have been identified. Included among these are mountain pennyroyal, spreading phlox, and bleeding heart. Climbers and hikers headed for the Mt. Shasta Wilderness use these camps as staging areas for assaults on the mountain.

Sims Flat Campground, along the Sacramento River at the southern end of the district, is the favorite put-in spot for white water boaters who go splashing down the Sacramento in early season. Fishermen, too, like Sims Flat because of the great trout action on the river. Bigleaf maples, oaks, and pines, as well as Douglas firs, shade the camping places, which are easy to get to from I-5.

Castle Lake Campground, west of I-5, is immediately north of Castle Crags Wilderness. Campers here can fish in Castle Lake or hike into the high country. The Pacific Crest Trail can be accessed here, and there are two more smaller lakes within short walking distance. The camping spots are over 5,000 feet and incense cedars, Jeffrey and ponderosa pines, and white firs grow in scattered groups around the lake.

McCloud Ranger District Camping

The McCould District covers the "back side" of Mt. Shasta, the McCloud River drainage, and the immense shield volcano country of Medicine Lake Highlands Volcanic Area. It's popular with both hunters and fishermen, as well as those who like to camp away from the I-5 corridor.

Fowler Campground (called Fowler's Camp) is situated right on the Upper McCloud River between the Lower Falls of the McCloud and the Middle Falls. The two loops of the camp are in a savannah of ponderosa pines and white firs with big manzanita shrubs making up most of the understory. Lava rocks protrude between shrubs and trees, and make up the bed of the river flowing at the edge of camp. A trail upstream along the river will take you through pink and white wild azalea and under ancient volcanic cliffs to the Middle Falls of the McCloud. The river bursts over the lip of hardened lava and plunges more than seventy feet into the deep, clear pool between cliffs that contain the falls.

Follow Highway 89 east of Fowler's Camp to Cattle Camp Campground, where generations of mushroom hunters have gathered each year to harvest the musty fare. Drying racks are spread in the sun, and the fleshy fungi are sliced to be dried and saved for savory sauces. Anglers, too, like to camp here, and it's always full during deer season. Broad meadows, and manzanita-ponderosa combination describe the campsites along the upper McCloud.

On the Lower McCloud, below McCloud Reservoir, Ah Di Nah Campground waits for you at the end of a long, dirt road. This exquisite camping place is perched at the edge of the river. A wide, green meadow filled with the yellows, reds, blues, and purples of gentians, Indian paintbrushes, marsh marigolds, and mountian asters, sits in the center of what used to be a resort back in the horse-and-wagon days. Each camp unit looks out over the perfect harmony of trees, grass, and flowers.

A different camping experience waits for you at Harris Springs Campground in the Medicine Lake Highlands Volcanic Area. Volcanic formations, such as glass and lava flows, pumice deposits, lava tubes, cinder cones, craters, and faults are found throughout the vicinity. Harris Springs is right at the western edge of the broad, flat region. Junipers, manzanita, and western white pines grow up among the spatter cones and other volcanic debris.

Weaverville Ranger District Camping

Of the twenty-two improved campgrounds on the Weaverville District, seven are along the shores of Trinity Lake, and an additional four are at the edge of Lewiston Lake. The others are scattered in the back country, or along the access roads to the Trinity Alps. In addition, there are three more boat access only campgrounds on the shores of the lake.

Family campers like to go to Tannery Gulch and Hayward Flat campgrounds on Trinity Lake, both big, handsome camping places with campfire programs, nature walks, and other interpretive programs. Tannery Gulch is perched in a thick grove of firs and pines above its own swimming beach and launch ramp. The sun's rays filter down through the overhead branches to dapple the shaded understory with every-changing light. Hayward Flat is on the upper reaches of the Stuart Fork Arm of Trinity Lake. The firs, cedars, and pines that surround the campsites provide shade and homes for squirrels, jays, and nuthatches.

Similar to Hayward Flat, Alpine View Campground is across the bay on Guy Covington Road, just beyond the Bowerman boat ramp. Boaters and anglers both like to use Alpine View, because the ramp is normally open all year long.

Located on East Weaver Creek about five miles north of Weaverville, East Weaver Campground is closest to the town and its attractions, including the State Historical Park.

Below Trinity Dam on the Lewiston Reservoir, Ackerman Campground is at the north end of the lake, spread out over an open, rocky flat. Campsites are widely spaced under the sparse cover of oaks and pines. At the south end of the Lake, Mary Smith Campground attracts tent campers to stay at the very edge of the lake. Willows and cottonwoods mix with the firs at the margin of the water. Canoes and rowboats, along with inflatables, can be launched right from the campground.

One of the most attractive camping spots in the area is actually on neighboring Klamath National Forest, but just barely, and the road to it is entirely Shasta-Trinity. Consequently Big Flat Campground is administered by the Weaverville District. It's toward the very end of Coffee Creek Road adjacent to a meadow and the Salmon River. Ponderosa pines that surely challenge the largest of these trees anywhere are spaced widely across the flat. Pileated woodpeckers, America's largest, make their homes here among the snags, and their resounding "whacks" can be heard a long way as they make the bark fly in their search for supper.

On the river north of Trinity Lake, Trinity River Campground sits on the hillside, and campers can look out over the river to the tangled thicket in the floodplain beyond. As the sun starts down behind the Trinity Alps behind the camp, deer begin to make their way through the thickets to the water's edge.

Rush Creek, Bridge Camp, Goldfield, and Big Flat all serve as jumping off points for entry into the Trinity Alps Wilderness, as do Horse Flat and Scott Mountain. The Shasta-Trinity, like the Klamath and Modoc national forests, is a long way from the population centers of the west, and these campgrounds are seldom full, even on the busiest weekends.

Big Bar Ranger District Camping

Three of the Big Bar District's improved campgrounds are on tributaries of the main Trinity, and the rest on the big river itself. Ripstein Campground, on Canyon creek, is the most popular jumping off place for backpackers

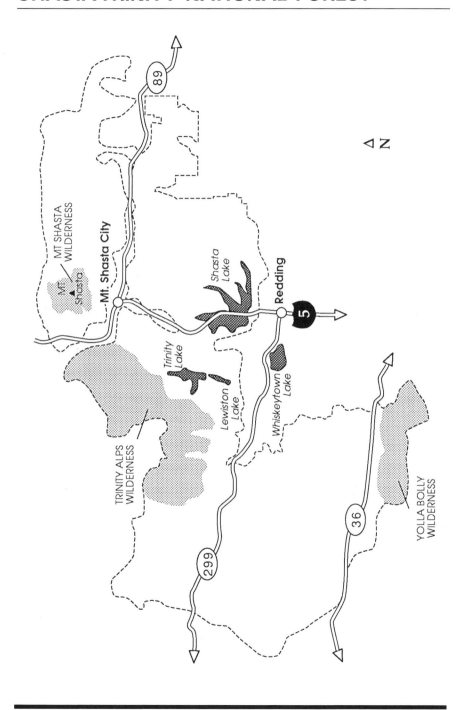

heading into the Trinity Alps. The canyon is steep-sided and rather narrow at the campground and the creek can be heard as it plunges down over the boulders in its bed.

Hobo Gulch Campground is on the North Fork of the Trinity, and like Ripstein, a famous starting point for trips into the wilderness. Equestrians and hunters use Hobo Gulch as a gathering place prior to forays into the backcountry. The campsites are strung out along the stream under firs and ponderosas, along with incense cedars and willows down close to the water. White-crowned and fox sparrows share the willows with Oregon juncos and yellow warblers.

Deep in the New River backcountry, Denny Campground waits for campers who want to try this new-old territory. Immense Douglas firs make up the bulk of the forest, but interspersed you'll find Pacific yew and madrones hidden away in the side canyons leading up from the river. Steelhead use much of the New River and its tributaries for spawning and rearing habitat, and native rainbows abound in both.

Along the main Trinity River, Big Flat, Burnt Ranch, and Pigeon Point campgrounds fill with overnighters late in the day during the summer season but could be almost empty in the middle of the day. All three are close to the river, and willows, oaks, and alders share the growing space with Douglas

Houseboats are a common sight on Shasta Lake.

firs. Ceanothus blooms blue for much of late spring and early summer all along the hillsides on the Big Bar District and east on the Weaverville District. Each of the main Trinity camps has its share of this exhuberant shrub.

Hayfork Ranger District Camping

Forest Glen and Hell Gate campgrounds are your best bets for access to the South Fork of the Trinity Wild and Scenic River. Both are in the little community of Forest Glen in the far southwest region of the forest. Hunters, anglers, berry pickers, hikers, in fact anyone who enjoys being out-of-doors without a lot of people around will enjoy these two sites. The river doesn't stop for any pauses, and its murmuring sound will lull you to sleep.

Other camping spots of the Hayfork District are at Big Slide Campground on the South Fork of the Trinity west of Hyampom, a steelheaders haven, and Philpot Campground, near the community of Peanut off Highway 3. Big Slide is one of the few access points for the Wild and Scenic South Fork and affords camp sites sheltered under Douglas firs, giant madrones, and bay trees. Lewis's woodpeckers have been spotted here, along with the more common acorn and downy woodpeckers, and trying to identify all of the different warblers that flit busily in and around the streamside shrubbery is lots of fun.

Yolla Bolly District Camping

At the extreme southern end of the Shasta-Trinity National Forest, Tomhead Saddle Campground serves as an entry point for the Yolla Bolly-Middle Eel Wilderness. Tomhead has corrals for horses, and equestrians heading for the Wilderness frequently use them. From Tomhead, high up on the slope of Tomhead Mountain, you have access to the Humbolt Trail, which will take you across the wilderness to the Kelsey Peaks on the boundary with Six Rivers National Forest.

Closer to the little town of Platina, where the district ranger station is located as two slightly larger units, Basin Gulch and Deerlick Springs campgrounds. Early season campers and deer hunters in the fall use both sites. From Deerlick Springs in the chaparral country, you can hike or ride into Chanchelulla Wilderness for a shot or two at a trophy blacktail.

On The Trail

There are more than 1,300 miles of trails on the Shasta-Trinity National Forest, and most of these are in the five wildernesses that bless the forest. Major hiking areas are on Mt. Shasta, around Shasta and Trinity lakes, and in the Trinity Alps Wilderness, along with trails that follow the major rivers and climb into the Yolla Bolly.

Pacific Crest Trail

Just over 150 miles of the Pacific Crest Trail are available to you on the forest The trial enters the forest on the northwest from Klamath National Forest and travels in a west to east direction through the Trinity Alps, Castle Crags State Park, and on to the McCloud Ranger District before leaving the forest near Lake Britton and MacArthur Burney Falls State Park. The elevations along this stretch of the trail range from 2,400 to 7,200 feet, and the scenery changes constantly as it crosses the forest. Mt. Shasta and Castle Crags dominate the view from many points along the way, and Mt. Lassen can frequently be seen.

Boaters enjoy Lewiston Lake for fun and fishing.

A section-by-section map of the PCT through the Shasta-Trinity is available from the forest showing access points, and explaining highlights of the trip.

National Recreation Trails
The two National Recreation Trails on the Shasta-Trinity National Forest are so different one from another that it's really worth trying them both

The Sisson-Callahan National Recreation Trail features spectacular mountain scenery along the entire route of its nine-mile length. Mt. Shasta rises to the east and Mt. Eddy to the north, and the southern horizon features the Castle Crags. From the final summit on the trail, the magnificent Trinity Alps rise in the west. The trail travels from the Parks Creek Summit high on the Trinity Divide to Lake Siskiyou just outside Mt. Shasta City on I-5. The first four miles of the trip are on the PCT from Parks Creek Summit to Deadfall Lakes, and from there it's all downhill to Lake Siskiyou. Spring hikers will probably run into some snow, and be able to smell the wild azaleas along the North Fork of the Sacramento River which the trail follows.

South Fork National Recreation Trail follows the South Fork of the Trinity River from Forest Glen upstream seven miles to the confluence with Smokey Creek under Chinquapin Butte. Douglas firs, giant ferns, alders and willows line the stream and golden-mantled ground squirrels and bright chipmunks scurry across your path as you go.

Shasta Lake Hiking Trails

The casual hiker will find a number of short trails at Shasta Lake. Many follow the shoreline offering plenty of opportunity for sightseeing as well as fishing. Three of these shoreline trails, Bailey Cove, Packers Bay, and Clikapudi, make loops and return to their original starting points. Of these, Bailey Cove is the shortest and easiest; Clikapudi requires at least a half day to complete.

At Hirz Bay, a trail connects Hirz Bay Campground with Dekkas Rock Picnic Area. It's an easy trail through lush growth of madrones, firs, pines, and ferns, and it especially pleasant to take on a warm evening or in the cool of the morning hours. Dead snags along the route are home to woodpeckers and raccoons.

The Clikapudi Trail passes through an area rich in Wintu Indian history. The name "Klukapusa" meaning "to kill" refers to a battle between the Indians and local traders. At Clikapudi Bay, excavations of a Wintu village site are visible—take only pictures, leave only footprints, please. Where the trail follows the edge of the water, there are places where you can fish, or just enjoy the view of the lake.

Trails on the Mt. Shasta District

Mt Shasta is a big mountain, and there are lots of places to walk, hike, or climb. But most people just drive up the Everitt Memorial Highway to Panther Meadow or Bunny Flat to start their treks. Consequently, to avoid the traffic, use one of the other trail heads. On the east side of the mountain, for example, you'll find the Brewer Creek and Clear Creek Trails. The Brewer Creek Trail provides access to the Wintun and Hotlum Glaciers on the northeast side of Mt. Shasta, while the Clear Creek Trail affords access to several outstanding waterfalls. Both give you the opportunity to explore the breathtaking subalpine environment.

From Highway 97 out of the city of Weed, you can get to four more trailheads, Black Lava, Graham Creek, Bolam and North Gate. From the Bolam trailhead, for example, you can get to Coquette Falls and Whitney Falls. The scenery includes Shasta red fir, whitebark pines, and hemlock.

If you plan to go all the way to the top of the mountain, make sure you register with the sheriff's office and with the Forest Service at the ranger station in Mt. Shasta City. In June and July, you'll be climbing over snow and ice, so crampons and ice axes are a necessity. Late in the year, most of your way will be over scree and rock. At any time of the year you have to watch the weather very closely. This mammoth of a mountain makes its own weather, and a perfectly clear day can give way to a blinding snowstorm without warning.

Another really interesting climb will take you to the top of Black Butte west of Mt. Shasta. From the 6,300-foot summit, you will get striking views of Mt. Shasta as well as the surrounding area, including Mt. McLaughlin's snow-covered volcanic cone in southern Oregon, the Klamath Mountains, and Mt. Eddy. This steep, nearly treeless dome of horneblende andesite was formed about 10,000 years ago, and the trail loops around from the bottom on the east to the north, west, and finally back to the east side again before reaching the top.

Trinity Alps Wilderness Hiking

The map of the Trinity Alps Wilderness produced by the Forest Service gets perfect marks. It's a contour map, so you'll know what kind of country you're getting into, it's on a very large scale, so details show up perfectly, and it has a list of the lakes on the wilderness and how to get to them.

The Trinity Alps Wilderness contains the headwaters of both the Trinity and Salmon rivers and several smaller rivers and creeks. High, jagged ridges with peaks ranging from 7,000 to 9,000 feet, deep water-and-wind carved canyons, and green meadows in glaciated alpine cirques are features of the wilderness. Wildflowers abound. Tiger lilies, pitcher plants, columbines, shooting stars, and bleeding hearts turn moist spots into a riot of color. After the first frosts of fall the big leaf and vine maples, the various oaks, and dogwood turn brilliant yellows and reds. Some say this is the best time of the year to be here.

The eastern half of the wilderness contains almost all of the lakes and high, glaciated peaks, while the western half tends to be more rounded and forested. Consequently, the eastern part receives more visitors by far than the western part. The wild, rugged and remote New River drainage accounts for much of the western portion of the wilderness and can be accessed from trailheads near Denny. This is the part of the wilderness to get into if it's solitude that you're looking for. Hunters, especially, will enjoy this "wild west." Both deer and bear hunters are successful each fall in bringing home their quarry.

Yolla Bolly District Hiking Trails

The northern extremes of the Yolla Bolly-Middle Eel Wilderness extend into the southern portions of the Shasta-Wilderness extend into the southern portions of the Shasta-Trinity on the Yolla Bolly Ranger District, and some excellent early season hiking can be had here in almost complete solitude. This least-used of all parts of the forest will reward you with views out over the Sacramento Valley, to Mt. Shasta and Mt. Lassen, and with close-up views of foxtail pines as well as more common western white pines and Jeffreys. Black Rock and Yolla Bolly Lakes and several springs along the trails are the only source of water. Any time you go into this country, you'll have to take your own drinking water or a water purifier.

Castle Crags and Chanchelulla Wildernesses

Castle Crags Wilderness lies adjacent to Castle Crags State Park just west of I-5 and contains a twelve-mile section of the Pacific Crest Trail within its boundaries. You can access the trail where it crosses the interstate, or by a side trail from the State Park.

The **Chanchelulla Wilderness** has limited maintained trails, although deer hunters and others make their way into the region by way of Deerlick Springs as well as from a series of jeep roads around its perimeter.

Touring, Sightseeing and Special Programs

There is so much to see on this huge forest that it will take a lot more than one trip to visit it all. One long automobile drive has been designated a "Scenic Byway" and another is being nominated by the forest. The first of these circumnavigates Mt. Shasta, and the second takes you on a tour from Weaverville to Weed via Trinity Lake and the Trinity Divide.

Every view you get of Mt. Shasta while driving around its base is different. There are five glaciers at the top, and you can sometimes distinguish them from the ordinary snowfields by the rough-appearing areas and cracks running across them. Some of the sights you'll see on this drive aren't visible any other way. For example, "the Whale Back," a volcanic cone northeast of the mountain, sticks up from the surrounding flat forest like an intruder—which it is. Its clinkery surface contrasts sharply with the juniper and manzanita that surrounds its base. Get the printed interpretive sheet "Around the Mountain" at either the McCloud or Mt. Shasta Ranger District office.

The other route proposed for Scenic Byway status leaves the gold rush community of Weaverville northbound on Highway 3. You'll drive through miles of Douglas fir and ponderosa forests laced with ceanothus blooming a brilliant blue before arriving at Trinity Lake's Stuart Fork Arm. The highway dips down to the lake and then away from it until you reach Trinity Center. Beyond Trinity Center, the road follows the lake shore where remains of mining activity is visible all around you. Giant piles of boulders moved by the dredges to get at the gold under them remind you of the tremendous and prodigious labors of Heracles the miners had to go through.

The road climbs steeply toward the top of Scott Mountain, but before you reach that point, you turn right on Primary Forest Route 17 which follows up the Trinity River and finally crosses the divide at Parks Creek Summit, before dropping swiftly down to I-5 just north of Weed.

Other interesting drives on the forest include following Highway 299 down the Trinity River to Burnt Ranch, and Highway 89 from Mt. Shasta City to Lake Britton and MacArthur Burney Falls State Park.

The most diverse and least visited of those places in California that have been volcanically active in historical times is the **Medicine Lake Highlands Volcanic Area** in the far northeast section of Shasta-Trinity National Forests and adjacent portions of Modoc and Klamath National Forests. A drive through this unique region will expose you to all kinds of volcanic formations: Glass and lava flows, pumice deposits, lava tubes, ice caves, cinder cones, spatter cones, craters and faults. Get the "Visitor Guide. . . Medicine Lake Highlands Volcanic Area" from the ranger station in McCloud and take this drive.

Sightseeing at Shasta Lake

Most of the sightseeing around Shasta Lake is best done by boat, but there are some roads, too, that make it a paradise for explorers. The four major arms of the lake offer wondrous scenery as well as unusual geological and historic areas of interest.

The dam, itself, is the first thing to see. From I-5 it's a short drive west to the damsite. Here a visitor center contains everything you'll ever want to know about the dam and its construction and purpose. The modern center contains a theater where a film about the dam and the Central Valley Project, of which it's a part, is shown on demand. Before the film is shown, you are seated facing an immense glass wall through which the dam, the lake and the mountain are all visible—The Three Shastas.

Two limestone caves are open for you to visit at the Lake. First is **Shasta Caverns** on private property, where tours are offered year round. The second is **Samwel Cave** high up on one arm of the lake. It takes a little exploring on your part to find.

To minimize vandalism to the cave the Forest Service maintains a locked gate across the entrance to the rear portions. A free permit and key is available at the Shasta Lake Ranger Station in Mountain Gate—next to I-5. Because of the extremely dangerous passages in the cave, the Forest Service advises that you never attempt exploration without highly experienced spelunkers as your guides.

Campers at Ski Island Campground on Shasta Lake. Royal Mannion photo.

The cave is believed to have been sacred to the Wintu, and the approach is over limestone rocks which have been metamorphosed into marble. Thus the approach to the cave is over a marble path, much like the approach to the sacred Oracle of Delphi in Greece, half a world away.

Besides caves, there are the remains of old mining towns to be explored around the lake. The town of Delamar and the Bully Hill Mine rests halfway up the Squaw Creek Arm, and boaters have the easiest approach to it. A jeep road will take you there, too, from the Fenders Ferry Road northeast of the lake.

A two page interpretive brochure is available from the visitor center which contains directions for finding all kinds of things along the four major arms of the lake.

Sightseeing and Programs at Trinity Lake

Interpretive campfire programs are scheduled by the Forest Service each weekend at Tannery Gulch and Hayward Flat campgrounds. In addition, each Wednesday during the summer season, at the historical Bowerman Barn, you can have a chance to experience a part of Trinity County history. The barn is a 110-year-old hand-crafted relic now on the National Register of Historic Places. A thirty-minute tour will show you how the barn was used in the early days, and some of the details of its construction.

The **Trinity River Fish Hatchery**, located immediately below Lewiston Dam, was built to help compensate for the loss of spawning grounds when the two dams were built. Today, the hatchery produces about 40 million fingerling and yearling salmon and steelhead each year. Drive up the right-hand side of Trinity River from the bridge below the dam and tour the hatchery. Millions of little fish will follow you as you walk along the rearing ponds expecting a hand-out.

Historic Weaverville is worth spending a day to look around. The Jack Jackson Museum in town has a fine collection of items and photographs depicting the growth of northern California. The Trinity County Historical Society keeps the museum open during the summer months and over Easter vacation. The **Joss House** in Weaverville is the oldest continuously operated Chinese temple in the New World. Now a State Historical Park, although still used for worship, guided tours are available all year round.

Sports

Boating, including whitewater rafting and kayaking, and fishing and hunting are the major sports on the Shasta-Trinity National Forest. Lake Shasta and Trinity Lake attract boaters and water skiers from all over the west. A wonderful brochure, paid for by the Whiskeytown Natural History Association, called "Sightseeing on Shasta Lake (and Some Underwater History About It)" should be read by everyone who launches a boat on the lake. You can pick one up at the Forest Service Visitor Center on I-5.

Other brochures and maps available here give lists of marinas and launch ramps, motels, campgrounds, stores, and restaurants around the lake—too many to include here. Similar kinds of information regarding the Trinity Lake vicinity can be picked up at information stations around the lake.

Other lakes on the Forest also offer boating of various kinds. McCloud Lake provides room to water-ski early in the season and outstanding trout fishing. Whiskeytown Lake, outside the Forest also has room for water skiers and speedboats, too.

Houseboating is a favorite vacation on both Trinity and Shasta Lakes, and lists of houseboat rentals can be obtained from Lake Shasta Infromation Center, 6547 Holiday Road, Redding, CA 96003, or Trinity County Chamber of Commerce, P.O. Box 517, Weaverville.

There is one alpine ski resort on Mt. Shasta, **Mt. Shasta Ski Park**, and another in the planning stage. Two chairs serve fifteen runs at the ski park.

Cross-country ski enthusiasts have lots of room to roam on the forest, especially on the Mt. Shasta, McCloud, and Weaverville ranger districts. Nordic skiers are free to go anywhere they want on the forest, of course, but rangers have made an attempt to describe some of the best places to ski.

On Mt. Shasta, three ungroomed trails have been specifically marked for beginners and intermediate skiers just off the Everitt Memorial Highway.

Castle Lake Cross Country Ski Area, on the Castle Lake Road, has access to about thirty miles of groomed trails with routes for every degree of skill.

On the Weaverville District, rangers have identified eighteen trails near Trinity Lake and the Trinity Alps for Nordic enthusiasts, ranging from very easy to very difficult.

Off Highway Vehicle travel

Except for the wilderness areas and the Pacific Crest Trail, jeepers and trail bikers have hundreds of miles of forest roads on which to roam. A free map is available from the Shasta-Trinity, which describes the full ranges of OHV opportunities.

Forest roads are sometimes closed to public use to prevent rutting of soft roadbeds during wet weather; to reduce disturbance to wildlife species during critical periods; to insure public safety and other national forest management requirements. Such closures are indicated by posted signs or gates.

Both Yolla Bolly and Hayfork Districts have routes that OHVs like to use. **Bear Wallow Meadow** region and **Pine Root Springs** area both give drivers a wide variety of roads to explore. Both areas are available from Highway 36 which crosses the southern end of the forest.

In the north, primitive roads and trails radiate from Iron Canyon Reservoir northeast of Shasta Lake. Many are suited only for four-wheelers and offer numerous opportunities for challenging extended loop trips. Deadlum campground at the lake can be used as a headquarters while you explore the surrounding mountains and canyons.

On both the Mt. Shasta and Shasta Lake Ranger Districts, OHVs have to watch carefully for sections of private property that checkerboard much of these districts. Further, the forest doesn't put up road signs on private holdings, so be especially alert and carry a good map if there's a chance you'll be driving off the forest.

Fishing and Hunting

Deer hunting accounts for a high number of visitor days on the Forest, especially on the McCloud Ranger District. Lots of hunters want to get a "lava buck," and the rolling country east of Mt. Shasta is one of the best places in the state to get one.

Other favorite hunting sports are in the Trinity Alps Wilderness, especially the western, or New River, portion.

A number of bears are bagged each year on the Shasta-Trinity, mostly on the Big Bar and Hayfork Districts near the western edge of the forest. Because the territory is so rough, most successful bear hunters use dogs to locate and chase down their quarry.

Pigeon Point, Junction City, and high mountain saddles provide challenging pass shooting opportunities for the shotgun enthusiast who wants to pursue the hard-to-get band-tailed pigeon.

The fishing on the forest probably attracts more sports enthusiasts than any other. Shasta, Trinity, and Lewiston Lakes are literally filled with fish—trout, bass, kokanee, and some pan fish are regularly included in the catches brought ashore at these big impoundments.

Hundreds of miles of clear, cold running streams provide anglers with the opportunity to hook into salmon, steelhead, and several kinds of trout. Especially good are the Lower McCloud and Upper Sacramento rivers.

Whitewater Rafting and Kayaking

Nine outfitters have permits to guide whitewater trips on the forest. Favorite runs are on the Upper Sacramento from Sims Flat campground downstream to Lake Shasta, and on the Trinity River almost its entire length on the Forest. Like the Klamath River to the north, the main stem of the Trinity has controlled flow and consequently offers year long whitewater and a full range of rapids from expert to inner tubers.

Rafters and kayakers also like to take on the Lower McCloud River early in the year when the water is high enough, although there are no outfitters on this river. The McCloud below McCloud Dam runs through many miles of private land, but there's just enough Forest Service land to provide camping spots. The Upper McCloud, fed by extensive springs, offers year round white water boating from Lower Falls at Fowler's Camp to McCloud Reservoir. Check with the rangers at the town of McCloud before you attempt these.

SHASTA-TRINITY NATIONAL FOREST CAMPGROUNDS

	Piped Water	Camp Sites	Trailer Space	Fishing	Boating	Swimming	Store	RV Dump Station	Reservations	Special Attractions
Big Bar Ranger District										
Big Bar	•	3		•			•			
Big Flat	•	10	•	•						
Burnt Ranch	•	16	•	•			•			
Denny	•	16	•	•						
Hayden Flat	•	35	•	•		•	•			
Hobo Gulch		10		•						
Pigeon Point		10	•	•	•					
Ripstein		10		•						
Hayfork Ranger District										
Big Slide	•	8		•						
Forest Glen	•	16		•			•			
Hell Gate	•	17	•	•			•			16' trailer
Philpot	•	10					•			
McCloud Ranger District										
Ah-Di-Nah	•	16		•						PCT Trailhead
Algoma		8	•	•						
Cattle Camp		11	•	•						
Fowler's Camp	•	39	•	•						
Harris Springs	•	15	•							
Mt. Shasta Ranger District										
Castle Lake		6		•	•	•				
McBride Springs	•	9								10' trailer

SHASTA-TRINITY NATIONAL FOREST CAMPGROUNDS

	Piped Water	Camp Sites	Trailer Space	Fishing	Boating	Swimming	Store	RV Dump Station	Reservations	Special Attractions
Panther Meadows		4	•							16' trailer
Sims Flat	•	17	•	•	•					
Toad Lake Walk-in		6								¼ mile hike
Shasta Lake Ranger District										
Antlers	•	41	•	•	•	•	•			
Bailey Cove	•	15	•	•	•	•				16' trailer
Deadlun	•	30	•	•	•	•				
Ellery Creek	•	15	•	•	•	•				
Gregory Creek	•	16	•	•	•	•				
Hirz Bay	•	38	•	•	•	•				
Lakeshore East	•	23	•	•	•	•	•			
Lower Jones Valley	•	14	•	•	•	•				
Madrone		13	•	•	•					16' trailer
McCloud Bridge	•	20	•	•	•	•				16' trailer
Moore Creek	•	12	•	•	•	•				
Nelson Point	•	8	•	•	•	•				16' trailer
Pine Point	•	21	•	•	•	•				
Upper Jones Valley	•	13	•	•	•	•				
Weaverville Ranger District										
Ackerman	•	66	•	•	•	•	•	•		
Alpine View	•	66	•	•	•	•				
Big Flat		5		•						
Bridge Camp	•	10		•						corrals
Clear Creek		8	•	•						22' trailer
Cooper Gulch		9	•	•						16' trailer
Eagle Creek	•	17	•	•						
East Weaver	•	15		•						16' trailer
Goldfield		6		•						
Hayward Flat	•	94	•	•	•	•				
Horse Flat		16		•						
Jackass Springs	•	21	•	•	•	•				
Mary Smith	•	18		•	•	•				
Minersville	•	21	•	•						18' trailer
Preacher Meadow	•	45	•	•						
Scott Mountain		7								PCT Trailhead
Stoney Point	•	22		•	•	•				
Tannery Gulch	•	83	•	•	•	•			•	
Trinity River	•	7	•	•						
Tunnel Rock		6		•	•	•				

SHASTA-TRINITY NATIONAL FOREST CAMPGROUNDS

Yolla Bolly Ranger District	Piped Water	Camp Sites	Trailer Space	Fishing	Boating	Swimming	Store	RV Dump Station	Reservations	Special Attractions
Basin Gulch	•	16	•	•						
Beegum Gorge		3		•						
Deerlick Springs	•	15	•							
N. Fork Beegum		3		•						
Tomhead Saddle		5								
White Rock	•	3								

SIX RIVERS
NATIONAL
FOREST

Sacramento

San Francisco

Los Angeles

Six Rivers National Forest

This long, narrow forest in the far northwestern corner of California is the newest of all the State's National Forests. It gets its name from six of the mighty north coast salmon and steelhead streams, the Smith, Klamath, Trinity, Van Dusen, Mad, and Eel rivers. It stretches from the Oregon border south for more than 140 miles along the west slopes of the Coast Ranges a few miles inland from the coastal state and national redwood parks.

Covered from head to toe in dense forests of Douglas fir, and shrouded in mists and fog much of the year, it's an ideal vacation place for those who like to spend time away from the hurried pace of civilization.

Because it is so near the moderating influence of the ocean, the Forest has a mild climate, and at least one of the campgrounds in each of the ranger districts is open all year long.

Camping

All of the campgrounds on the Smith River National Recreation Area are on the main (Middle) fork of the Smith River on Highway 199 from Crescent City, California to Grants Pass, Oregon, except **Big Flat** Campground on the South Fork. This rustic spot serves as a staging point for kayaking trips on the South Fork, hiking trips on the South Kelsey National Historical Trail, and fishing the South Fork and its tributaries.

The use of the campgrounds along the Smith River generally falls into a pattern of overnight occupation by travelers from Oregon and California. During the summer season, the sites will often be almost empty at high noon, but full to overflowing by nightfall. **Grassy Flat, Panther Flat**, and **Patrick Creek** campgrounds are close to the river on benches that provide sites high above the stream.

The Smith is the "crown jewel" of the forest, and camping along its banks is reason enough to stay here. Camping is in a mixed forest with Douglas firs, madrones, and oaks. The trees are close enough to each other that privacy in the campground is assured. Hawks, especially the redtail and the kestral, dominate the skies over the Smith, and in the underbrush you can spot Bewick's wrens, golden-crowned kinglets, vireos, and several different warblers.

Orleans Ranger District

The pattern of use for the Orleans Ranger District is just about the opposite of the Smith River National Recreation Area and Lower Trinity Districts. This is a region for anglers who come to the forest to stay for the steelhead and salmon on the Klamath River.

Unique is **Aikens Creek** Campground, about six miles east of Weitchpec. Both Aikens Creek and **Bluff Creek** campgrounds a mile upstream have fourteen-day camping limits from the first of August through the middle of October. Otherwise, there aren't any limits.

The campground at **Fish Lake**, just north of Aikens Creek, provides good lake access for anglers in the early season. The Forest Service has built

An environmental education weekend for kids on Fish Lake in the Orleans Ranger District includes a fishing derby and campout. Stephanie Gomes photo.

wheelchair access for fishing here, and handicapped campers are urged to take advantage of it. There are partially wheelchair accessible camp sites at Aikens Creek. Both Aikens Creek and Bluff Creek campgrounds are in low elevations—below 1,000 feet—and the forest cover is made up of Douglas firs, ponderosa pines, madrones and canyon live oaks. The Klamath flows by the camps, and this big river, the largest on the north coast, has the highest catch each year for both steelhead and salmon. The camps at Fish Lake offer magnificent views out over the lake and to the surrounding tree-covered ridges. It's not a highly used camping place, and with very little effort you can get off by yourself to enjoy the forest.

Lower Trinity Ranger District

On the Lower Trinity District, as on the Smith River National Recreation Area, most of the campsites are used by overnighters traveling along Highway 299 to and from the Sacramento Valley, and in the fall by anglers. In the summer season, they are full frequently at night, but if you arrive during the middle of the day, you will just about have your choice of sites.

This is especially true for two of the very pretty campgrounds, **Boise Creek** and **Grays Falls**, which are both just off Highway 299. Boise Creek has special units for the physically challenged, cyclists, and hikers. The campground is on a bluff overlooking Willow Creek in a mixed growth of ponderosa pines, Douglas firs, madrones and oaks. Some of the madrones have been there

SIX RIVERS NATIONAL FOREST

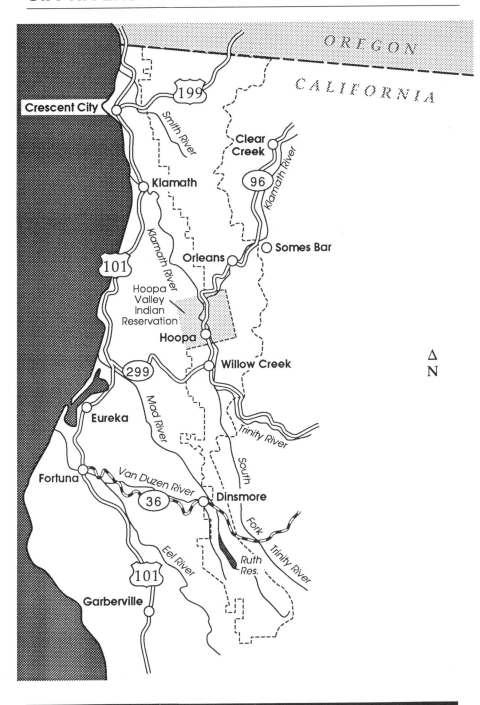

a long time and are probably two feet in diameter at chest height, among the largest anywhere. Huckleberry lovers come to Boise creek to gather their favorite berries for pies and jams every fall.

Grays Falls Campground is at a slightly higher altitude—just over 1,000 feet—than the others along the river, and the forest is not quite as thick, giving a more savannah-like appearance to the campground and surrounding area. Like Boise Creek, Grays Falls has units for the physically challenged. In addition, there is a mile-long nature trail. Grays Falls is a favorite camping place for salmon anglers each fall and winter. In the summer, rafters, kayakers, and float-tubers splash in the warm season pools.

Tish Tang Campground is north of the town of Willow Creek along Highway 96, just at the edge of the Hoopa Indian Reservation. This is an angler's campground, and a berry picker's paradise. The units are tucked away beneath branches in shady glens, making camping cool and sheltered on all but the hottest September days.

A campground host will greet you in all three of these campgrounds. They'll know where to fish and what to use when the big ones are hitting. They're knowledgeable about the region, too, and can answer your questions about the history—both human and natural—of the Trinity River country.

Mad River Ranger District

Little-visited Mad River Ranger District has a beautiful forest environment with spectacular views, wilderness lands, hiking trails, and excellent fishing, boating, camping, and hunting.

The national forest operates three campgrounds on the district, and the Ruth Lake Community Services District two more. On the Mad River itself is **Mad River** Campground. Open year round, this site is on the Mad River halfway between Highway 36 and Ruth Reservoir. Smaller than the Klamath or Smith, the Mad is nevertheless a great fishing stream, and summer trout fishermen, as well as steelheaders enjoy this region. At 2,500 feet, this campground spreads out along the banks of the river under a canopy of tall ponderosas.

On Ruth Reservoir, the two Forest Service campgrounds are operated very differently. **Fir Cove** Campground is for group camping *only* from mid-May through mid-October, and you can reserve sites for your family and friends through the Mad River District Office in Brideville. Fridays, Saturdays, and Sundays, the sites are for single family use.

Bailey Canyon Campground, also on the shores of Ruth Reservoir, is for family camping and opens mid-May each year, closing down about the middle of October. Both Fir Cove and Bailey Canyon campgrounds are located near the water, and Bailey Canyon has restroom facilities for the phscially challenged. The parking spurs are probably the most level of any on the Forest, and are ideal for trailers to twenty-two feet, even though narrow and steep Highway 36 makes it tough to haul a trailer to the lake.

On The Trail

Partly because of its long, narrow shape, and partly because its more famous neighbors to the east take much of the crowds, a lot of the Six Rivers National Forest's 200 miles of developed trails are vacant much of the time. For a weekend getaway, the forest offers opportunities on each of its four Districts for hikers to spend some quiet time in pondering the ills of civilization.

National Recreation Trails

High in the Trinity Alps Wilderness east of Hoopa Valley Indian Reservation, you'll come across **Horse Trail Ridge National Recreation Trail**. It offers marvelous scenery of valleys, meadows, rock outcroppings, and peaks of northern California's Salmon Mountains. There are perennial streams, conifer forests, and some steep going. The trails's history goes back some 4,000 years, and Indians, gold miners, and ranchers have used the trail as an important route. You can access it from Hawkins Bar on Highway 299, and from Hoopa Valley via Forest Roads 8NO1 and 10NO2.

In the same general area is the **Salmon Summit National Recreation Trail**. This trail is eighteen miles southeast of Orleans, and leads to Redcap Lake, popular for its fishing, and the Trinity Alps Wilderness. Beginning at 5,200 feet, it follows ridgeline open to long, sweeping views of the Salmon Mountains. There are lots of deer in the area and the quiet hiker may be rewarded with sight of a pine marten.

Third of three National Recreation Trails on the Six Rivers is **South Kelsey National Historical Trail**. This 16.5-mile trail is the remains of an historical route that joined Crescent City on the coast with Fort Jones in Siskiyou County. The Purpose of the trail was to supply the army post at Fort Jones, constructed in 1851. Eventually, much of the gold mined in the Fort Jones area was shipped over this trail to be sent by boat to San Francisco and the rest of the world. The first seven miles of the trail follow the Wild and Scenic South Fork of the Smith River. It is covered in old-growth Douglas fir, with scattered tanoak and madrones. As it climbs to the forest boundary above Harrington Lake, the route passes through cool forests of tall pines and firs, alternating with green meadows and chaparral. Finally breaking out on the west aspect of Baldy Peak, you'll be rewarded with a 360-degree panoramic view from the Pacific Ocean to the rugged Siskiyou mountain backbone.

Smith River National Recreation Area Hiking Trails

This ranger district has many miles of hiking trails to choose from, ranging from easy one-day hikes to the more challenging ones into the Siskiyou wilderness. An information sheet, "Gasquet R.D. Forest Trail Guide," can be obtained at the office at Gasquet. It lists nineteen trails that can be accessed on the district.

Among the most exciting of the trails is the backpackers' loop involving the **Boundary, Summit Valley**, and **South Kelsey trails**. Access is near Buck Creek Camp south of Big Flat on the South Fork of the Smith, and hikers get an interesting variety of terrain to experience. There will be craggy, steep peaks above you as you cross forested ridges, and hike along Harrington Creek and the swift waters of the South Fork of the Smith. Harrington Lake, Buck Camp Ridge, Sawtooth Mountain, and Chimney Rock are landmarks on this thirty-five-mile loop through the Siskiyou Wilderness.

One of the very best day-hikes on the Smith River National Recreation Area is the **Myrtle Creek Trail**. This nature trail follows the creek northward from Highway 199 for a mile from the hamlet of Hiouchi. The region is arresting to botanists and nature lovers because its location is almost exactly at the edge of the fog-dominated coastal weather and the interior weather. Consequently, the plant species that occur along the trail are a brilliant mixture of types adapted to both climates. Thirteen different trees, six different ferns, and twenty-five distinct shrubs and vines have been identified. A checklist

A ranger working on a reforestation project.

of the plants along the trail can be obtained at the Smith River National Recreation Area office.

Lower Trinity District Hiking Trails
   Much of the walking on the Lower Trinity District is in what's called the "Trinity Summit High Country." The Trinity Alps Wilderness and adjacent areas east of the Hoopa Valley Indian Reservation are interlaced with trails, some them left-overs from pre-wilderness times. Trails in the area are challenging and worthy of adventure. Climbing in and out of the headwaters of three creeks, **Tish Tang, Horse Linto**, and **Mill**, they lead to summer trout fishing and fall deer and bear hunting. Personnel at Lower Trinity Ranger Station will point you in the right direction for these trailheads.

Mad River District Hiking Trails
   There are angler's streamside trails along most of the tributaries of the Mad and Van Dusen rivers on the Mad River District. However, on many of the district trails, hikers and off-highway vehicle operators have to share the right-of-way. For hikers only, the trails in the Yolla Bolly-Middle Eel Wilderness can be accessed from Jones Ridge Road (FR 27N02) about 12 miles upstream from Ruth Reservoir. This is deer country; south-facing slopes that grow little or no timber. Instead, grass, manzanita, and scrub oak dominate. North Fork

Wilderness, in the same general area, is similar, and like the Yolla Bolly attracts many deer hunters each fall.

Touring, Sightseeing, and Special Programs

For hikers, there are two or three really special areas on the Six Rivers National Forest. Deep in the Mad River Ranger District, is the proposed **Lassic Botanical Area**. Follow County Road 511 south from the Mad River Ranger station to FR 1S07 which climbs the ridge west between Black Lassic and Shanty creeks into what at first looks like an alpine area at much too low an altitude. Bent and twisted trees, and bare rock make it seem like timberline in the Trinities. However, the cause is serpentine rock and soil, which lacks nourishment and causes dwarfing in plants, especially pines. The walking is easy, and you'll find yourself at the top of Black Lassic Peak in no time. Around you, the bare serpentine soils have had their effect on all of the plant life, making it appear shriveled and twisted. These serpentine soils are extremely erosive, so tread lightly when visiting this unique area.

Bear Basin Butte, near the Siskiyou wilderness on the Smith River NRA will be designated a "Botanical Area," too, to help preserve the native plants, especially the firs—noble, red, and white—as well as wild flowers such as the trillium, golden buckwheat, wild parsley, and lupine. Take FR 17N05 south from Highway 199 upstream from Patrick Creek directly to Bear Basin.

While you're at Patrick Creek, look for a new nature trail along the Middle Fork of the Smith where a lot of fish habitat work has been done to improve fishing on the river.

If you walk up **Bluff Creek** from the Klamath river for a couple of miles, you'll come to Wright Ranch. Here, members of the Karuk Tribe working with the State Department of Fish and Game, have been working to improve salmon fishing in Bluff Creek. Through a process known as "imprinting," where water from Bluff Creek was washed over the salmon eggs before they hatched at a hatchery, the memory of "Bluff Creek" was imprinted in the fishes' make-up, and for the first time in more than twenty years there's a run of salmon in Bluff Creek.

Bluff Creek has another claim to fame, too. It was here that the first reported sighting of "Big Foot"—California's Sasquatch—took place, so look sharp when you're on the trail around here. Be especially careful just at dusk, for this is the time of day when Big Foot roams the shadowy depths of the forest.

For these of you who like automobile touring, the Six Rivers has some great routes. On the Lower Trinity District, the rangers have described four tours for Autumn color. Black oak, Oregon oak, big leaf maple, vine maple, dogwood, and poison oak all grow in abundance in the region. Some of the drives are as short as a half hour, some as long as a half day. One of the most interesting is the Waterman Ridge and Grove Prairie trip. From Willow Creek, you drive north on Patterson Road to FR 7N02. Travel east and south to FR 7N04 to Grove Prairie. The return is via FR 7N04 to Highway 299 above Salyer.

A long and scenic trip is to take County Road 1 south from Berry Summit on Highway 299. The road will take you circling to the top of Last Chance Ridge and South Fork Mountain and finally hitting Highway 36 near Mad River Ranger Station. South Fork Mountain, incidentally, is the highest continuous ridge in the United States. You'll reach an altitude of 5,800 feet at Blake Mountain, and be able to see east into the Hayfork region of Trinity National Forest

The Six Rivers National Forest gets its name from six major salmon and steelhead streams which cut through it to the Pacific Ocean.

and beyond. Clear days will bring mighty snow-covered Mt. Shasta into focus far across the intervening ranges and valleys. The canyon of the South Fork of the Trinity River will be right below you, and the shining peaks of the Trinity Alps will mark the northeastern horizon.

The Six Rivers National Forest is one of the very few in the state that offer Christmas tree cutting permits. They cost $5 and each person is allowed one per household. Families by the thousands come into the forest just after Thanksgiving to get their trees, and youngsters and oldsters alike have a great time picking and cutting just the right tree.

Sports

Horse Mountain, just inside the forest east of Eureka, attracts cross-country skiers to its snowy slopes and trails. The high points of all the major roads and highways get their share of Nordic skiers whenever conditions permit. The best cross-country region of the forest is along South Fork Mountain. It can be accessed by Highway 36 from either Mad River Ranger Station, or Berry Summit on Highway 299.

There aren't any specified snowmobile areas, but miles of unplowed forest roads criss-cross the forest, and unless specifically shut down, are open for you to use.

Boating and Water Skiing

Boating as such is mostly confined to the larger streams such as the Klamath and the Trinity where anglers search for steelhead and salmon, although Ruth Reservoir is becoming popular for both sailing and water skiing despite the difficulties in towing a boat up there.

However, rafting in all its dimensions, including kayaking and inner-tubing, is rapidly gaining the status of major sport along all of the "Six." Perhaps one of the wildest experiences in white water in the state is on the **South Fork** of the **Smith**. Kayakers put in at Big Flat campground and go crashing down to the junction with the Middle Fork at Hiouchi. Although the road parallels the river the whole time, it doesn't affect the white water, and the experience is for good kayakers only; it's not a beginner run.

For some easier and more family-oriented rafting, the **Klamath** and **Salmon rivers** are very popular, as are the main and south forks of the **Trinity River**. Trips on both of these streams begin in neighboring Klamath or Shasta-Trinity National Forest and continue into the Six Rivers.

On the Trinity River near the town of Willow Creek, many summer visitors enjoy innertubing. The put-in point is near the community of Salyer. Entire families come scooting down the stream, having a great time. Water fights are the order of the day. The Trinity in this section is basically a beginners river, with most of the water being class I and II. The three-hour run from Salyer to Wiillow Creek, for example, has only one Class II rapid, with all the rest Class I.

Off Highway Motoring

Almost all off-highway motoring on the Six Rivers is carried on in association with deer hunting. Hunters use the rough forest roads to get away from the busy highways and points of civilization. There are some designated routes on the Mad River District to the north of Mad River Ranger Station. These are easy routes, and good for learning the skills required for off-highway driving. **Pilot Creek** and **Skull Camp trails** are two of the best.

Fishing and Hunting

The Six Rivers National Forest straddles the six best steelhead and salmon streams in California, with only the Sacramento River and its tributaries offering competition. Among these, the Klamath sees the most fish caught. There are licensed guides who will take you on the river, and while they won't guarantee a catch, it's surely the best way to put the odds in your favor.

Several of the small lakes in off-the-beaten-track locations offer good fishing for trout, especially early in the season. Among them are **Island** and **Harrington Lakes** in the Siskiyou Wilderness; **Fish, Twin**, and **Red Mountain Lakes** on the Orleans Ranger District; and several just over the boundary on Klamath National Forest that are easiest to reach from the Six Rivers side.

Hunting

Deer and bear hunting make up most of the big game hunting on the Six Rivers National Forest, and hunters are quite successful each year, with a larger-than-state-average record for number of kills to number of licenses sold ratio.

Best record for deer comes from the Mad River District, especially along **South Fork Mountain**, and in both the Yolla Bolly-Middle Eel and the North Fork wildernesses. The South Fork Mountain area is most popular because of its accessibility, while the wildernesses necessitate pack animals to set up a deer camp and to haul out your buck.

Hot spots for bear hunters are farther north, and what was a hot spot one year may be empty the next. Personnel at Smith River NRA and Orleans ranger stations can usually tell you where you're most likely to have some success with brother bruin.

SIX RIVERS NATIONAL FOREST CAMPGROUNDS

	Piped Water	Camp Sites	Trailer Space	Fishing	Boating	Swimming	Store	RV Dump Station	Reservations	Special Attractions
Smith River NRA										
Big Flat		30	•	•						
Grassy Flat	•	19	•	•						
Panther Flat	•	42	•	•						
Patrick Creek	•	17	•	•						
Lower Trinity Ranger District										
Boise Creek	•	16	•	•						
Grays Falls	•	33	•	•						
Tish Tang	•	40	•	•						
Mad River Ranger District										
Bailey Canyon	•	23	•	•	•	•				
Fir Cove Family Group	•	21		•	•	•			•	Reservations through Mad River Ranger Station
Mad River	•	40	•	•						
Orleans Ranger District										
Aikens Creek	•	29	•	•						
Bluff Creek	•	11	•	•						
Fish Lake	•	23	•	•						
Pearch Creek	•	11	•	•						

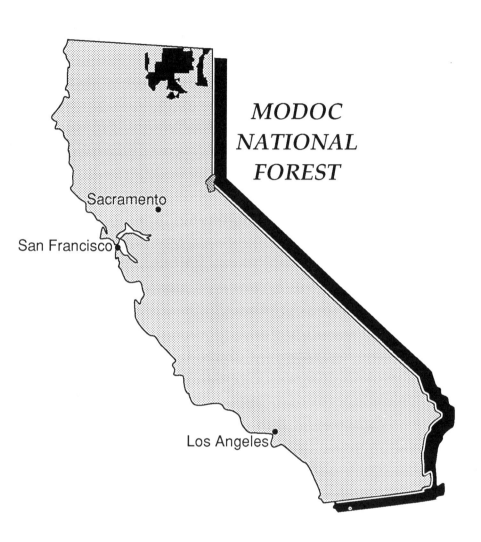

MODOC
NATIONAL
FOREST

Sacramento

San Francisco

Los Angeles

Modoc National Forest

The Modoc National Forest is California's most remote in terms of distance from larger centers of population. Located in the northeastern corner of the state, it's about a three-hour drive from Reno, Nevada, on Highway 395 and about the same distance from Redding, California, on Highway 299.

The forest is bordered on the east by a spur of the Cascades known as the Warner Range, and to the west by a plateau region of forest and meadows, western juniper timber, lakes, rolling hills, lava beds, and open range land.

The forest was the scene of many bloody wars between settlers and Native Americans. The most famous was the Modoc War of 1873, which took place in the northwestern part of the forest and the Lava Beds National Monument. Although it seems tiny, even insignificant, with its eighty-nine killed and only a few hundred wounded, the six-month war virtually ended the 10,000-year-old Modoc civilization, one of the oldest cultures documented by archaeologists in North America.

Camping

There are twenty developed campgrounds on the forest with a total of 277 individual campsites. Of these, almost half are at Blue Lake in the South Warner Range or at Medicine Lake. These are the only ones on the forest where fees are charged. The four campgrounds at Medicine Lake and the one at Blue Lake are all suitable for trailers, too. Because of the type and condition of roads to some of the other campgrounds, there are limits to the size of recreational vehicles for some of them. Be sure to check the campground chart for restrictions.

South of Highway 299 from Adin along Highway 139 is Willow Creek Campground and picnic area. Much of the year this is an overnighter's stopping place for people on their way to some other place. But during hunting seasons, it becomes a center for hunters and explorers.

Ash Creek Campground off county road 527 out of Adin serves the same purpose as Willow Creek, with the added attraction of pretty good trout fishing in Ash Creek. The campsites are close enough to the creek that its splashing sounds become a part of the experience, along with the songs of both wrens and flycatchers. North of Adin along Highway 299 are the Rush Creek campgrounds. The lower campground has easy access to the highway, while the upper camp is a little more difficult to get into. Both are right along Rush Creek in a well-timbered valley. Pine needles and black oak leaves give off a musty aroma as you crush the duff under foot.

West of Canby three campgrounds attract campers—Howard's Gulch, Cottonwood Flat, and Lava Camp. Howard's Gulch, just off Highway 139, is a mixed grove of pines and firs with aspens circling the edge of two interconnecting meadows. In the fall it's like camping in a postcard picture, with the fluttering gold of the dollar-sized aspen leaves contrasting with the forest-green conifers and the gray-brown autumn grass in the meadows. Birders often stay here and drive to the wetlands to the north in Devil's Garden.

Cottonwood Flat and Lava Camp are more remote and Lava Camp has no drinking water. Both camps are little used except during the hunting seasons,

Aspens at Parsnip Springs herald the approach of fall weather.

although both are attractively located on smooth-surfaced dirt roads at about 4,500 feet in plateau country. Junipers dot the lava-strewn flats surrounding the camps, and deer are regular visitors. Cottonwood Flat is about three miles from good fishing on the Pit River.

Ten of the forest's twenty campgrounds are in the Warner Mountains along the eastern edge of the region. Of these, Blue Lake is the most fully developed. The lake is a 160-acre natural body of water surrounded by massive ponderosa pines, moss-hung white firs, and small pocket meadows. It has a good population of both rainbow and brown trout, and a launching ramp for boaters. The forty-eight units of the campground are all situated to take advantage of the view out over the lake and the ridge beyond. In the evening, as shadows creep across the lake, the water becomes as still as a painting, and the rippling circles of rising trout spread across the surface.

Mill Creek Falls Campground, located at the edge of the South Warner Wilderness, rests close enough to both stream and lake fishing that you can use it for a base camp and walk easily to the water. Mill and Poison creeks and Clear Lake are all within walking distance, and Mill Creek Falls are only a quarter-mile from camp. These falls drop vertically over a cliff channel set into a mixed forest of oak and pine trees and evergreen shrubs.

Parsnip Springs is just to the north of Blue Lake on the Patterson Meadow road. Here an undeveloped campground with sites in the aspens attracts campers almost all summer long. A bubbling creek tumbles down through the meadows and groves of white-barked quaking aspens, their leaves set quivering by the slightest breeze. As with all of the dispersed camping sites on the forest, a campfire permit is needed and you are responsible for all of your own garbage.

Where Highway 299 crosses the Warners at Cedar Pass is **Cedar Pass** Campground. More alpine than other auto camping sites on the forest because of its altitude, this camp has granite boulders, willows, and Jeffrey pines between the sites. Thomas, Cedar, and Deep creeks are nearby, and so are the trails into the Warner back country.

One of the least improved of all "improved" campgrounds on the forest is halfway between Cedar Pass and the Oregon border at **Plum Valley**. Even though it has no piped drinking water, the camp sites are frequently full. It is a drawing card for rockhounds who come to collect obsidian "needles" and "bombs." Nearby Lassen Creek's dispersed camping sites also attract rockhounds for these special forms of volcanic glass.

On The Trail

The Warner Mountains are the best place for hikers and backpackers to enjoy the Modoc National Forest. All of the maintained trails on the entire forest are in the Warners, and all but two of these are in the South Warner Wilderness.

In the far northern reaches of the Warners, north of Buck Creek on Forest Road 47N72 about five miles is the trailhead for the **Higrade National Recreation Trail**. This 5.5-mile walk through the heart of the northern Warner Range takes you through the old mining town of Highgrade. At one point along the trail you can look out to the east across Surprise Valley into Nevada, and then turn to the west and see Goose Lake Valley in California and Oregon. The trail is through a pine forest almost the entire distance, with breaks at just the right time for the breathtaking views to the valleys below. The contrast between the cool pines along the trail and the shimmering rock of the high Nevada desert makes the hike really special.

Another hike that is really a stroll, is on **Blue Lake National Recreation Trail**. The trailhead is in the Blue Lake campground, and it continues around the lake for about 2.4 miles. Practically the entire distance is in the shade of enormous ponderosa pines and old-growth white firs. The little-used trail often has as many deer tracks as hikers' on it. Take your camera or binoculars with you when you make this hike, because you're apt to see gray squirrels, Douglas squirrels, loons, hawks, ducks, and geese.

Trailheads for the South Warner Wilderness are mostly on the western and southern sides of the region. The northernmost four are all within an hour of Alturas, and the southern six are no more than two hours from Alturas. **Pine Creek** and **Pepperdine** trailheads probably will get you into the high country the fastest, and **Emerson** on the east side is the steepest. **Patterson,**

MODOC NATIONAL FOREST

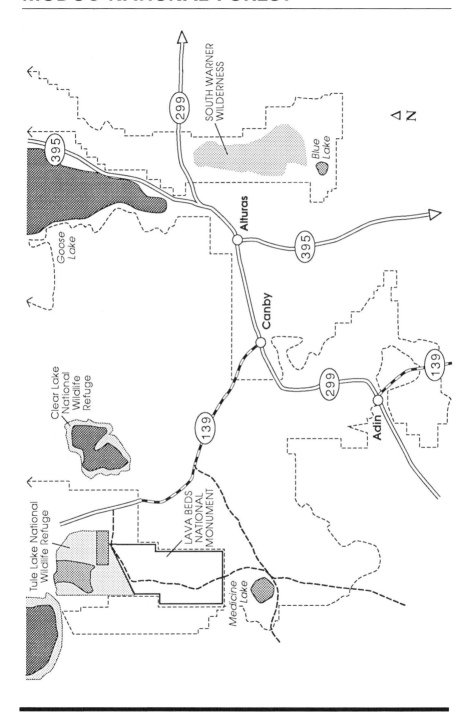

Mill Creek and **Soup Springs** trailheads all have developed campgrounds, as does Pepperdine. Emerson and **Bear Camp** are the hardest to get to, and you don't even want to try Bear Camp without a high clearance vehicle.

The **South Warner Wilderness** consists of about 77,385 acres of high alpine country, criss-crossed with an extensive trail system covering more than seventy-five miles. The trail system, indeed the entire wilderness is little used when compared with the larger and more famous examples in the Sierra to the south.

This is a wilderness to get away by yourself. No permits are required to enter; there is no quota system for visitors. The wilderness contains mountain peaks, glacial lakes, canyons, creeks, meadows, and aspens. All of them home to an astounding variety of wildlife. You can count on getting glimpses of mule deer, pronghorn, porcupines, and blue grouse, as well as the usual ground squirrels birds, and chipmunks.

Being a wilderness, naturally all motorized vehicles are barred from the region. Horsemen, however, find the trails in the wilderness well-suited for pack trips, and there are public corrals at Pepperdine trailhead. Stock is not permitted at Mill Creek Falls campground.

Touring, Sightseeing, and Special Programs

While there are no campfire or interpretive programs on the Modoc, nor any signed educational trails, there are still lots of special things to see and do. The wildlife refuges, especially, are fascinating places to visit.

Tule Lake National Wildlife Refuge in the far northwest is one of the centers of the semiannual migration of birdlife along the Pacific flyway. Many waterfowl nest on the lakes of the Klamath Basin, and especially on Tule Lake. In late spring the waters are covered with thousands of ducklings, goslings, and the offspring of other water fowl.

Despite the magnificence of the springtime numbers however, the fall gathering is even more spectacular, for approximately two million ducks and a million geese stop here to rest and feed on their way south, some birds coming from as far away as Siberia. There are times when the sky is literally blackened by the arrival of a very large flock of birds, an increasingly rare event in North America. From vantage points along the road you can watch more than twenty species of ducks, plus many varieties of geese, grebes, pelicans, herons, cormorants, gulls, coots, terns, avocets, and other birds.

An unusually large concentration of raptors dwells in the forest near Lava Beds National Monument and the Tule Lake Refuge. Each meadow adjacent to the refuge seems to be patrolled by a specific northern harrier searching for one of the many rodents that also make this area their home. Chief among the hunting birds is the bald eagle that winters here in numbers greater than any place outside Alaska. More than 900 eagles were counted in the winter of 1987-88.

Clear Lake National Wildlife Refuge, just to the east of Tule Lake also hosts thousands of water fowl annually, but the surroundings aren't as conducive to nest safety because nest sites are easily reached from land. Consequently, the numbers are not as great as those at Tule Lake.

In the Medicine Lake Highlands is a wonder of geology and three sections of the area have been set aside as "Special Interest Areas." First of these is **Burnt Lava Flow**, which is one of the youngest flows in the area, estimated

234

to be only about 200 years old. It's jet-black lava is in clear contrast to near-by **Medicine Lake, Glass Flow**, a stony grey dacite obsidian. **Glass Mountain** is the most spectacular of the three special interest sections.

Adjacent to the Forest, between Medicine Lake Highlands and Tule Lake, is **Lava Beds National Monument**, a fascinating area of lava flows, caves, and historic sites connected with the Modoc Wars of the 1870s. An exquisite campground, well-composed museum, and both ranger-led and self-guided hikes and tours are featured in the monument.

Sports

Except for boating and waterskiing on Medicine Lake and boating on Blue Lake, summer sports on Modoc National Forest are pretty much confined to the traditional outdoor sports such as fishing and hunting. In the winter, despite limited access, snow enthusiasts are finding more and more to do on the forest.

At **Cedar Pass** the Modoc Ski Club maintains a surface lift in the Warners. There are easy slopes for beginning downhillers as well as more advanced runs. There are miles and miles of territory open for both cross-country skiers and snowmobilers, too.

At **Mammoth Crater** near Medicine Lake, a snowmobile route loops around the lava flow and back to the crater. The snow seems to make a silent white blanket over the countryside, and the small trees and shrubs look like snowmen standing guard.

Hunting

The Modoc National Forest is very popular as a hunting area, especially for the "lava buck," the Rocky Mountain **mule deer** . It's one of the few areas in California where the mule deer, noted for its large body and immense antlers can be hunted.

Large herds of **pronghorn antelope** roam throughout the forest, and hunting for them has become a "must" during the August season for a growing number of hunters.

There are opportunities for hunting both **ducks** and **geese** early in the season on the numerous wetlands and reservoirs throughout the forest, especially in the Devil's Garden Ranger District. However, as one of the rangers said, "Once it starts to rain, the roads turn to glue," and access becomes very difficult.

Hunting opportunities for **blue grouse** are good early in the season. They are often found near wet meadows and springs, and are fairly common ear or above the 6,000 foot level.

Both **morning doves** and **quail** are found in heavy concentrations on the forest at the start of the season. The doves are especially common in recently disturbed areas, such as burned over or logged regions, and where ponds or springs or other watering holes are available to them. Both doves and the California and mountain quail can be disturbed by cold fronts that begin passing through in early to middle September, and their patterns of use will change or they may even head south for the winter.

Fishing

Anglers are attracted to the Modoc for the variety of species available. Fishing is good from boats on most of the reservoirs and shore fishermen get their catches along the many creeks. Many of the waters are stocked with rainbow, brook, and brown trout. Bass and catfish also are found in several of the reservoirs. For a change, arctic grayling have been planted in Little Medicine Lake.

Off Highway Vehicles

The South Warner Wilderness, Special Interest Area, and the Devil's Garden Research Natural Area are off limits to off-road travel, but the rest of the forest is open and available. Occasionally, an area will be closed or restricted and off-highway vehicle fans should always check with a ranger station for temporary closures or restrictions.

MODOC NATIONAL FOREST CAMPGROUNDS

	Piped Water	Camp Sites	Trailer Space	Fishing	Boating	Swimming	Store	RV Dump Station	Reservations	Special Attractions
Big Valley Ranger District										
Ash Creek		7	•	•						
Lava Creek	•	12	•							
Upper Rush Creek	•	13	•	•						
Willow Creek Camp	•	8	•							
Lower Rush Creek	•	10	•	•						
Devil's Garden Ranger District										
Cottonwood Flat		10	•							
Howard's Gulch	•	11	•							Barrier free restrooms
Doublehead Ranger District										
Headquarters	•	9	•	•	•	•				
Hemlock	•	19	•	•	•	•				
Medicine Camp	•	44	•	•	•	•				
A. H. Hogue	•	24	•	•	•	•				
Warner Mountain Ranger District										
Blue Lake	•	48	•	•	•	•				Wheelchair accessible, fishing pier and restrooms
Cave Lake	•	6	•	•	•	•				No motor boats
Cedar Pass	•	17	•	•						
Emerson		4		•						
Mill Creek Falls	•	19	•	•						
Patterson		5	•							
Plum Valley		7	•	•						
Soup Springs	•	14	•							
Stough Reservoir		8								
Pepperdine	•	5								Corrals

*KLAMATH
NATIONAL
FOREST*

Sacramento

San Francisco

Los Angeles

Klamath National Forest

The Klamath National Forest invites recreationists of every kind to enjoy its boundless resources. Unparalleled white-water rafting, more than a thousand miles of trails, beautiful picnicking and camping spots, outstanding fishing and hunting, and stunning vistas make the Klamath a quality vacation paradise.

All or part of five wilderness areas are on the 1,700,000-acre forest, and four of its rivers are National Wild and Scenic Rivers.

The Klamath is between the coast ranges and the Cascades, and consists of the Marble, Salmon, Scott Bar, and Siskiyou mountain ranges. The rivers of the forest are among the largest in the state, and along with the steep and high mountain ranges, dominate the geography of the five contiguous ranger districts. Because of its remoteness, the Klamath National Forest is seldom crowded.

Camping

A variety of campgrounds, from cool, secluded forest sites to sunny streamside locations, can be found on the Klamath National Forest. There are twenty-six campgrounds with more than 350 units. Most of the sites are along the major rivers off Highway 96, the Salmon River and Scott River roads, plus three on the Goosenest District.

Goosenest District Camping

Most frequently visited of the three campgrounds on the Goosenest District is exquisite Juanita Lake. This serene, twelve-acre lake offers fishing for rainbow and brown trout, as well as small-mouth bass. No motors are allowed on the lake, but its size makes it ideal for small rowboats or canoes. At over 5,000 feet, you'll be high above the volcanic lands to the east under widely-spaced Jeffrey pines. The campsites are distributed over about forty acres with manzanita and ceanothus between the units.

Martin's Dairy Campground is a favorite of those who like a peaceful, remote campsite high in the mountains. The Little Shasta River flows through a lush, green meadow beside the units. Each campsite looks out over the meadow from pine clad hillsides. A picturesque split-rail fence at the upper end of the meadow separates the campground from private property beyond.

Oak Knoll District Camping

Tree of Heaven Campground, named for the special trees introduced into California from China during the gold rush days, sits on the banks of the Klamath River. The flat camping place is part of an early homestead, and you'll stay under introduced fruit and nut trees, as well as the typical conifers of northern California. A broad lawn spreads over the fault between the campsites.

In front of you, the swift Klamath flows westward making homes for muskrats and river otters in its banks. Mergansers and their chicks paddle busily downstream, and great blue herons stalk the shallows. Boaters and rafters launch here, and steelhead and salmon anglers make it headquarters in the fall and winter.

Near the community of Klamath River, Beaver Creek flows into the Klamath from the north. Turn up the road that parallels the creek about five miles to Beaver Creek Campground. Sheltered in the riparian alders, the individual camp units are spread out along the creek bank. The creek itself splashes over volcanic basalt boulders through brushy banks.

Farther on down the Klamath River, just before the little community of Hamburg, Sarah Totten Campground rests by the side of the river. Big Douglas firs grow from tremendous mounds of tailings left behind by miners who seemingly turned over every rock in the river in their search for the precious golden flakes. Fishermen enjoy staying at Sarah Totten for access to the Klamath and Scott rivers and Horse Creek within a short distance of each other.

O'Neil Creek and Fort Goff campgrounds are right on the river downstream, and Grider Creek is five miles up-stream of that name near Seiad Valley. Grider Creek Campground is the number one jumping-off place for hikers and horseback riders on the Pacific Crest Trail. From Seiad Valley, the PCT goes north into Red Butte Wilderness and Oregon, or south to the Marble Mountain Wilderness. The campground also provides a stopping place for people who just want to make some day hikes or fish the stream.

Happy Camp District Camping

West Branch Campground, a few miles up Indian Creek from the town of Happy Camp, provides anglers with a place to stay away from the Klamath River. Port Orford cedars and big leaf maples grow along Indian Creek and help make this family campground a truly harmonious place to camp.

The only other developed campground on the Happy Camp District is fifteen miles south of Happy Camp on Elk Creek Road near the boundary of Marble Mountain Wilderness. Sulphur Springs Campground is a walk-in campground and is a favorite with backpackers heading into the wilderness. Elk Creek Trail leaves from the upper end of the campground and enters the wilderness after four easy miles.

Ukonom District Camping

Dillon Creek and Oak Bottom campgrounds are the most used camping places along the rivers on the western part of the forest. Oak Bottom Campground is just two miles up the Salmon River from its juncture with the Klamath at Somesbar. The Wooley Creek entrance to the Marble Mountain Wilderness is a mile upstream, and several handy boat launch ramps and river access points are nearby. Berry pickers and fishermen gather at both Oak Bottom and Dillon Creek in season. The rivers are big here and river guides conduct steelhead and salmon anglers on float trips after their quarry. Mouth-watering huckleberry pies pop out of ovens all over the north state after a stay at these camps.

These two campgrounds provide good swimming on the big rivers, which slow down enough to make for excellent family fun in the water.

Scott River District Camping

Scott River District has six campgrounds and two day use picnic areas. The river flows through a wide valley with farms and ranches surrounded by mountains and is used for rafting, kayaking, swimming and fishing.

KLAMATH NATIONAL FOREST

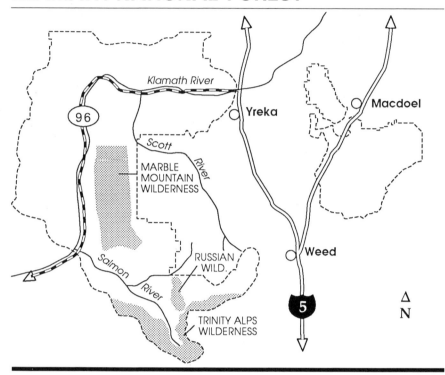

Closest to the Klamath River is Bridge Flat Campground. From this point, kayakers and rafters head down the Scott during spring floods. The canyon is narrow here, and the sound of the stream's musical notes reverberates through the camp sites.

Upstream a few miles, Indian Scotty Campground is across the river from the main road under cover of some fine old Douglas firs with moss-encrusted branches drooping overhead. Anglers have access to the Scott River here and are near Canyon Creek. From both Bridge Flat and Indian Scotty, you're within a couple of miles of Marble Mountain Wilderness.

Lover's Camp Campground, reached by road from Indian Scotty, is a walk-in camping place, and a major entry point for the wilderness. From here, backpackers and horsemen reach the complex of alpine lakes in the shelter of Red Mountain. They can also connect with the Pacific Crest Trail high up on Marble Mountain itself.

Kangaroo Lake Campground is at 6,000 feet, east of Scott Mountain near the boundary of the forest. Recently completely renovated, this cool, summer spot is just the place for some evening trout fishing. Forest Service personnel have provided wheelchair fishing access to the shore of this granite-bound lake as a part of the renovation project. It is near timberline under the sharp peaks of South China Mountain and Cory Peak.

Salmon River District Camping

Two of the Salmon River District's campgrounds are the major southern entry point for Marble Mountain Wilderness. At Little North Fork Campground, corrals have been provided for equestrians who bring their own stock. Idlewild is at a somewhat higher elevation than Little North Fork and there are some wonderful places for kids to play along the stream. Both are located on the banks of the North Fork Salmon River with access to fishing. The Russian Wilderness is also accessible from Idlewild following a short drive up Russian Creek or to Etna Summit.

Three more Salmon River District campgrounds are spread along the South Fork Salmon River-Mathews Creek, East Fork, and Shadow Creek campgrounds. All three are near the northern boundary of Trinity Alps Wilderness. Thompson Peak's glaciers and snowfields dominate the southern horizon from Shadow Creek and East Fork, while Mathews Creek's views are up toward Dees Peak and Mary Blaine Mountain. Tumbling creeks follow each canyon down from the Trinities, each adding its bit to the South Fork Salmon River. This Wild and Scenic River follows its rambunctious path beside campsites, adding to the attractiveness of the place. Mathews Creek Campground sits near a half-dozen good berry-picking spots, and both blackberries and huckleberries ripen in their turn.

On The Trail

The Klamath is beyond all doubt a quality setting for hikers, backpackers, and riders. There are 450,000 acres of wilderness, three National Recreation Trails, and 120 miles of the Pacific Crest Trail. Because it is remote, hikers have the chance for long periods of solitude.

Pacific Crest Trail

The Pacific Crest Trail first enters the Klamath National Forest near Mt. Ashland in Oregon where the forest pushes up across the state border. The trail follows the Klamath-Rogue River boundary all the way down into California and to the edge of Red Butte Wilderness before turning south to Seiad Valley and crossing the Klamath River.

From Seiad Valley the trail climbs up into the Marble Mountain Wilderness, crosses to the Russian Wilderness at Scott Mountain.

Sources of water are nearby for almost the entire trip through the Klamath except for one seventeen-mile stretch between Payne Lake on the Russian Wilderness and Shelly Meadows on the Marble Mountain Wilderness. Horses are allowed on the trail but equestrians must bring all their feed prior to July 1. Even after that date, supplementary pellets should be added to the list of supplies.

The trail can be accessed at either end of the forest—Mt. Ashland or Scott Mountain. In between these spots, paved roads lead to trail crossings at Seiad Valley, Etna-Sawyer's Bar Road, and Callahan-Cecilville Road. Several other access points can be reached by short hikes from trailheads throughout the length of the trail.

National Recreational Trails

The newest National Recreation Trail on the forest is the Kelsey Historical Trail. It traverses the entire forest from the confluence of Kelsey Creek and Scott River to tie in the the South Kelsey National Recreation Trail on Six Rivers

National Forest. The Trail follows the approximate route of the original army trail built to supply soldiers stationed at Fort Jones during gold rush times.

Boundary National Recreation Trail is located in the high mountainous terrain of the Siskiyou Mountain crest along the California-Oregon border. Impressive geological formations abound in the volcanic butte country along this steep and rugged trail. The trail is clear of snow from June to October and use is very light. It intersects the PCT near Kangaroo Mountain and travels west and into the Red Butte Wilderness on the Rogue River National Forest.

Clear Creek National Recreation Trail follows Clear Creek from about six miles southwest of Happy Camp. The creek is aptly named, having sparkling pools 20 to 30 feet deep. A rich mosaic of life exists around the near-pristine trail through the Siskiyou Wilderness. The stream supports its own distinct environment. Springtime brings multi-colored flower displays including tiger lilies, pitcher plants, and columbine. A special treat is the majestic Port Orford cedar. Notice the ends of the branches look like they've been ironed flat, and how you can rub a sort of whitish bloom from the foliage with your fingers. The trail is an easy climb with a top elevation of 4,600 feet. There are a number of camping places along the stream to enjoy the wilderness.

Goosenest District Hiking Trails

The Goosenest Ranger District has not been known as a hiking region, but trails are being developed rapidly for both walkers and mountain bicycle riders.

The district has built a handicap-access loop trail at Juanita Lake with built-in handicap fishing access as well. Associated with this trail is a new trail to Ball Mountain which serves as a mountain bike route and a cross-country ski route in the winter.

Most of the Goosenest District is relatively flat, and both hiking and bike trails are mostly on unpaved Forest roads until you get to the far southern part of the district along Antelope Creek. This is the closest to alpine scenery on the district with sharp peaks and cones along Hemlock Ridge, Rainbow Mountain and Stevens Butte. A short trail leads from Stephens Pass on Forest Road 43N13 to the top of Stevens Butte. The back side of Mt. Shasta and the colorful volcanic formations of the Medicine Lake Highlands are visible along the way.

Marble Mountain Wilderness

The Marble Mountain Wilderness, which is entirely within the Klamath National Forest, has within its boundary a wide variety of nearly 100 lakes, meadows, craggy peaks, and many interesting geological formations. At lower elevations, Douglas firs and some ponderosa pines mixed with oaks and madrones predominate. These gradually give way to stands of white and then red firs along with weeping spruce at higher elevations. Trails of the wilderness connect camping spots along the river systems and beside the many alpine lakes.

Virtually all the trailheads are at the end of dirt or gravel roads except at Wooley Creek and Etna Summit. The $4 wilderness map can be obtained from Forest Service offices showing all the trailheads.

Logging trucks are a familiar sight on roads on the Klamath National Forest.

One feature of the wilderness that gets little publicity because of the dangers involved is limestone caves. Six or more of the top twenty caves in length and depth west of the Mississippi are in the Marble Mountain Wilderness. Experience in caving is highly stressed before attempting these caves.

Packers, both horse and llama, are used to take you into the Marbles. It's a favorite place for both deer and bear hunters in the fall and winter and has all the potential for a high quality outdoor experience.

Siskiyou Wilderness

The Siskiyou Wilderness, which the Klamath shares with the Siskiyou and Six Rivers National Forests, is the least-visited of all the forest's wilderness areas. Located in the northwest corner of the forest, there is lots of space and trees. Some of the streams, Clear Creek especially, have good runs of steelhead as well as year round rainbow trout populations. Blacktail deer and bears roam the back country, and hunters come in the fall to try their skills.

An interesting loop trip is between Clear Creek National Recreation Trail, the West Fork Trail, and the Kelsey Historical Trail. There are deep pools along the streams, and the Bear Lakes high up under Bear Peak provide stunning campsites.

Russian Wilderness

The high granite country of Russian Wilderness straddles the Salmon-Scott Divide along the eastern edge of the forest between the Marble Mountains and the Trinity Alps. It's little-visited, but has the potential to attract many more hikers and campers once it becomes better known. More than twenty lakes sit in glacial cirques above timberline sparkling in the sunlight reflected from the perennial snow fields.

Entrance to the wilderness is via the little communities of Callahan or Etna. Hikers along the PCT will cross this wilderness along its long axis, passing near 8,100-foot Russian Peak and Paynes Lake.

Trinity Alps Wilderness

While most of this wilderness is on the neighboring Shasta-Trinity National Forest, the part that is included on the Klamath has some charming lake and creekside camping places. Included among these are Long Gulch and Trail Gulch lakes on the crest of the Scott Mountains. One good loop trip to both of these lakes begins at Trail Creek campground on the Callahan-Cecilville Road. From the campground, go up Fish Lake Creek and cross the ridge to Trail Gulch Lake. From there the trail flanks Deadman Peak and down into Long Gulch Lake and back down to Trail Creek Campground, about 14 miles in all. Both lakes lie in open granite basins tucked under the crest of the Scott Mountains surrounded with green meadows.

Touring, Sightseeing, and Special Programs

Some auto tours make the Klamath National Forest accessible. First is the drive down Highway 96 from I-5 to SomesBar along the length of the Klamath River on the forest. From high desert to deepest, moss-hung forest, this drive will show perhaps better than any other the variety of woodlands in these mountains.

A second tour has been nominated by the forest for "Scenic Byway" status and gives an alternate route to the Pacific Coast. Turn off Highway 96 at Happy Camp and proceed up Indian Creek to Grayback Road. This goes to Illinois Valley on the Siskiyou National Forest in Oregon, and from there down US 199 to Crescent City. Lots of different ecosystems prevail along this route, from riverine to subalpine to middle altitude conifer forest.

A third auto tour makes a loop from forest headquarters in Yreka, and includes Fort Jones, the Scott Valley and Scott River and back up the Klamath River Highway to Yreka. Fort Jones was the center of a vast gold-mining area, now devoted to growing grains and alfalfa. The Scott River Canyon from Indian Scotty Campground on down to the confluence of the Klamath is dramatic. High cliffs and sharp escarpments contain the swiftly flowing river at the bottom.

An auto tour of the Goosenest District to the east if I-5 will take you out into the Medicine Lake Highlands Volcanic Area. Spatter cones, craters, glass flows, and rocks that float, are all part of the scenic east side. Junipers and manzanitas dominate the foliage, and rough lava rocks are scattered everywhere.

The Goosenest District is a birder's paradise. The Pacific flyway crosses the district and literally millions of migratory wildfowl rest here in the spring and fall as they make their way between summer nesting spots in the far north and wintering grounds. Meiss Lake, immediately adjacent to the district ranger station near MacDoel, is the center of a state wildlife area. The Klamath Basin National Wildlife Refuges northeast of the Goosenest Ranger District.

Sports

Fishing, hunting, river boating, and hiking are the biggest sports attractions on the Klamath National Forest. More steelhead and salmon are caught each year in the Klamath River than in any other California waterway. The deer harvest on the forest is among the top two or three each year without fail.

Fishing and Hunting

Generally speaking, the lakes of the high country are free of ice by the first of July, but a few patches of snow may remain beside some of the trails. The streams of the low and middle altitudes flow heavily all year long and support large populations of trout both native rainbows and introduced browns and brook trout.

Four big game animals are successfully hunted on the Klamath: Deer, bears, elk, and pronghorn antelope. The elk is the second largest deer on the continent, and the largest in California. Best place to get a look at this magnificent animal is on the Goosenest Ranger District near MacDoel.

But it is deer, and particularly the mule deer, the so-called "lava buck," that brings the hunters out in record numbers every year. The harvest is a good one, but because of the large number of hunters, it is sometimes difficult to find a place to hunt.

Canoeists have their pick of several fine rivers in the Klamath National Forest.

Boating, Rafting, and Kayaking

The Klamath River offers year round boating opportunities. Winter and fall driftboat fishing, spring and summer rafting, canoe and kayak runs from Class I through IV. The Scott and Salmon Rivers, too, both have breathtaking Class V whitewater runs, available in spring only. Both rivers are much more difficult than the Klamath.

The Salmon River, like the Scott, is not controlled, and flows vary widely from spring highs to late summer and fall lows. Here, too, high canyon walls and crashing rapids interspersed with quiet pools make for eye-popping kayak and raft trips, definitely advanced whitewater runs.

Mountain Bicycling

So much of the Goosenest District is relatively flat, that travel by mountain bike is possible for miles over Forest Service roads. Especially interesting, as well as something of challenge is the Martin's Dairy-Ball Mountain loop. This trip visits the green meadows at Martin's Dairy, the quiet, placid water of Juanita Lake, and the high lookout atop Ball Mountain.

Altogether there are 3,000 miles of dirt roads on the forest and excellently arranged for biking.

Winter Sports

Cross country skiing, snowmobiling, and snow play all account for many visitor days on the Klamath National Forest. Snowmobiling is very popular on the Goosenest District. It has two snowmobile parks. One is at Deer Mountain on the back side of Mt. Shasta, and one is at Four Corners near Medicine Lake. There are marked and groomed trails at both places with terrain ranging from almost flat for beginners, to some very challenging. The Scott Mountain Snowmobile Trail offers access to several square miles of national forest. Routes are marked to the east of Highway 3 from Scott Mountain Summit to Carmen Lake.

Nordic skiers also find the Scott Mountain Summit area to be excellent for their sport. Cross-country skiers stay west of Highway 3 and snowmobilers east of the highway. Up on the Goosenest District, cross country specialists like the trails around Juanita Lake. They travel from Meiss Lake on groomed trails, and have the entire area to roam.

KLAMATH NATIONAL FOREST CAMPGROUNDS

	Piped Water	Camp Sites	Trailer Space	Fishing	Boating	Swimming	Store	RV Dump Station	Reservations	Special Attractions
Beaver Creek	•	8	•	•						
Big Flat		9		•						Through Shasta-T
Bridge Flat	•	8	•	•						Rafting
Curly Jack	•	15	•	•	•		•			
Dillon	•	21	•	•	•	•				
East Fork		9	•	•						
Fort Goff		5		•						On Klamath R.
Grider Creek	•	10	•	•						PCT trailhead
Hotelling		5		•		•				S. Fork Salmon R.
Idlewild	•	23	•	•						
Indian Scotty	•	32	•	•						
Juanita Lake	•	23	•	•	•	•				No motor boats
Kangaroo Lake	•	14	•	•	•	•				
Little North Fork		4		•						Corrals
Lover's Camp	•	10		•						Walk-in
Martin's Dairy	•	8	•	•						
Mathews Creek	•	14	•	•						
Mt. Ashland		9	•							
Mullbridge		4		•						Horse corrals
Norcross		6	•	•						Horse corrals
Oak Bottom	•	35	•	•	•	•				
O'Neil Creek		18	•	•						
Red Bank		4		•		•				N. Fork Salmon R.
Sarah Totten	•	17	•	•						On Klamath R.
Scott Mountain		6		•						Near PCT
Shadow Creek	•	10	•	•						Small trailers
Shafter	•	10	•	•		•				
Sulphur Springs		7		•		•				Walk-in
Trail Creek	•	15	•	•						
Tree of Heaven	•	21	•	•						On Klamath R.
West Branch	•	15	•	•						

Glossary

Backcountry: Remote, wilder part of a forest.

Bureau of Land Management: Public administrative unit charged with overseeing federal land outside of national parks, monuments, and forests.

Bureau of Reclamation: Public administrative unit charged with building and maintaining dams for flood control, irrigation, etc.

Campground Host: Volunteers who serve as campground patrons; they greet visitors, provide information, and help with grounds upkeep.

Catchable: Term used to describe the trout released into streams and lakes of California by the State Department of Fish and Game.

Chaparral: Dense thicket of shrubs containing one or more dry-land species such as manzanita, sagebrush, chamise, or ceanothus.

Developed Campground: One that has such amenities as a fire-ring, picnic table, parking spur, vault or flush toilet. Has garbage pick-up.

Dispersed Camping: Camping away from developed campgrounds. There are no improvements and you must carry out your own refuse.

Endangered Species Act: Passed by Congress to protect those species thought to be in danger of extinction.

Forest Association: Volunteer groups that assist the Forest Service with such tasks as interpretive programs, tree planting, trail maintenance, etc.

Front Country: Nearer, more domesticated portions of a national forest.

FR 21S34: (An example) Designation for a forest road. Both developed roads and trails have numerical designations.

Giardia lamblia: Microscopic parasite responsible for an intense intestinal disorder. It has spread widely through America and even the clearest-appearing waters may be contaminated.

"Green Sticker": License sticker applied to an off-highway vehicle by the State of California. Vehicles so marked are not "street legal."

Group Camping: Organizations—formal or informal—of more than six persons reserve special group campgrounds through ranger districts.

Interpretive Program: Information program to introduce or instruct forest visitors.

Interpretive trail: One that serves to introduce forest visitors to specific aspects of the forest, such as kinds of trees, minerals, uses of the forest.

Mountain Bicycle or Bike: Pedal-powered bicycle, not to be confused with a *Trail Bike*, which is a type of motorcycle.

National Forest: Agency of the U.S. Department of Agriculture charged with multi-use management of the nation's forest resources for sustained yields of water, forage, wildlife, wood, and recreation.

National Monument: Place of specific interest such as a natural wonder or historic site. Usually under the aegis of the National Park Service, but occasionally operated by the Forest Service.

National Park: Agency of the Department of Interior charged with maintaining the national parks and monuments in pristine condition.

National Recreation Area: Region established by the Congress to provide for public recreation. Can be managed by any federal bureau.

National Scenic Area: Area established by the Congress to preserve extraordinarily scenic places.

Nature Conservancy: Organization dedicated to preseving flora and fauna of the world.

ORV, OHV: Initials stand for Off-Highway Vehicle and Off-Road Vehicle. Sometimes used interchangeably, the Forest Service prefers the appelation "Off-Highway" rather than "Off-Road," because the use of such vehicles off designated roads and trails is prohibited.

Passport Program: Golden Eagle, Golden Age, and Golden Access programs whereby persons can obtain free or low-cost entry to national parks, monuments, forest campgrounds.

Penny Pines Plantation: Section of reforested land paid for by donations from the public.

Permit: A license required on the national forests to allow certain things, such as campfires away from developed campgrounds, cut firewood for home use, enter a wilderness, cut Christmas trees.

Primitive Campground: Usually units contain table and fire-ring only, and no garbage pick-up.

Rare Species: Designation under California Endangered Species Act. A "rare" species is one that is in decline.

Riparian: Land near a stream. In California typical "riparian" woodlands contain cottonwoods, aspens, certain oaks, alders, and chokecherries.

Sno-Park: Parking area for persons using winter sports areas. Permits are required for their use.

Threatened Species: Designation under Federal Endangered Species Act. A "threatened" species is one that may become extinct if corrective measures are not taken.

Trail Bike: Motorcycle designed for use on mountain trails. Not to be confused with *Mountain Bike*, which is a bicycle.

Wetlands: Lands developed with water for the protection of migrating waterfowl.

Addenda

ANGELES NATIONAL FOREST
Forest Supervisor
Arcadia, CA 91006
(818) 574-5200

Mt. Baldy District
110 N. Wabash Avenue
Glendora, CA 91740
(818) 335-1251

Tujunga District
12371 N. Little Tujunga Cyn. Road
San Fernando, CA 91342
(818) 899-1900

Arroyo Seco District
Oak Grove Park
Flintridge, CA 91011
(818) 790-1151

Saugus District
30800 Bouquet Canyon Road
Saugus, CA 91350
(805) 296-9710

Valyermo District
34146 Longview Road
Pearblosson, CA 93553
(805) 944-2187

CLEVELAND NATIONAL FOREST
Forest Supervisor
10845 Rancho Bernardo Rd.
Suite 200
San Diego, CA 92127-2107
(619) 673-6180

Palomar District
1634 Black Canyon Rd.
Ramona, CA 92065
(619) 788-0250

Descanso District
3348 Alpine Blvd.
Alpine, CA 91901
(619) 445-6235

Trabuco District
1147 E. 6th Street
Corona, CA 91720
(909) 736-1811

ELDORADO NATIONAL FOREST
Forest Supervisor
100 Forni Road
Placerville, CA 95667
(916) 622-5061

Georgetown District
7600 Wentworth Springs Road
Georgetown, CA 95634
(916) 333-4312

Placerville District
4260 Eight Mile Rd.
Camino, CA 95709
(916) 644-2324

Amador District
26820 Silver Drive
Pioneer, CA 95666
(209) 295-4251

Pacific District
Pollack Pines, CA 95726
(916) 644-2349

INYO NATIONAL FOREST
Forest Supervisor
873 N. Main Street
Bishop, CA 93514
(619) 873-5841

Mono Lake District
P.O. Box 429
Lee Vining, CA 93541
(619) 647-3000

White Mountain District
798 N. Main Street
Bishop, CA 93514
(619) 873-2500

Mt. Whitney District
P.O. Box 8
Lone Pine, CA 93545
(619) 876-6200

Mammoth District
P.O. Box 148
Mammoth Lakes, CA 93546
(619) 924-5500

KLAMATH NATIONAL FOREST
Forest Supervisor
1312 Fairlane Road
Yreka, CA 96097
(916) 842-6131

Goosenest District
37805 Highway 97
MacDoel, CA 96058
(916) 398-4391

Happy Camp District
P.O. Box 377
Happy Camp, CA 96039
(916) 493-2243

Scott River District
11263 S. Highway 3
Fort Jones, CA 96032
(916) 468-5351

Ukonom Ranger District
P.O. Drawer 410
Orleans, CA 95556
(916) 627-3291

Oak Knoll District
22541 Highway 96
Klamath River, CA 96050
(916) 465-2241

Salmon River District
P.O. Box 280
Etna, CA 96027
(916) 467-5757

**LAKE TAHOE BASIN
MANAGEMENT UNIT**
870 Emerald Bay Rd.
Suite 1
South Lake Tahoe, CA 96150
(916) 573-2689

LASSEN NATIONAL FOREST
Supervisors Office
55 South Sacramento Street
Susanville, CA 96130
(916) 257-2151

Almanor District
P.O. Box 767
Chester, CA 96020
(916) 258-2141

Eagle Lake District
55 South Sacramento Street
Susanville, CA 96130
(916) 257-2151

Hat Creek District
P.O. Box 220
Fall River Mills, CA 96028
(916) 336-5521

LOS PADRES NATIONAL FOREST
Forest Supervisor
6144 Calle Real
Goleta, CA 93117
(805) 683-6711

Mt. Pinos District
HC1 Box 400
34580 Lockwood Valley Rd.
Frazier Park, CA 93225
(805) 245-3731

Santa Barbara District
Star Route
Santa Barbara, CA 93105
(805) 967-3481

Monterey District
406 S. Mildred
King City, CA 93930
(408) 385-5434

Ojai District
1190 E. Ojai Avenue
Ojai, CA 93023
(805) 646-4348

Santa Lucia District
1616 Carlotti Drive
Santa Maria, CA 93454
(805) 925-9538

MENDOCINO NATIONAL FOREST
Forest Supervisor
420 E. Laurel Street
Willows, CA 95988
(916) 934-3316

Covelo District
Route 1, Box 62C
Covelo, CA 95428
(707) 983-6118

Upper Lake District
P.O. Box 96
Upper Lake, CA 95485
(707) 275-2361

Corning District
P.O. Box 1019
22000 Corning Road
Corning, CA 96021
(916) 824-5196

Stonyford District
5080 Ladoga Road
Stonyford, CA 95979
(916) 963-3128

MODOC NATIONAL FOREST
Forest Supervisor
441 N. Main Street
Alturas, CA 96101
(916) 233-5811

Big Valley District
P.O. Box 159
Adin, CA 96006
(916) 299-3215

Devil's Garden District
P.O. Box 5
Canby, CA 96015
(916) 233-4611

Doublehead District
P.O. Box 369
Tulelake, CA 96134
(916) 667-2246

Warner Mountain District
P.O. Box 220
Cedarville, CA 96104
(916) 279-6116

PLUMAS NATIONAL FOREST
Forest Supervisor
159 Lawrence Street
Quincy, CA 95971
(916) 283-2050

Beckwourth District
P.O. Box 7
Blairsden, CA 96103
(916) 836-2575

Greenville District
P.O. Box 329
Greenville, CA 95947
(916) 284-7126

LaPorte District
P.O. Drawer 369
Challenge, CA 95925
(916) 675-2462

Milford District
P.O. Box 369
Milford, CA 96121
(916) 253-2223

Oroville District
875 Mitchell Avenue
Oroville, CA 95965
(916) 534-6500

Quincy District
39696 Highway 70
Quincy, CA 95971
(916) 283-0555

**SAN BERNARDINO
NATIONAL FOREST**
Forest Supervisor
1824 S. Commercenter Circle
San Bernardino, CA 92408-3430
(714) 383-5588

Big Bear District
P.O. Box 290
Fawnskin, CA 92333
(714) 866-3437

San Gorgonio District
Mill Creek Ranger Station
34701 Mill Creek Rd.
Mentone, CA 92359
(714) 794-1123

Arrowhead District
P.O. Box 7
Rimforest, CA 92378
(714) 337-2444

Cajon District
Lytle Creek Ranger Station
Star Route, Box 100
Fontana, CA 92336-9704
(714) 887-2576

San Jacinto District
P.O.Box 518
Idyllwild, CA 92349
(714) 659-2117

SEQUOIA NATIONAL FOREST
Forest Supervisor
900 W. Grand Avenue
Porterville, CA 93257
(209) 784-1500

Hume Lake District
35860 E. Kings Canyon Road
Dunlap, CA 93621
(209) 338-2251

Hot Springs District
Route 4, Box 548
California Hot Springs, CA 93207
(805) 548-6503

Greenhorn District
800 Truxton Avenue, Room 322
P.O. Box 6129
Bakersfield, CA 93386-6129
(805) 871-2223

Tule River District
32588 Highway 190
Porterville, CA 93265
(209) 539-2607

Cannell Meadow District
P.O. Box 6
Kernville, CA 93238
(619) 376-3781

SHASTA-TRINITY NATIONAL FORESTS
Forest Supervisor
2400 Washington Avenue
Redding, CA 96001
(916) 246-5222

McCloud District
P.O. Box 1620
McCloud, CA 96057
(916) 964-2184

Mt. Shasta District
204 West Alma
Mt. Shasta, CA 96067
(916) 926-4511

Shasta Lake District
14225 Holiday Rd.
Redding, Ca 96003
(916) 275-1587

Big Bar Ranger District
Star Route 1
Box 10
Big Bar, CA 96010
(916) 623-6106

Hayfork District
P.O. Box 159
Hayfork, CA 96041
(916) 628-5227

Weaverville District
P.O. Box 1190
Weaverville, CA 96093
(916) 623-2121

Yolla Bolly District
Platina, CA 96076
(916) 352-4211

SIERRA NATIONAL FOREST
Forest Supervisor
Supervisor's Office
1600 Tollhouse Rd.
Clovis, CA 93612
(209) 487-5155

Pineridge District
P.O. Box 300 Shaver Lake, CA 93664
(209) 841-3311

Kings River District
34849 Maxon Rd.
Sanger, CA 93657
(209) 855-8321

Mariposa District
41969 Highway 41
Oakhurst, CA 93644
(209) 683-4665

Minarets District
North Fork, CA 93463
(209) 877-2218

SIX RIVERS NATIONAL FOREST
Forest Supervisor
1330 Bayshore Way
Eureka, CA 95501-3834
(707) 442-1721

Orleans District
Drawer B
Orleans, CA 95556
(916) 627-3291

Gasquet District
P.O. Box 228
Gasquet, CA 95543
(707) 457-3131

Mad River District
Star Route, Box 300
Bridgeville, CA 95526
(707) 574-6233

Lower Trinity District
P.O. Box 68
Willow Creek, CA 95573
(916) 629-2118

STANISLAUS NATIONAL FOREST
Forest Supervisor
19777 Greenley Road
Sonora, CA 95370
(209) 532-3671

Mi-Wok District
P.O. Box 100
Mi-Wuk Village, CA 95346
(209) 586-3234

Summit District (Pinecrest)
Number 1 Pinecrest Lake Rd.
Pinecrest, CA 95364
(209) 965-3434

Calaveras District
P.O. Box 500
Hathaway Pines, Ca 95233
(209) 795-1381

Groveland District
24545 Old Highway 120
Groveland, CA 95321
(209) 962-7825

TAHOE NATIONAL FOREST
Forest Supervisor
P.O. Box 6003
Nevada City, CA 95959-6003
(916) 265-4531

Downieville District
Star Route Box 1
Camptonville, CA 95922
(916) 288-3231

Foresthill District
22830 Foresthill Road
Foresthill, CA 95631
(916) 367-2224

Sierraville District
P.O. Box 95
Sierraville, CA 96126
(916) 994-3401

Nevada City District
Highway 49 & Coyote Street
Nevada City, CA 95959
(916) 265-4538

Truckee District
P.O. Box 399
Truckee, CA 95734
(916) 587-3558

TOIYABE NATIONAL FOREST
Supervisors Office
1200 Franklin Way
Sparks, NV 89431
(702) 355-5302

Bridgeport District
P.O. Box 595
Bridgeport, CA 93517
(619) 832-7070

Carson District
1536 So. Carson Street
Carson City, NV 89701
(702) 882-2766

Guide to Packers

Inyo National Forest
Frontier Pack Train
   Box 18, Star Route 33
   June Lake, CA 93517
   (619) 648-7701

Agnew Meadows Pack Train
   P.O. Box 395
   Mammoth Lakes, CA 93546
   (619) 934-2345

Red's Meadow Pack Train
   P.O. Box 395
   Mammoth Lakes, CA 93546
   (619) 934-2345

Mammoth Lakes Pack Outfit
   Box 61
   Mammoth Lakes, CA 93546
   (619) 934-2434

McGee Creek Pack Station
   Route 1, Box 162
   Mammoth Lakes, CA 93546
   (619) 935-4324

Rock Creek Station
   Box 248
   Bishop, CA 93514
   (619) 935-4493

Pine Creek Saddle and Pack Station
   P.O. Box 968
   Bishop, CA 93514
   (619) 387-2747

Schober Pack Station
   Route, 1, Box AA-4
   Bishop, CA 93514
   (619) 873-4785

Rainbow Pack Outfit
   P.O. Box 1791
   Bishop, CA 93514
   (619) 873-8877

Glacier Pack Trains
   P.O. Box 321
   Big Pine, CA 93513
   (619) 938-2538

Onion Valley Pack Trains
P.O. Box 1791
Bishop, CA 93514
(619) 873-8877

Mt. Whitney Pack Trains
P.O. Box 1514
Bishop, CA 93514

Cottonwood Pack Station
Star Route 1, Box 81-A
Independence, CA 93526
(619) 878-2015

Kennedy Meadows Pack Train
P.O. Box 1300
Weldon, CA 93823
(619) 378-2232

Klamath National Forest
Lane's Pack Station
P.O. Box 31
Orick, CA 95555
(707) 488-5225

Kleaver Pack Station
8033 Big Springs Road
Montague, CA 96064
(916) 459-5426

Heart D Guide & Pack Station
356 Bridge Street
Fort Jones, CA 96032
(9160 468-5548

Quartz Valley Pack Outfit
12712 Quartz Valley Road
Fort Jones, CA 96032
(916) 468-2592 or 468-5511

Shasta Llamas
P.O. Box 1137
Mt. Shasta, CA 96067
(9160 926-3959

Burton's Guide Service
15432 Quartz Valley Road
Fort Jones, CA 96032
(916) 468-2279 or 468-2966

Jim Payne
3505 Coffee Lane
Santa Rosa, CA 95401
(707) 542-6992

Kidder Creek Orchard Camp
P.O. Box 208
Greenview, CA 96037
(9160 467-3265

Wilderness Packers
P.O. Box 764
Happy Camp, CA 96039
(916) 493-2793

Wilderness Experience on Horseback
P.O. Box 23
Fulton, CA 95439

Sequoia National Forest
(Most of the packers on the Forest also
have permits to operate within the
National Parks adjacent.)

Horse Corral Pack Station
P.O. Box 135
Sequoia Nat'l Park, CA 93262
(209) 565-3404

Dan Shew's Pack Station
P.O. Box 756
Springville, CA 93265
(209) 539-2744

Mineral King Pack Station
P.O. Box 61
Three Rivers, CA 93271
(209) 561-4142

Cedar Grove Pack Station
Kings Canyon Nat'l Park,
CA 93633
(209) 565-3463

Shasta-Trinity National Forests
Junius Ammon
P.O. Box 13
Salyer, CA 95563

Llama Backpacking
Rt. 1, box 168
Mt. Shasta, CA 96067

Six Pak Packers
P.O. Box 301
Weaverville, CA 96093

Shasta Llamas
P.O. Box 1137
Mt. Shasta, CA 96067

Coffee Creek
Trinity Center, CA 96091

Sierra National Forest
(Most of those listed also have permits
to operate on adjacent National Parks.)

Clyde Pack Outfit
12267 E. Paul
Clovis, CA 93612
(209) 298-7397

High Sierra Pack Station
Mono Hot Springs, CA 93642
(209) 299-8297

Minarets Pack Station
c/o Watson Moore
8648 E. Shaw
Clovis, CA 93612
(209) 299-3229

D. & F. Pack Station
P.O. Box 156
Lakeshore, CA 93634
(209) 893-3220

Lost Valley Camp Pack Station
P.O. Box 288
Lakeshore, CA 93634

Stanislaus National Forest

Toiyabe National Forest
Little Antelope Pack Station
P.O. Box 179
Coleville, CA 96107
(702) 782-4528

Leavitt Meadows Pack Station
P.O. Box 124-a
Bridgeport, CA 93517
(916) 495-2257

Virginia Lakes Pack Outfit
HC Route 1, Box 1076
Bridgeport, CA 93517
(702) 867-2591 (winter)

Kerrick Corral
Winter: P.O. Box 154, Jamestown, CA 95327 (209) 984-5727
Summer: Kerrick Corral, Box 1435, Pinecrest, CA 95364 (209) 965-3561

Cherry Valley Pack Station
Winter: P.O. Box 1339, Sonora, CA 95370, (209) 532-2961
Summer: PO Groveland, CA 95321, Phone Cherry Valley No. 2, through Stockton
operator - Tuolumne County

Kennedy Meadows Resort
Winter: P.O. Box 4010 Sonora, CA 95370 (209) 532-9096
Summer: Star Route, Box 1490 Sonora, CA 95370, Phone Kennedy Meadows #1,
through Stockton Operator - Tuolumne County

Mather Pack Station
Winter: 12942 Highway 120 Oakdale, CA 95361, (209) 847-5753
Summer: Mather (via Groveland), CA 95321, (209) 379-2334

Forest Associations

BIG SANTA ANITA HISTORICAL SOCIETY   Angeles NF
7 North 5th Avenue, Arcadia, CA 91006

BIG SUR NATURAL HISTORY ASSOCIATION   Los Padres NF
P.O. Box 189, Big Sur, CA 93920

EASTERN SIERRA INTERPRETIVE ASSOC.   Inyo NF
Drawer R, Lone Pine, CA 93545

ELDORADO NAT'L FOREST INTERP. ASSOC.   Eldorado NF
3881 Many Oaks Line #33, Shingle Springs, CA 95682

FRIENDS OF THE FOREST   San Bernardino NF
P.O. Box M21-7, Big Bear Lake, CA 92315

LAGUNA MOUNTAIN VOLUNTEER ASSOC.   Cleveland NF
3348 Alpine Blvd., Alpine, CA 92001

LOOMIS MUSEUM ASSOCIATION   Lassen NF
P.O. Box 100, Lassen Volcanic National Park
Mineral, CA 96063-0100

LOS PADRES INTERPRETIVE ASSOC.   Los Padres NF
P.O. Box 3502, Santa Barbara, CA 93105

PACIFIC NORTHWEST NATIONAL PARKS &
FORESTS ASSOCIATION   Shasta-Trinity NF
83 S. King St., Suite 212, Seattle, WA 98104

RIM OF THE WORLD INTERPRETIVE ASSOC.   San Bernardino NF
P.O. Box 1958, Lake Arrowhead, CA 92352

SAN GABRIEL MOUNTAIN INTER. ASSOC.   Angeles NF
P.O. Box 1216, Wrightwood, CA 92397

SAN GORGONIO INTERPRETIVE ASSOC.   San Bernardino NF
4297 Mt. View Avenue, San Bernardino, CA 92407

TAHOE TALLAC ASSOCIATION   Lake Tahoe Basin
P.O. Box 1595, So. Lake Tahoe, CA 95705

THREE FORESTS INTERPRETIVE ASSOC.   Sequoia NF
13098 East Wiregrass Lane   Sierra NF
Clovis, CA 93612   Stanislaus NF

SOUTHWEST PARKS & MONUMENTS ASSOC.   Shasta-Trinity NF
221 North Court Ave.
Tucson, AZ 85701

Additional Agencies

Army Corps of Engineers
Natural Resource Management
650 Capitol Mall
Sacramento, Ca 95814
(916) 551-2112

Bureau of Land Management
2800 Cottage Way, Room E-2841
Sacramento, CA 95825
(916) 978-4754

California Department of Fish and
  Game
1419 Ninth Street
Sacramento, CA 95814
(916) 445-3531

California Department of Forestry and
  Fire Protection
1416 Ninth Street
Sacramento, CA 95814
(916) 445-9921

California Department of Parks and
  Recreation
P.O. Box 2390
Sacramento, CA 95811
(916) 445-4624 or 1-800-444-7275

Department of Boating and Waterways
  (California Boating)
1629 S Street
Sacramento, CA 95814
(916) 445-2615

National Park Service
Fort Mason, Building 201
San Francisco, CA 94123
(415) 556-4122

State of California Office of
  Tourism
1121 L Street, Suite 103
Sacramento, CA 95814
(916) 322-1397 or 1-800-862-2543

United States Geological Survey
555 Battery Street, Room 504
San Francisco, CA 94111
(415) 556-5627

PRIVATE AGENCIES

Mistix
P.O. Box 85705
San Diego, CA
  92138-57051-800-444-PARK

Eastern High Sierra Packers
  Association
690 N. Main Street
Bishop, CA 93514
(619) 873-8405

High Sierra Packers Association,
  Western Unit
P.O. Box 1362
Clovis, CA 93613

About The Author

George Stratton is a history teacher and free-lance writer who specializes in outdoor and travel subjects. A native Californian, he has camped, hiked, and fished in every National Forest in the state. His travel articles have been published about the western states as well as Austria, Italy, and Canada.